The Power
of Mature Empathy

The Power of Mature Empathy

In Response to Sexual Violence in Faith Communities

Sung Hyun Lee

☙PICKWICK *Publications* • Eugene, Oregon

THE POWER OF MATURE EMPATHY
In Response to Sexual Violence in Faith Communities

Copyright © 2025 Sung Hyun Lee. All rights reserved. Except for brief quotations in critical publications or reviews, no part of this book may be reproduced in any manner without prior written permission from the publisher. Write: Permissions, Wipf and Stock Publishers, 199 W. 8th Ave., Suite 3, Eugene, OR 97401.

Pickwick Publications
An Imprint of Wipf and Stock Publishers
199 W. 8th Ave., Suite 3
Eugene, OR 97401

www.wipfandstock.com

PAPERBACK ISBN: 979-8-3852-0290-4
HARDCOVER ISBN: 979-8-3852-0291-1
EBOOK ISBN: 979-8-3852-0292-8

Cataloguing-in-Publication data:

Names: Lee, Sung Hyun, author.

Title: The power of mature empathy : in response to sexual violence in faith communities / Sung Hyun Lee.

Description: Eugene, OR: Pickwick Publications, 2025. | Includes bibliographical references and index.

Identifiers: ISBN 979-8-3852-0290-4 (paperback). | ISBN 979-8-3852-0291-1 (hardcover). | ISBN 979-8-3852-0292-8 (ebook).

Subjects: LSCH: Empathy. | Sexaul ethics. | Pastoral theology. | Violence—Religious aspects—Christianity. | Sex crimes—Religious aspects—Christianity.

Classification: HQ71 L25 2025 (print). | HQ71 (ebook).

VERSION NUMBER 04/28/25

Scripture quotations are from the New Revised Standard Version Bible (NRSV), copyright © 1989 National Council of the Churches of Christ in the United States of America. Used by permission. All rights reserved worldwide.

To my mom and dad,
Kyung Soon Kim and Yong Dae Lee,
who planted in me the faith in the goodness of God
and the courage to hold onto hope and joy
in the midst of the dark tunnel life endows;

and to my spouse, Ted Rohe,
who loves me so much
and who willingly chases after stray dogs for hours with me
without being grumpy
so that my empathy is fully realized.

Contents

Acknowledgments | ix

Introduction | 1

1 A History of the Scholarship of Empathy | 14
2 Mature Empathy and Its Moral Implications | 58
3 Case Study: Sexual Violence in Faith Communities and the Role of Empathy in Digital Activism | 93
4 Building Blocks of Mature Communal Empathy | 136

Bibliography | 167

Index | 175

Acknowledgments

In this seemingly disconnected and polarized world, there are still many people who willingly sacrifice their time and proactively share others' agonies through empathy. Those were the ones who made this book possible. Thus all the thanks goes to them who struggle with their lives but still do not give up on empathizing with others, striving to fully imagine the others' pains and losses. They are the reason why this world that is full of agonies and aggressions still has hope.

Special thanks need to go to those who participated in the #MeToo Movement as the supporter of the victim-survivors and those victim-survivors who took immense courage to speak up and broke the silence. Because of their courageous action and caring empowerment, this book had stories to share and to prove that mature empathy is possible and hence so is a moral society.

The mentorship my dissertation committees showed me was foundational for this book. I express my gratitude especially to Dr. Kate Ott and the committee members, Drs. Traci West and Merel Visse, who trusted in me even when I doubted myself. The concepts and theories were born and refined thanks to your provocative, inspirational, patient, and empathetic guidance and mentorship!

There are many other people who inspired me and gave me honest feedback as I contemplated on empathy and its caring power including my family, my dear friends, and my spouse Ted Rohe who had to deal with my messy sentences and thoughts, and mulled over them with me. Lastly, I give my special thanks to everyone on my publishing team, especially the editor in chief, Dr. K. C. Hanson. It is impossible to include every single

ACKNOWLEDGMENTS

name that I owe thanks to for this work. Thank you *all* who have helped me, supported me, and inspired me through this journey.

Introduction

> "I want us to organize, to tell the personal stories that create empathy which is the most revolutionary emotion."
>
> —Gloria Steinem

THIS WORK AIMS TO encourage communities to build a social and communal imaginary based on mature empathy. Out of this imaginary—"the ways that ordinary people "imagine" their social surroundings,"[1] which also brings about ordinary praxis—the majority of members of the society think, feel, understand, and act accordingly. It is a society in which mature empathy—a morally nuanced and psychologically developed form of empathy—is one of the most prevailing emotional, political, social, and cultural values. With mature communal empathy as central, members will be able to communally challenge and change unjust systems, cultures, and practices to a great degree, trying hard to make unheard voices heard and to question the immoral problems that have never been questioned *enough*.

Across the international borders of our societies, we face compelling and excruciatingly complex social issues at stake such as racism, sexism, poverty, violence against humanity, gender inequality, distributive injustice, environmental issues, child/sexual/animal abuse, refugee issues, and interreligious violence, just to name a few. Yet, these various issues are complicatedly intermingled together. Not one type of social injustice stands alone by itself. Statistics bear witness to the fact that a black girl in the

---

1. Steele, "Social Imaginaries," 1047.

United States with a single mother from a low wealth community is more vulnerable to sexual abuse; this one case exemplifies the intersectionality of race, gender, economy, and other social factors.

My initial interest in empathy as a moral resource began with a general concern for caring for the marginalized who is exposed to various types of social injustices. This concern led me to wonder: what can we do to help socially marginalized people? What is the most rudimentary altruistic motivation to encourage people to participate in empowering the vulnerable? There is a variety of answers to these questions. For me, empathy is one of the answers due to its potential as a powerful moral resource for resistance that all human beings can use. There are many claims about the limitations and risks of empathy by ethicists and psychologists as it relates to morality. Despite the concerns on the moral use of empathy, we can easily find examples of empathy foundationally accelerating diverse social movements.

This book is led by some rudimentary questions: How can we use empathy for making a more just, caring society? What is the role of empathy as people are motivated to take action to participate in helping others to create a just, caring society? How do we recognize the actualized form of mature communal empathy as it appears when collective people share the agonies of the marginalized?

With these driving questions in mind, in the following section, I first propose the significance of the research academically as well as practically. Then, I share my primary methodologies and introduce the overview of each chapter in the last section of introduction.

The Significance of the Project

Over the last two decades, empathy has drawn special attention from scholars in varied disciplines primarily philosophy, biology, evolutionary anthropology, primatology, care ethics, and moral, developmental, psychoanalytic, and neurological psychology, just to mention a few. Yet, there has been no single scholarly consensus on its definition, function, developmental line, or its impacts on morality of human and non-human lives. One of the reasons for this extraordinary attention given to empathy is its multilayered and intersubjective nature and the interdisciplinary issues derived from varied notions of empathy. Among extensive controversies, significant discussions in the scholarship of empathy directly or indirectly related to this book are as follows: what is empathy? Is empathy inherent in the nature of human beings or a socially cultivated skill? Is empathy necessary for moral deliberation, development, or behavior? What are the moral benefits and problems of empathy? How do we understand the moral and political dimensions of empathy? What are the motivations that lead people to making empathic responses to others? What are the political and moral roles of mature empathy? Exploring these questions will lay a foundation for my study of communal empathy, especially a mature form.

This extensive range of discussions on empathy is helpful as I study the moral implications of empathy, specifically how mature empathy can be utilized as a motivational resource for justice-seeking activity. I insist that empathy is a rich cognitive and emotional asset, not only as a private or person-to-person emotion but also in public, political, and communal forms. It has potential as a motivational source to generate inner response and eventually ethical action, which can contribute to building a better caring society. The feeling and cognitive process of empathy positions the self in relation to the other and can motivate individuals and communities to try to understand and imagine others' feelings and situations based on intersubjectivity and diversity without losing themselves. The knowledge and experience obtained through the emotional and cognitive empathic process also have the potential to lead us to solidarity and social activism. As a minority Korean immigrant woman scholar, studying the intersubjective nature of empathy that may be a source of solidarity has a special meaning for me; for I often receive the benefit of and contribute to acknowledging the richness of diversity, which may be a stepping stone for solidarity and a moral society.

However, some scholars from diverse fields, even among care ethicists, hold conflicting positions on the concept of empathy and the various degrees to which empathy is a necessary component of justice and morality. There are groups of scholars who are either extreme proponents of or critics against empathy such as Michael Slote as a representative proponent of empathy or Paul Bloom as a notorious critic. However, most scholars seem to agree on the fact that empathy has both its own problems and prosocial benefits. Feminist philosopher, Julinna C. Oxley, who also is one of the proponents of the moral importance of empathy, argues that empathy can be "part of the story of morality but by no means the whole of it."[2]

The core issue is *how* we utilize empathy and *what kind* of empathy is needed for moral purposes while avoiding empathy's manipulative and

---

2. Oxley, *The Moral Dimensions of Empathy*, 4.

biased tendency. I argue that despite potential risks and limitations of empathy as it relates to morality, the problems do not outweigh the benefits of its rich social and political value. Empathy has potential to be *developed* into a morally nuanced and psychologically developed mature form. Depending on the ways in which empathy is directed, delivered, taught, and actualized by multi-factors such as culture, politics, and the ethos of each society, it embodies a wide spectrum of moral implications. Therefore, my central concerns relate to how we can *direct* empathy to be used for a more just caring society rather than exploiting it in appropriated, biased, gendered, or manipulative forms; what ethical model of empathy can promote solidarity and ignite justice-seeking movements; and lastly, how do we cultivate a mature form of empathy for it to be used communally as a motivational source of resistance? My thesis is that empathy has enriching moral potential for justice-seeking movements when it is in a morally nuanced and psychologically mature form. It will be even more powerful if we can find ways to *communally* actualize mature empathy. As Frans de Waal implies in his book *The Age of Empathy*, empathy has "produced the glue that holds communities together."[3] It provides a powerful resource for solidarity and has potential to promote social change for a morally mature society, that is, I claim in this book, a just and caring society.

In order to understand mature communal empathy, I intend to focus on the political and ethical problems and potentials of mature communal empathy related to sexual violence against women. Victim-survivors of sexual violence are oftentimes in the oppressed and/or marginalized group in heteropatriarchal society. In 2006, social activist Tarana Burke used the key phrase "empowerment through empathy"[4] as she starts the #MeToo movement for victim-survivors of sexual violence. Feeling understood and connected based on empathy has great healing power for the marginalized in "a white supremacist and heteropatriarchal" society[5] as well as the power to form solidarity as a resistance to social injustice.

My intention in examining the stories of sexual violence victim-survivors in Christian communities is to call attention to the current immoral atmosphere in Christian communities, rather than to limit the moral role of mature communal empathy to this particular community or context.

---

3. De Waal, *The Age of Empathy*, 45.

4. Murray, "Everyone Meet Tarana Burke."

5. West, "Is Christian Political Theology too Conservative to Undermine Sexual Violence?"

Introduction

Christian communities, in my observation, have a particular severity and cruelty in how they react to sexual violence victim-survivors, revictimizing them by hurting their dignity. In the aftermath of sexual violence, the survivors in the faith community are often asked to be empathically associate with the agony of the community, to stay in silence and to *forgive* the offender, *sacrificing* oneself for the sake of the whole faith community. As feminist and womanist theologians point out including Marie Fortune, Traci West, Rita Nakashima Brock, and Rebecca Ann Parker, doctrines and theologies can be easily distorted and exploited in heteropatriarchal and white supremacist society to be used against women and subalterns. I argue that this type of manipulative and distorted theology often generates a range of negative emotional reactions in sexual violence victim-survivors such as shame, guilt, and humiliation. In addition, it also coerces women into certain behaviors such as forced self-sacrifice and forgiveness. By keeping silent, they forcibly sacrifice themselves to keep an unethical peace in their community. This leads to "virtual" empathic guilt[6] for the community, which means the victim-survivor thinks that she has caused a moral transgression and thus she is the sinner. In turn, the community empathizes with the offenders and *forgives* them for their sins. This is one of the paradigmatic cases of evil that can come from gendered and manipulated empathy.

I attribute one of the fundamental problems of these immoral responses to dysfunctional and manipulated empathy, which feeds off of unjust heteropatriarchal and hierarchical socio-cultural and political systems and practices. In this vein, this book challenges empathy when it is misunderstood as limited to a personal and private emotion. In addition, more importantly, the book offers a new understanding of empathy as a moral source of resistance against all of the immoral contexts where dysfunctional empathy is manifested and used as a primary tool for injustice through systems by varied communities. *One* of many examples includes the perception of and responses to sexual violence victim-survivors in Christian communities.

As I develop how communal empathy is realized as a social movement for seeking justice, I scrutinize the #MeToo movement as a rich example of the realization of communal empathy. In exploring the #MeToo movement, I illustrate how empathy can be realized by the community in the public sphere as moral motivation on behalf of known and unknown

---

6. Hoffman, *Empathy and Moral Development*.

victim-survivors. The examination of stories of #MeToo aids not only to develop the idea of communal empathy, but to obtain a perspective on how members of Christian communities can engage in an ethical healing process of care with empathy. Probing mature communal empathy is an attempt to find ways in which empowering the vulnerable is sought through the action of solidarity and social activism by fellow humans in transnational community. Effectuating communal empathy assists us to appreciate the in-between place of I and Thou where we can realize the power of hospitality to strangers without losing the dignity and worth of the self/selves or the other(s).

Methods and Resources

This book is written as a praxis based on the foundational belief that an individual is a subject who constantly *unfolds*[7] and develops their identity in radically intricate relational networks, learning through mutuality with other fellow human and non-human beings. Thus, my research philosophy relies on the understanding of creatures, e.g. humans, as interdependent and intersubjective beings. One individual is one part of a relational and caring network rather than an autonomous and independent being. Therefore, this study starts from a belief that the moral power of mature empathy should be studied from a heuristic and interpretive approach as opposed to a positivistic and impartial research philosophy as multifaceted relational networks ceaselessly create new and different relational particularities among individuals. In this vein, qualitative research methods will be more effective and appropriate as a primary methodology than quantitative research, while quantitative research can be used at times as a supportive role, mainly sourced from existing data sets. As Merel Visse and Tineke Abma argue, "we can learn from evidence" but solely depending on an "evidence-based approach" to understand moral encounters simply will not work.[8]

---

7. I use this term in the same way that Merel Visse and Tineke Abma use it in their work. Visse and Abma note, "Praxis focuses on a particular kind of human engagement that involves one's dealings with, or interactions with, others that *unfolds* in view of some particular understanding of substantive rationality appropriate to the practice in question" (Schwandt, 2005, p. 98). We stress the word unfold in italics because it illustrates that we cannot steer or control human engagement or understanding through a rational (evidence-based) approach. We can learn from evidence, but it is impossible to simply transfer evidence gathered in one context to another." Visse and Abma, *Evaluation*, 227.

8. Visse and Abma, *Evaluation*, 227.

Introduction

My assumption based on developmental psychology is that empathy is a universal capacity of human beings, who are innately equipped with an empathizing ability whether it is in a primordial or developed form.[9] The problem is to know *what* moral potentials *mature* empathy holds and *how* we prompt our communities to realize the potential by encouraging members to develop their empathic ability to a mature degree. The question of how we promote *mature communal empathy* will be investigated by using case studies as my research strategy. It will be helpful to examine people's collective responses to two particular cases of the #MeToo movement as an effort to better understand the realization of communal empathy.

Due to the constraints of space and time, I will limit my focus only to *mature* empathy, mentioning immature empathy only when it is necessary to look at the immature aspects to better understand mature empathy. This study is a valuable attempt, considering the need for research specifically in ethical and moral psychological domains, to understand the moral value of mature communal empathy especially as a motivational resource for social justice movements.

As to relevant academic disciplines, this book is an interdisciplinary work built upon an existing body of scholarship on empathy. It is an attempt to find the ethical, political, and psychological value of empathy for making a better just caring society from intercultural, transnational, religious, social, and gender perspectives. In order to discover the valuable moral assets of empathy in relation to social and gender justice, the primary conversation partners are feminist care ethicists. These thinkers from care ethics have contributed to gender justice and the ethical and philosophical development of care as an important factor as opposed to impartial or deontological ethics. Other significant conversation partners are from the domain of moral, developmental, and social psychology, who examine the psychological understanding of empathy in relation to society, developmental processes, and the morality of human beings. Also, Christian feminist ethics and digital humanities are significant domains as they help me to build a lens to investigate current social, ethical, and theological issues that need to be examined further in relation to empathy and sexual violence.

As to care ethics on empathy, unfortunately not many care ethicists solely give attention to empathy in the process of discussing caring and morality. For this reason, it will be one of my primary scholarly attempts to

---

9. I note that there might be absence of empathic ability due to neurological issues at times.

engage care ethics where we find direct reference to empathy. In that, I primarily use the work of Joan Tronto, Virginia Held, Elena Pulcini, and Inge van Nistelrooij along with other care ethicists. Scholars such as Virginia Held see empathy as a moral emotion[10] unlike other care ethicists who understand empathy as a risky resource for morality such as Sevenhuijsen who argues that empathy has "some serious drawbacks" which need to be distinguished from moral "active attention."[11] Held acknowledges that empathy is one of the important elements that practices of care involve. Also, Joan Tronto's and Elena Pulcini's[12] political approaches to care ethics are beneficial as I try to constructively explore the building blocks of mature empathy from a care ethical perspective to envisage a morally mature society and the political usefulness of empathy in moral encounters.

The work of psychologists with a focus on the development and manifestation of empathy in human behavior and relationships is a necessary lens to better define empathy. It also provides a significant lens to understand why empathy is important to human nature and society, and how it functions as a significant moral affect for justice in society. Along with several psychologists on empathy such as Nancy Eisenberg, Daniel Batson and John Gibbs, my primary conversation partner is Martin Hoffman, a developmental moral psychologist, whose work is considered substantial to the scholarship of empathy. Also, the work of Julinna Oxley, a feminist ethicist and moral psychologist, is critical in providing dialectical thinking on empathy's moral dimension from psychological and ethical perspectives. Finally, scholars from the domain of philosophy of psychology and emotion provide insights about empathy from philosophical and moral perspectives such as Heidi Maibom and Amy Coplan.

Among the rich literature in psychology on this discussion, Martin L. Hoffman is one of the most important psychologists on the scholarship of empathy. As a developmental psychologist, he wrote, *Empathy and Moral Development: Implications for Caring and Justice*. In the book, defining empathy as "the vicarious affective response to another person,"[13] Hoffman researches the psychological development of empathy. In addition to studying its contribution to altruism for the "distressed group" as well as feelings such as guilt, anger, sympathy, and the feeling of injustice, he insists these

---

10. Held, *The Ethics*.
11. Sevenhuijsen, "Care and Attention," 7.
12. Pulcini, *Care of the World*.
13. Hoffman, *Empathy and Moral Development*, 29.

feelings are derived from and developed in the empathizing process with someone in diverse contexts. His study of the relationship between empathy and morality is to be used for understanding empathy and its nature, development, and roles in society as it relates to morality.

Secondary, yet significant, disciplines include political and philosophical feminism, and clinical psychology on emotions, as well as studies of digital humanities. Important feminist theorists are included, who raise concerns about the politics of emotions and the ways in which affect including empathy plays out on private, public, political and communal levels. Furthermore, I will engage Christian theological resources for critically analyzing current social issues related to sexual violence in church communities. Feminist/womanist ethicists and theologians such as Traci West, Beverly Wildung Harrison, Kwok Pui-Lan, and Rita Nakashima Brock provide a helpful lens for ethical analysis on the ways in which church communities respond to sexual violence survivors as well as on social and communal burden to victim-survivors. For these matters, we ultimately need help from mature communal empathy to foster moral responses from the communities, and lead Christians to have morally directed theological and doctrinal understandings of sexual violence and other injustice issues. In the discipline of digital humanities, I draw on Lisa Nakamura's work who is one of the precursors of the studies of digital humanities. In addition to that, the work of Kate Ott, a Christian social ethicist who draws on the study of digital humanities is a helpful resource for engaging Christian ethics with digital humanities.

Thus, this is an interdisciplinary work that attempts to promote a new moral and developmental psychological understanding of empathy as a primarily social care ethics project that can be used, but not exclusively, in Christian communities to respond to sexual violence. While it is a significant part of this book to explore the issues of sexual violence in Christian communities as well as (im)migrants' particularities whose voices are often missing in the public discourses especially in chapter 3 and 4, it is my intention not to limit the psychological and ethical understanding of empathy's political and moral role only to Christian communities or sexual violence cases. Rather, it is my intention to disrupt any social justice problems by offering a new understanding of applicable mature communal empathy across boundaries of nationality, religion, (im)migration/citizenship status, gender, race, culture, and any affiliations.

Overview of Chapters

In addition to the introduction, this book has four chapters. The first two chapters provide the theoretical groundwork related to empathy and how to envisage a mature moral society. The third chapter provides a case study analysis of mature communal empathy in practice. The final chapter robustly details the elements of mature communal empathy upon which I call for radical imagination of the moral society where mature communal empathy provides a moral compass to the members.

In chapter 1, I bring these two primary disciplines, developmental and moral psychology with feminist care ethics, into a dialectic and complementary conversation with each other about empathy's moral value. Psychological scholarship needs to be tested against applied matters of justice; and care ethics is needed to understand the nature and development of human empathy in order to properly utilize the potential of empathy as an empowering and justice-seeking moral asset. Moreover, Hoffman's theory on empathy needs to be engaged in dialogue with feminism and care ethics to gain gender, cultural, contextual, and ethical perspectives which cannot be neglected in the discourse on empathy and morality.

In this chapter, I consider the limitations and potential risks of empathy as well as its benefits and moral potentials as a moral affect. I compare both sides of existing arguments on the moral implications of empathy. Only with sufficient exploration of contemporary controversies on empathy will it be possible to see how a notion of empathy can be developed into a psychologically and ethically mature form for seeking justice. It is not my position to defend against all the critiques of empathy that have been made. Rather, I focus on how we can overcome the limitations and avoid the moral risks that empathy involves for the sake of making a just caring society. The examination of the moral risks and limitations of empathy will help me to grasp a balanced perspective on the moral value of empathy and to find ways in which we can properly utilize empathy for seeking social and gender justice while avoiding the dangerous aspects of empathy for morality.

After examining current scholarship on empathy and its relation to morality in chapter 1, I invite the reader to envisage a morally mature society and to a theoretical exploration of moral implications of empathy that can contribute to building a moral society. This process of building a social and communal imaginary will be a necessary foundation to conceptualize mature communal empathy and to imagine its moral features, which will also be examined in chapter 2.

Introduction

  This chapter starts by envisioning a morally mature society that, I hope, mature empathy can contribute towards building. Defining mature empathy as a normative moral faculty, I argue that mature empathizers are those who cannot countenance social injustice thanks to the moral features of mature empathy they embody. After this brief understanding of mature empathy as a normative moral faculty, I attain insights from feminist care ethics to imagine a moral society that has never fully come into being, yet is possible to actualize. Especially I argue that we need a complementary view on justice and care for such a moral society. Then, based on this vision of society, I provide features of mature empathy from psychological and care ethical findings from the previous work, which may contribute to establishing a morally mature society that I just envisaged. The chapter is concluded by recapitulating moral implications of empathy.

  I turn to digital activism cases of the #MeToo movement as my case studies in chapter 3. Before analyzing two #MeToo stories from church settings, I explore the social implications of sexual violence and its social, citizenship status, cultural, religious, and spiritual impact on victim-survivors and the hardships that they face as they try to break their silence. Three primary factors will be demonstrated, which perpetuate sexual violence and victim-survivors' suffering. Based on this research, I use case study analysis as my method in order to provide a careful appraisal of the dominant responses in church communities to sexual violence victim-survivors. Then, I turn to investigate the responses in digital spaces, trying to see the moral roles of empathy and how mature empathy is utilized in the #MeToo movement. As a commitment to drawing attention to minority groups, I focus on transnational settings, and (im)migrants' and relatively more vulnerable people's stories throughout the chapter as their stories are often missing even in the #MeToo movement. This focus will help us attend to the distinctive vulnerability and invisibility of (im)migrants, and the stories coming out of transnational settings. Stories that often involve immigration/citizenship status, vulnerable to institutional and legal systemic evil and xenophobic/racist cultural practices highlight intersectional struggles. These stories show the bare face of our current society in which marginalized people suffer from the absence of a care network, striving to maintain their human dignity. Particular attention to these stories is truly significant since the stories of survival of those alienated in a foreign land are often unheard unless we proactively seek to listen.

The particular contemporary context and the socio-political dynamics generated from the case studies display noteworthy manifestation of a certain form of empathy, i.e. communal empathy, and its relevant caring action such as solidarity. The use of this case study offers a helpful method to illumine the problem of exploiting religious doctrines to cover up sexual violence. As a primary method of this book, the case study approach is designed to help me illustrate a notion of communal empathy stemming from the concrete lived experience of victim-survivors as the socially marginalized distant others. The particular socio-cultural contexts I will assess are at the intersections of gender, race, religion, and nation, e.g. (im)migrant women in the United States. Looking to the particular socio-cultural contextuality of sexual violence and victim-survivors in heteropatriarchal society unveils the bare face of oppression and how the society manipulates the emotions of the marginalized.

Given the uniqueness of this recent movement, online journals, newspapers, social networking sites as well as academic literature will be utilized to collect and reflect on responses to sexual violence and its survivors. Additionally, this method explores how online platforms can be employed for dismantling social injustice and promoting communal empathy. This book is mainly founded upon narrative and qualitative research methods, given that the aim of this book is not to measure the severity of the injustice in numerical data; rather, it is to see how people listen to the living narratives of the marginalized with empathy and promote people's communal empathic response to the injustice.

I intend to illuminate the ethical importance of mature communal empathy within the movement as it allows me to observe how empathy is or is not working to provide insights on gender and social justice-seeking action. Also, through this methodological approach, I expect to uncover how gender justice can be sought by people who are motivated by mature communal empathy. In sum, there are four reasons to employ this movement in the Christian faith community as my lens in this book. First, I seek to ground this book in the situatedness of people's concrete lived experiences and, hence, to prevent this work from being a disciple of the abstract. Second, it helps me to show how theology and gender discrimination perpetuate the exploitation of empathy. Third, these particular case studies reveal how empathy as a moral resource functions in the context of an unjust and malfunctioning society as it brings attentiveness of people to the isolated experience of sexual violence against women; and, therefore, presents a new way for us to foster a better caring society as the movement continues to grow. And finally, this lens helps me to examine the praxis and significant components of communal empathy revealed in the movement which is formed by responsiveness of people to the sufferings of others. Communal empathy shown in the movement motivates members of the community to desire a caring community. Through the meta-synthesis of the two responses from church communities and digital spaces, I look closely at the findings to see how mature empathy can motivate bystanders to participate in the justice-seeking activism, and can hinder pseudo-empathy that is a product of an unjust and immoral society and community.

In chapter 4, I explore mature communal empathy and its elements as well as how mature communal empathy as a praxis can be fostered in our daily life. In this final chapter, I try to weave the findings together from previous chapters to evoke our radical imagination of a society, a practice to build a just caring society, as a *beginning* step. I suggest building blocks of a communal form of mature empathy, its ethical aspects, and the role for social and gender justice movement. In this chapter, a few aims will be achieved: Psychological and care ethical findings from the case study will be identified, which ultimately exhibits mature communal empathy. In addition, the elements of communal empathy will be explored. What are the factors that make people form communal empathy? To answer this question, I offer five primary elements of mature communal empathy based on my findings from the analysis of the #MeToo movement, engaging the cases and stories that were presented in chapter 3.

After exploring these significant aspects of communal empathy, I call for a radical imagination of a just caring society that is founded on mature communal empathy. In this section, I offer examples of the praxis of mature communal empathy. First of all, I illustrate, engage, and exemplify mature communal empathy as a resistance to pseudo-empathy and describe the elements of mature communal empathy. In the following section, I also provide examples of the use of mature communal empathy in partnership with Christian values such as anger, love, and sacrifice. These Christian values need a new understanding so they can be strengthened through mature empathy. Then, I challenge the reader to imagine a society where mature communal empathy is one of the most significant bedrocks. The final chapter concludes by summarizing and recapitulating each chapter and presenting final claims and the need for future research.

1

A History of the Scholarship of Empathy

> Humans would be totally lost without empathy.[1]
>
> —E. Ann Kaplan

IMAGINING A SOCIETY WHERE no empathy exists gives us a glimpse of how *essential* empathy is for humankind. Researching human cruelty in history, some scholars find the source of inhumanity to be the *absence* or underdeveloped state of empathy.[2] A newborn baby may not be able to survive, if parents do not have the empathic ability to read the baby's needs; it is less likely that victims in a terrorist attack get help from civilian bystanders if empathic motivations did not exist. Empathy is the source of humanity, which makes humans attentive to the distress or pain of others.[3] Reason

---

1. Kaplan, "Empathy and Trauma," 256.

2. Baron-Cohen, *Zero Degrees*. In this book, Baron-Cohen finds the reason for human cruelty throughout history from the lack, absence, or distortion of empathy.

3. I interchangeably use the term "another" and "the other" for the one who is to be observed and possibly receives empathy from the "observer," instead of using the term "victim"(Martin Hoffman) or "target"(many scientific researchers including Daniel Batson). Martin Hoffman uses the term, "victim." However, considering that offenders also

and other human faculties may play a role but reason without empathy loses its power to motivate bystanders to engage with and take action for distant others. Empathy is the fundamental human asset to make people imagine other people's intricate emotional states of suffering, grief, pain, anger, agony, fear, pride, shame, joy, satisfaction, happiness, and so on. It is the most essential communicative tool that encourages people to be prosocial and altruistic. Empathy gives a different set of perspectives that make people put their own interests aside and take on others' as a priority. Empathy is one of the essential elements needed to form community and solidarity.

Given empathy's essential value for humankind, scholars in the field of psychology and ethics continue to research the value and prosocial role of empathy in society. To understand the major debates on empathy and morality, I provide a relevant theoretical background of empathy in this chapter that contributes to conceptualizing mature communal empathy. In the first section, definitions of empathy among diverse scholars will be introduced, out of which I suggest my own definition of empathy. In the following section, I introduce a few significant concepts and related debates in the scholarship of empathy, which will be utilized in later chapters to build the concept of communal empathy. In the third section, I explore the work of Martin Hoffman on empathy in relation to morality. By looking into Hoffman's work, I attempt to understand the development of empathy and its moral role in human life, which later will be engaged with empathy's moral implications and roles at a communal level. In the final section, I examine and categorize the alleged weaknesses of empathy as a moral resource to grasp the potential problems empathy might present for moral life and I suggest probable solutions to them. Hoffman's work in particular and this chapter's introduction to a history of scholarship on empathy provides a foundation for chapter 2 where I more deeply explore the features of mature empathy and envisage a morally mature society from the perspective of feminist care ethics.

---

can attain empathy from people, the term "victim" can cause confusion between victims of social injustice and those who are observed by people and gain empathy. There should be a complete distinction between the two terms. Hoffman, *Empathy and Moral Development*; Batson, *A Scientific Search*.

Definitions of Empathy

The historical development of the concept of empathy begins with the term *einführung* grounded in German aesthetics, literally meaning 'feeling into.' The word *einführung* was coined by Robert Vischer in 1873 according to art critic Edgar Wind (1963).[4] Edmund Tetchener later translated *einführung* into the English word *empathy* in 1909 as he introduced the concept of *einführung* from the work of Theodor Lipps whose work was based on the aesthetics of psychology. However, this conceptual understanding of empathy was preceded by David Hume and Adam Smith under the term *sympathy*.[5] Since then, the concept of empathy or sympathy used by Hume and Smith has been interdisciplinarily developed, revised, and broadened.[6]

Sympathy vs. Empathy

Despite the diverse opinions on the notions of sympathy and empathy, one of the most agreed upon distinctions between the two is based on the availability of an affect match. Empathy which includes both cognition and emotion tends to involve an affect match or, at least, congruent feelings with the other. Whereas sympathy does not demand an affect match or congruent feelings; sympathy is feeling concerned *for* someone, especially those who are in problematic situations. In her article "Empathy and Sympathy,"[7] social developmental psychologist Nancy Eisenberg defines sympathy:

> I define "sympathy" as an affective response that consists of feeling sorrow or concern for the distressed or needy other (rather than feeling the same emotion as the other person). Sympathy is believed to involve other-oriented, altruistic motivation. . . . Although sympathy probably stems primarily from empathy in many contexts, it may also result from cognitive processes such

---

4. Wispé, "History of the Concept," 18.

5. Wispé, "History of the Concept," 18; Batson, "These Things Called Empathy," 3–15; Stueber, "Empathy"; Oxley, *The Moral Dimensions of Empathy*.

6. I will ignore the origin and its historical development of the term empathy here. I do not think the origin of the concept is significant to conceptualizing communal empathy. For reference on this term, see Coplan and Goldie, *Empathy*; Wispé, "History of The Concept."

7. Eisenberg, "Empathy and Sympathy," 677–91.

as perspective taking and accessing of information encoded in memory that is relevant to the other person's condition.[8]

Sympathy, for her, involves mourning or a concerned response to another in distress and, most importantly, comes out of empathy in many cases. Her definition has a shared ground with the work of moral developmental psychologist Martin Hoffman. He develops his notion of sympathetic distress which he argues is a later developmental stage of empathy. I revisit this in a later section of this chapter.[9]

The simple definition suggested by Amy Coplan and Peter Goldie articulates the difference between empathy and sympathy. They argue that "in morality . . . we make a very straightforward distinction between" the two concepts.[10] Empathy, according to them, can be defined as "feeling the suffering of another person," whereas sympathy is "feeling *for* that person's suffering"[11] There are controversies over this distinction. Yet, there seems to be an overarching consensus among scholars that empathy in a general sense can be understood as "feeling *into*," whereas sympathy is "feeling *for*."[12]

Definitions of Empathy

Many scholars from diverse disciplines have tried to create a definition of empathy. Yet, no single agreed upon definition has arisen due to the wide range of involved disciplines.[13] Definitions of empathy and the range of empathic phenomena tend to be delineated based on the author's subject and the discipline. There is a group of scholars who understand empathy broadly as an umbrella phenomenon under which other emotions are involved such as compassion, sympathy, empathic anger, guilt, and so on,[14]

---

8. Eisenberg, "Empathy and Sympathy," 678.
9. Hoffman, *Empathy and Moral Development*.
10. Coplan and Goldie, "Introduction," XLIII.
11. Coplan and Goldie, "Introduction," XLIII.
12. Coplan and Goldie, "Introduction," XLIII.
13. In order to map the broad working definitions of empathy in the scholarship of empathy, Batson's summary is helpful. Batson in his article, "These Things Called Empathy," distinguishes five other psychological states that are called as empathy in the scholarship to clarify more on his definition of the concept of empathy: (1) Knowing another person's thoughts and feelings. (2) Feeling as another feels. (3) Imagining how another feels. (4) Imagining how you would feel in another's place. (5) Feeling distress at witnessing another's suffering. Batson, "These Things Called Empathy."
14. Hoffman, *Empathy and Moral Development*.

whereas other scholars consider empathy as a mere emotion/affection or cognitive ability. One of the scholars who follow the narrower concept of empathy is Amy Coplan, a scholar in the field of philosophy of emotion and moral psychology. She argues that in the current scholarship "[w]e need more specificity, not more generality"[15] in making a definition because the general understanding of empathy would hinder the scholarly efforts to study the empathy-related processes and only generate "ambiguity and confusion."[16] However, most prominent scholars in the field hold the contrasting definition, which is broader and encompasses various relevant emotions. For example, Heidi L. Maibom holds the same view as Hoffman and Batson in terms of a wider definition of empathy. She describes empathy as "*a range of* emotional responses we have to what others feel or the situation they are in, such as sympathy, empathic anger, or compassion, in addition to some form of *appreciation* of their psychological state" [italics added].[17] My analysis is grounded in this understanding of empathy.

In the midst of the rich and diversely defined concepts and roles of empathy, my work takes major conversation partners such as Martin Hoffman, C. Daniel Batson, and Frans de Waal. Moral and developmental psychologist Martin Hoffman defines empathy as "the involvement of psychological processes that make a person have feelings that are more congruent with another's situation than with his own situation."[18] Hoffman's definition is very similar to that of Stephanie Preston and de Waal. In their article "Empathy: Its Ultimate and Proximate Bases,"[19] they explain the "perception-action" model. Based on this model, the authors define empathy as "any process where the attended perception of the object's state generates a state in the subject that is more applicable to the object's state or situation than to the subject's own prior state or situation."[20] They argue that whereas Hoffman focuses on *response,* their focus is on the *process.* The process model that Preston and de Waal suggest endows empathy as a "superordinate category" under which all phenomena of the empathic process are included as subcategories like emotional contagion, helping

---

15. Coplan, "Understanding Empathy," 5.

16. I will not explain Coplan's theory here since her definition of empathy does not match with mine. For more information, see Coplan, "Understanding Empathy," 3–18.

17. Maibom, *Empathy and Morality*, 1.

18. Hoffman, *Empathy and Moral Development*, 30.

19. For more discussion on the model, see Preston and de Waal, "Empathy."

20. Preston and de Waal, "Empathy," 4.

behavior, guilt, cognitive empathy, sympathy, and so on.[21] They maintain that their concept of empathy is designed to "unify" the variety of perspectives and definitions on empathy in the existing scholarship of empathy so that extensive notions of empathy in different fields may be incorporated.[22]

Another attempt to unify the nature and various aspects of empathic phenomena into the term empathy is made by C. Daniel Batson. Batson tries to incorporate the extensive empathic phenomena under the term empathy. He prefers to call empathy "empathic concern" since, to him, empathy as emotion is a "response to *another's need*" [italics added].[23] In other words, it is one of the other-oriented emotions such as sympathy, pity, compassion, etc. These emotions "react to seeing someone suffer" which later generate altruistic motivation.[24] Batson simply calls this emotional reaction to others' suffering empathy or empathic concern—"a source of altruism."[25] Based on his "empathy-altruism hypothesis," he interchangeably uses empathy and empathic concern.[26] For him, empathy is "elicited by and congruent with the perceived welfare of someone in need."[27] Then, does Batson mean that empathy always exclusively involves other people's *negative* situations or feelings from which empathy is aroused? Not exclusively. For him, empathy as a whole includes one's feelings for someone else's positive situation as well as negative situations. For example, he clarifies the differences by using the term "empathic joy" compared to "empathic concern," which is under the umbrella term of empathy for the congruent empathic feeling when the other is in a positive condition.[28] For Batson, feeling empathy involves both empathic concern and joy depending on another's current state of in-need (negativity) or in-joy (positivity).

For Martin Hoffman, as it is stated earlier, empathy is conceived as "an affective response more appropriate to another's situation than one's own."[29]

---

21. Preston and de Waal, "Empathy," 4.
22. Preston and de Waal, "Empathy," 3.
23. Batson, *A Scientific Search*, 29.
24. Batson, *The Altruism Question*, 58.
25. Batson, *The Altruism Question*, 58; Batson, *A Scientific Search*, 28.
26. Batson, *A Scientific Search*, 29–34; Despite the importance of Batson's empathy-altruism hypothesis, I will not explain further in detail due to the limited space in this book. For more information on the hypothesis, see Batson, *The Altruism Question*.
27. Batson, *A Scientific Search*, 29.
28. Batson, *A Scientific Search*, 29.
29. Hoffman, *Empathy and Moral Development*, 4.

To be empathic leads the person to put someone else's perspective first and allows the other's emotions to be placed in the person's own affective state. For Hoffman, however, empathy does not require an affective match between the observer and the other since empathy, according to his definition, is *reactional* feelings out of the psychological response to another person or the person's situation, that is more congruent with another's—or a "victim's" in Hoffman's term[30]—situation than one's own. Not requiring an affect match is a significant feature of Hoffman's understanding of empathy. He explains why: "The empathy-arousing processes often produce the same feeling in observer and victim but not necessarily, as when one feels empathic anger on seeing someone attacked even when the victim feels sad or disappointed rather than angry."[31] Hoffman acknowledges that accuracy of cognitive assessment—or "empathic accuracy" by William Ickes[32]—of another's situation or psychological state is important. Nonetheless, he states that "dropping the requirement of an affect match" has advantages as he studies the moral significance of empathy and empathic distress.[33] Empathic distress here is a key term in Hoffman's theory in relation to prosocial moral behavior, which is defined as "*one's reactional distress caused by observing a person who is in actual distress,*" which may generate various emotions such as sympathetic distress, empathic anger, an empathic feeling of injustice, and guilt.[34]

However, when we drop the requirement of an affect match between the observer and the other, an ethical question arises. Does that mean the perspective-taking[35] by someone such as a sadist or torturer of a victim should be understood as empathy if they can completely understand another's emotion without an affect match? Many ethicists and philosophers of emotion as well as psychologists take a very cautious approach to this ethical inquiry.

---

30. Hoffman, *Empathy and Moral Development*, 6.
31. Hoffman, *Empathy and Moral Development*, 30.
32. Ickes, *Empathic Accuracy*.
33. Hoffman, *Empathy and Moral Development*, 30.
34. Hoffman, *Empathy and Moral Development*, 4.
35. In the following section, I will explain the concept of perspective-taking in detail. To simply put it, perspective-taking is an ability or an action to take or adopt another's perspective, through which you view the world, the situation and the induced feelings and thoughts of the other.

First of all, Hoffman's definition of empathy "not requiring (though often including) a close match between observer's and victim's affect"[36] requires certain conditions. There are occasions in which empathy does not require a match and, indeed, may require a certain mismatch, as when the victim's life condition belies her feelings in the immediate situation. These are occasions in which verbal mediation and role-taking are likely to be paramount.[37]

For example, when a daughter just figured out that her mother is a final-stage cancer patient, which the mother herself did not know, the daughter will feel sadness as she empathizes with her, while her mother would not feel the matching emotion. Certain occasions may cause an affective mismatch between the observer and the other. For another example, consider how a pastor and congregant might experience empathy based on their past and immediate experiences. There is a Korean 1.5-generation[38] teenage girl who had grown up in a very conservative church denomination for most of her life in South Korea. The church educated her that losing purity (virginity) is a sin. She moved to the United States several years ago and was recently raped by a former church staff member in a Korean-congregation church in the United States. This young woman seeking care turns to a Nepali immigrant woman pastor who is a sexual violence victim-survivor as a kid and has overcome her spiritual, physical, and emotional struggles. The pastor will empathize with the teenage girl, feeling anger and disgust at the offender and feeling heartbroken, sympathetic, and compassionate for the teenage girl, while the teenage girl might only feel shame and guilt. In these cases, the affective mismatch is generated because of the particular circumstances of the empathized, i.e. the teenage girl, rather than because of the observer's own mindset or certain harm against another's will or wellbeing.

Alternatively, feminist philosopher Julinna Oxley defines empathy as "feeling a congruent emotion with another person, in virtue of perceiving her emotion with some mental process such as imitation, simulation, projection, or imagination."[39] She further articulates that "congruent emotions"

---

36. Hoffman, *Empathy and Moral Development*, 60.

37. Hoffman, *Empathy and Moral Development*, 61. I provide more explanations on verbal mediation and role-taking in the later section.

38. 1.5-generation immigrants refer to those who immigrated to the United States as children or in their teenage.

39. Oxley, *The Moral Dimensions of Empathy*, 32.

are the significant feature of empathy, which is beyond "a mere simulation."[40] Some scholars such as John Deigh or Martha Nussbaum consider a sadist's perspective-taking with the victim also as one kind of empathy to some degree, but not a mature one.[41] Oxley does not agree with their view. Oxley explains using a cognitive theory of emotion that the sadist's emotion does not match the other party's *cognitive content* and *emotion*. Emotion, for her, means "an *intentional stance* or propositional attitude *toward some state* or belief."[42] Empathy, for her, is "an *affective* response or attitude toward some state with cognitive content."[43] Oxley's view on empathy shares ground with Batson's definition stated above, i.e. "other-oriented emotion elicited by and congruent with the perceived *welfare* of someone in need"[italics added].[44] Thus, empathy in its nature involves one's cognitive and affective *intention* for the sake of another's well-being.

Nancy Sherman, a philosopher and an ethicist, suggests a distinctive definition of empathy: "[T]o be empathetic is to be a good listener, to imaginatively engage in another's thoughts and feelings without becoming overly enmeshed in them . . . it is to understand but also to let another know, in a supportive way, how and what one understands."[45] Sherman seems to emphasize the importance of sharing the feelings of the other while keeping the emotional boundary between the observer and the other.

I strongly agree with the view of Sherman and Oxley with one condition. Non-cognitive forms of empathy which may later develop into mature forms of empathy should be an exception. The non-cognitive forms of empathy include what Hoffman illustrates as primitive modes of empathic arousal, such as: (1) mimicry, (2) classical conditioning, (3) direct association.[46] These forms of empathy start from the newborn stage and develop into more cognitive and voluntary ones. Unless the observer holds an inevitable unavailability of cognitive development, empathy should contain the observer's "intentional stance" toward another's situation for the sake of the welfare of the other.

40. Oxley, *The Moral Dimensions of Empathy*, 24.
41. Oxley, *The Moral Dimensions of Empathy*, 24–25.
42. Oxley, *The Moral Dimensions of Empathy*, 25.
43. Oxley, *The Moral Dimensions of Empathy*, 25.
44. Batson, *A Scientific Search*, 29.
45. Battaly, "Is Empathy a Virtue?" 280.
46. These concepts are examined in the following section. For deeper understanding, see Hoffman, *Empathy and Moral Development*.

A History of the Scholarship of Empathy

Drawing on definitions of Hoffman, Oxley, and Sherman as well as other scholars, I describe empathy as *an observer's or observers'—as a community—cognitive and affective inner process and response to another or others in various negative and positive circumstances, which leads the observer(s) to feel congruent and oftentimes matching feelings with the other(s) through mimicry, perspective-taking, imagination, and/or simulation.*[47] If and only if emotions are aroused *out of* empathy, I consider them as *branches of empathic affect* such as empathic anger, disgust, sympathy, compassion, love, and joy.[48] Another element of empathy is *engagement and interaction* with another. This engagement and interaction should be accompanied with a stance that corresponds to the *well-being of the other*. In other words, any feelings or thoughts based on an empathic process and response should be on behalf of the person with whom one empathizes.

When empathy is transformed into an engaging action, i.e. *empathic action*, in order to seek the welfare of the other, it may form *solidarity* and reinforce *intersubjectivity*. However, a mature form of empathy must involve a morally-nuanced social cognition, which may direct the empathizer to moral deliberation and action. This idea of solidarity and intersubjectivity in relation to empathy is worth revisiting in later chapters when discussing the moral implications of empathy and communal empathy. For now, suffice it to say that the transformation of *empathy* as an inner response into an *empathic action* creates the space of reciprocity and "transitional space."[49] Out of this transformation, intersubjective relationships are created between empathizer(s) and the empathized, and even potentially between communities that are involved in the situation—or, even further, a new community may be formed in the empathic interaction. These empathic relationships are not unidirectional, but mutual. In other terms, empathizers can be the empathized at the same time or the other way around, as they intersubjectively interact through empathy.

At this point, I need to clarify two things regarding this notion of empathy. First of all, the intensity of empathy may vary depending on various

---

47. The concepts of mimicry, perspective-taking, imagination, and/or simulation are based on Hoffman's theory. These will be explored more later.

48. Martin Hoffman also theorizes four empathy-based affects, which will be discussed later in this chapter. Some of the empathic affects that I named here will also be explored further in detail in the final chapter of this book.

49. This term is coined by Donald W. Winnicott, a pediatrician and psychoanalyst. I will revisit this term in later chapters. For further exploration, see Winnicott, *Playing and Reality*.

factors such as the psychological and physical distance, semblance between observers and the others, the nature of the relationship between them, and so on. At any rate, however, being genuinely empathetic[50] cannot be against another's well-being since the subject holds emotions as congruent with those of the other as possible. Secondly, empathy based on this description does not necessarily represent that being empathic is being moral based on a two-fold requirement. First, this does not necessarily mean that to be empathetic leads the observers to actualizing empathy into any tangible actions.[51] Second, even if there is a sequential action out of empathy, there is no guarantee that the empathic motivation to help the other is necessarily moral. For example, a mother of a rapist who knows his past stories will likely empathize with her child in wanting to avoid any social accountability. She might even try to cover up evidence to avoid his legal punishment. Also, when a wife of a pastor from a very conservative denomination finds out that her husband has been sexually harassing women congregants, she might think of the scripture that demands wives to submit themselves to their husbands,[52] and feel sympathetic for her husband with whom her loyalty resides. Then, she may be committed to advocating for her husband rather than seeking justice, caring for the victims.

However, when a *mature* form of empathy meets with morally-nuanced social cognition through either direct or indirect exposure to the narrative of victims-survivors of injustice, empathy may transform into a very powerful moral motivation and conduct. As Nancy Eisenberg states, empathy can be a powerful "mediator or contributor to positive human interaction and altruistic behavior."[53] *Mature* empathy may lead the mother of the rapist to recognize the victim-survivor's suffering hence empathize

---

50. Genuine empathy here means the definition of empathy that I made earlier. The opposite type of empathy is pseudo-empathy. Coplan also uses the term "pseudo-empathy" in her article; however, I use this term in a different way. Pseudo-empathy in my usaage can be defined as the incongruent feeling of an observer whose intention is against the well-being of the other. A typical example of this is a torturer or a sadist who feels and knows how the victim feels but does not seek to relieve the victim's distress. Another example is the manipulated form of empathy, which the victim-survivors of sexual violence is forced to have. This will be explored more in chapter 2 and 3. For Coplan's use of pseudo-empathy, see Coplan "Understanding Empathy," 3–18.

51. Possible actions out of empathy could be canceled out for a range of reasons. This will be explored more in the following section. One of the typical reasons that Hoffman argues is "egoistic drift." See Hoffman, *Empathy and Moral Development*, 54–59.

52. Col 3:18.

53. Eisenberg and Strayer, *Empathy*, ix.

with her while she still empathizes with her rapist son. Then, she may take a morally nuanced action for the sake of the victim-survivor, i.e. just caring, as well as her son as her action also carries out a caring justice for him. When the wife of the pastor sees her church members suffering in the aftermath of sexual harassment, she might cognitively struggle with what she needs to do. Mature empathy then can remind her of the second commandment in the bible "You shall love your neighbor as yourself"[54] or "weep with those who weep."[55] When her empathic development is mature enough, her moral sight may be recovered, helping her to choose to stand with the victim-survivors. She then refuses her initial biased empathic response toward her significant other, i.e. her husband, practicing mature empathy for her husband in a form of caring *justice* and hopefully accountability.[56]

Understanding Significant Concepts in the Scholarship of Empathy

We have explored the definitions of empathy in the current scholarship and I have suggested my own. Empathy might seem to be a confusing concept at times due to its wide range of involved disciplines and the origin of the term, i.e., "sympathy." While some think that definitions of empathy need to be more precise and narrower such as Amy Coplan,[57] I have agreed with the broader definitions of empathy, which integratively involve other emotions such as sympathy, empathic anger, compassion, and so on; for emotions cannot be clearly distinguished from one another because of their complex nature. As I stated earlier, I understand empathy as *an observer's or observers'—as a community—cognitive and affective inner process and response to another or others in various negative and positive circumstances, which leads the observer(s) to feel congruent and oftentimes matching feelings with the other(s) through mimicry, perspective-taking, imagination, and/or simulation.* In this vein, empathy has the potential to ignite socially significant emotions against violence and injustice. At minimum, empathy is worth our time to explore as it can provide powerful moral motivation for prosocial behavior and justice-seeking movements. I intend to examine and develop the ways in which empathy and empathic moral conduct are

54. Mark 12:31.
55. Rom 12:15.
56. See Luke 4:18.
57. Coplan, "Understanding Empathy," 5.

realized in society. This idea will be gradually studied through the case of communal empathy in response to victim-survivors of sexual violence in chapter 3. Now I turn to three significant concepts in the scholarship of empathy, that are useful for developing communal empathy—mimicry, emotional contagion, perspective-taking. After examining the theoretical concepts and their implications, I will look into Martin Hoffman's theory that is relevant to the main concern of this book.

Mimicry

The first significant concept is mimicry. Hoffman theorizes mimicry, which leads to emotional contagion, as a significant human asset for developing mature empathy. As he draws on the theory of mimicry and feedback-hypothesis, he concludes that it is safe to say that there is the imitation-(afferent) feedback sequence. This means that mimicry as an empathy-arousing mechanism has two steps that are imitation and afferent feedback.

Afferent feedback is reactive "afferent neural pathways" to the cues that arouse certain emotions.[58] According to Hoffman, mimicry is "hardwired" with the nervous system, which has two significant implications: First, it gives "a quick-acting mechanism" which enables babies to empathize with another person with no previously experienced emotion. This is an involuntary and universal affective ability of human development. Second, mimicry is the only empathy-arousing mechanism that *guarantees* the affect match between the observer and the other at least in face-to-face circumstances. Drawing on research done by psychologists such as Janet Beavin Bavelas, Hoffman summarizes and carefully suggests that mimicry can be a powerful human asset for generating solidarity and prosocial act:

> [M]imicry is a communicative act, conveying a rapid and precise nonverbal message to another person. Specifically, they argue that people are communicating solidarity and involvement ("I am with you" or "I am like you") when they mimic . . . If Bavelas et al. are right, then mimicry may not just be another mechanism of empathic arousal that predisposes people to help others, but it may also be *a direct means of giving support and comfort to others*. That is, mimicry-based empathy may not only be a prosocial motive but also a prosocial act.[59]

---

58. Hoffman, *Empathy and Moral Development*, 41.
59. Hoffman, *Empathy and Moral Development*, 44–45; italics added.

I consider mimicry as *a crude* but powerful form of empathy. However, mimicry might be able to develop into an integrative mature form of empathy with the aid of cognitive empathy in the later developmental stage, which holds a significant moral implication for social activism. The subconsciously communicative and interactive aspect of empathy will be revisited in later chapters.

Emotional Contagion

The next significant concept is emotional contagion. Jean Decety and Andrew N. Meltzoff define emotional contagion as "the tendency to rapidly mimic and synchronize facial expressions, vocalizations, postures and movements with those of another person and, consequently, converge emotionally with the other" [italics added].[60] To simply put it, emotional contagion is others' emotional state being contagious to yours. Without awareness, you experience the involuntary transference of the matching emotions of others by observing or even by hearing the expression of the other's varied emotions such as joy, anger, sadness, disgust, and so on. The typical example of emotional contagion is that a newborn baby starts crying as an involuntary response to the sound of another baby's crying while not being responsive as much to a white noise or recorded crying sounds from a computer.[61] This means the reactive crying is induced from the involuntary interaction with the other baby rather than the baby responding to the disturbing sound.[62] Scholars interpret this phenomenon as sharing emotional distress or a state that later develops into "empathic concern."[63]

Because of its significant social implications, emotional contagion and mimicry are very important concepts in the study of empathy, involving developmental psychology as well as neuroscience, studying mirror neurons in particular. Regarding these concepts, scholars in the field hold various opinions on whether emotional contagion and mimicry need to be included in the range of empathy. The most striking feature of emotional contagion is its non-cognitive involuntariness. When emotional contagion happens, it is not through the observer's cognitive process but

---

60. Decety and Meltzoff, "Empathy, Imitation," 68.
61. Simner, "Newborn's Response"; de Waal, *The Age of Empathy*, 74.
62. Light and Zahn-Waxler, "Nature and Forms of Empathy," 111.
63. This term is based on the work of Batson. I will examine this concept in a later section. For more, see Batson, *The Altruism Question*.

purely through automatic emotional transmission. Some scholars such as Dan Zahavi and Soren Overgaard[64] hesitate to include emotional contagion as a type of empathy because it has no cognitive basis; it lacks space for the cognitive awareness or understanding of another's position due to its involuntariness. However, a number of major scholars such as Martin Hoffman and Frans de Waal, with whom I agree, consider emotional contagion as an entry point to developing empathy or an aspect of empathy.[65] Scrutinizing the empathy-related emotions including emotional contagion and sympathy, Heidi L. Maibom also states that scholars often perceive emotional contagion as "the most basic emotional reaction to the emotions of others that is still empathic in nature."[66] She continues to draw on other scholars on the subject, stating that "[m]any think that mature empathy develops out of this basic tendency to feel what others feel,"[67] despite the fact that it might not be a mature type. Whereas she does not clearly articulate her own opinion on whether emotional contagion is a part of empathy, she emphasizes the importance of emotional contagion for social interaction, for "people who mimic one another report liking each other more."[68]

The role of emotional contagion in social relationships has been studied by many scholars. De Waal explores involuntary empathy by drawing on the experiment done by Swedish psychologist Ulf Dimberg. Dimberg found out that people who were exposed to happy face pictures on a computer screen felt better than those exposed to the angry ones.[69] Hoffman includes this type of involuntary empathy or emotional contagion as the first three modes of his description of empathic arousal, i.e. preverbal, automatic, and involuntary, which will be explored later in the chapter.[70] Emotional contagion is an important concept in reference for its role as an entry point to further developmental courses. Furthermore, its ability to amplify

---

64. Overgaard and Zahavi, "Empathy without Isomorphism," 5–6.
65. De Waal, *The Age of Empathy*; Hoffman, *Empathy and Moral Development*.
66. Maibom, *Empathy and Morality*, 4.
67. Maibom, *Empathy and Morality*, 4.
68. Maibom, *Empathy and Morality*, 4.
69. De Waal, *The Age of Empathy*, 66.

70. Additionally, scholars also study gender differences in the phenomena of emotional contagion, in which women or baby girls are more prone to have sensitivity to others' feelings. De Waal argues from an evolutionary perspective that it is probable that empathy was an evolutionary part of parental care as the mothers of every species needed to respond to their babies immediately in order to proliferate their genes. See de Waal, *The Age of Empathy*, 67.

an emotional empathic reaction may play a significant role in communal empathy. When a community sees people suffering, they may initially feel emotional contagion that might later develop into mature empathy.

Self-oriented vs. Other-oriented Perspective-taking

In addition to mimicry and emotional contagion, self-oriented and other-oriented perspective-takings are significant concepts at the core of the debate as scholars study empathy and its moral function. Perspective-taking is an ability or an action to take or "adopt"[71] another person's perspective, through which you view situations and the world, and assume the induced feelings and thoughts of others. This ability is beyond the level of an egocentric mindset like a young baby who has not developed the sense of distinction between the self and the other. Through perspective-taking, individuals use a different vantage point to see the world. Batson, Shannon Early, and Giovanni Salvarani in their article argue that perspective-taking of others when they are in need arouses empathy:

> Encounter a stranger in need and—at least sometimes—you will feel empathy. Why? The most common answer among psychologists is perspective taking: Adopting the perspective of another perceived to be in need evokes empathy for that person (see Davis, 1994; Stodand, 1969) . . . There, you adopt another person's perspective—often a significant other—to see yourself as object through the other's eyes. Here, what is perceived is not yourself; what is perceived is the other's situation.[72]

In other words, when we find someone who seems to be in need of help, or I would include experiencing anger, joy, sadness, and so on, we adopt the other's perspective, i.e. perspective-taking, to understand the situation. By doing so, we gain a new epistemological advantage to comprehend the feelings and thoughts that the other is going through. That is when and how our empathy is evoked.

Scholars mostly believe that there are two different modes of perspective-taking, i.e. *self-oriented perspective-taking* and *other-oriented perspective-taking*. Self-oriented perspective-taking is to imagine *yourself* in the other's situation and correspondingly imagine how *you* would feel

---

71. Batson et al., "Perspective Taking."
72. Batson et al., "Perspective Taking."

in that situation. Other-oriented perspective-taking is to imagine yourself *being the other* and, consequently, imagine how the other would feel in that situation through their frame. Let us consider the following hypothetical scenario: Linda who has a husband and a big family with economic privilege is a friend to Jinhee. Unlike Linda, Jinhee, a 1.5-generation immigrant Korean American in the US, lost both her parents at the age of seventeen and is a single mom to her seventeen-year-old daughter without any other family members in the US. Jinhee just found out that she has inoperable stage-four cancer. With a self-oriented perspective-taking, Linda who is a different person with a different background than Jinhee would start simulating in her mind how it would be *for herself* to find out that she had an inoperable cancer. With an other-oriented perspective-taking, on the contrary, Linda imagines herself *being Jinhee*, who lost both her parents at the same age as her daughter, and simulates how *Jinhee* would feel as she found out that she was dying and her daughter would be left alone soon like she was. The intensity and the types of feelings and thoughts induced from the other-oriented perspective-taking would be different from the self-oriented. Other-oriented perspective-taking requires much more cognitive effort and a mature state of psychological development. Based on empirical research, Amy Coplan also states that other-oriented perspective-taking needs "greater mental flexibility and emotional regulation and often has different effects than self-oriented perspective-taking."[73]

    Scholars hold varied perspectives on the relation of the two forms of perspective-taking to the nature and concept of empathy. Each of these has its limits and strengths in relation to genuine or mature empathy. However, self-oriented perspective-taking is at the core of disagreements in relation to empathy. It has mostly three risks for contributing to genuine empathy.[74] The first is wrongful assumptions. According to Coplan, self-oriented perspective-taking as our "default mode of mentalizing"[75] is engaged with psychological phenomena such as "errors in prediction, misattributions, and personal distress."[76] We tend to assume too much similarity with the other, the "default mode of mentalizing" leads us to a self-centered bias or "egocentric bias" as Coplan calls it.[77] Thus, she holds a pessimistic view on

---

73. Coplan, "Understanding Empathy," 10.
74. For its definition, see n50 above.
75. Coplan, "Understanding Empathy," 10.
76. Coplan, "Understanding Empathy," 10.
77. Coplan, "Understanding Empathy," 10.

self-oriented perspective-taking in order to form genuine empathy. This bias leads to assumptions that the other would have the same or similar feelings, thoughts, and interpretations on the situation that may not be true.[78] Self-oriented perspective-taking is also related to the ability of self-other differentiation. Failing in the self-other differentiation can cause an enmeshed relationship between the self and the other, which causes empathic over-arousal.

The second limit is empathic over-arousal or personal distress. Self-oriented perspective-taking also may cause unintended personal distress. Because of the self-identifying process of perspective-taking, stress, pain, and emotions may come out of the process. Such a process can remind the observer of their own relevant experiences in the past that likely results in causing empathic over-arousal. In this state, empathic distress may transform into personal distress.[79]

The third is experiential limits. Self-oriented perspective-taking also has experiential limits. One can only have a limited overlapping range of related experiences with another person in order to put the self in another's situation. When the experience is out of the observer's experiential range, it is even harder for the observer to understand the other's situation from the other's perspective. At a socio-economic level, this limitation implies that those from socio-economically privileged groups have epistemological limits of empathy to understanding certain social issues to which they tend to be less vulnerable due to the systemic protection of their entitled group. Coplan even criticizes empathy based on self-oriented perspective-taking as a type of "pseudo-empathy,"[80] unless it involves other-oriented perspective-taking.[81]

---

78. Coplan, "Understanding Empathy," 12.

79. For more information, see Maibom, *Empathy and Morality*, 243–45; Coplan, "Understanding Empathy," 15–17; Hoffman, *Empathy and Moral Development*, 55–56, 63. Empathic overarousal will be discussed later in this chapter.

80. Coplan, "Understanding Empathy," 12.

81. There are, however, different evaluations on self-oriented perspective-taking. Hoffman introduces the experimental result which shows that empathy aroused by self-oriented perspective-taking is much more intense than other-oriented perspective-taking. This implies that strong prosocial motivation can be made out of self-oriented perspective-taking to help another. On the other hand, if the intensity of empathy is too strong, i.e., empathic overarousal, empathic distress may lead the observer to avoid the confrontation caused by another's distress. See Hoffman, *Empathy and Moral Development*, 55.

Contrary to self-oriented perspective-taking, other-oriented perspective-taking tends to be considered a more mature mental activity which may generate a mature level of empathy or empathic concern. Since it simulates the others' feelings and thoughts in their perspective, the result from the simulation can be more accurate. However, other-oriented perspective-taking requires information about the other. This aspect leads to a tendency to empathize more with similar or significant others. Other-oriented perspective-taking is also less likely to cause empathic over-arousal or intense personal distress, for the self can keep the psychological distance from the other as the observer tries to simulate the situation from the other's perspective rather than identifying oneself with the other in the simulation process.

Each type of perspective-taking has benefits and weaknesses for understanding other people's positions and having congruent reactive feelings for the other. Self-oriented perspective-taking has many risks such as enmeshment with the other, inaccurate affective and cognitive assessment, and possible wrongful reactions based on the inaccurate information. This inaccurate assumption in the process of self-oriented perspective-taking can generate misguided empathy since inaccurate assumptions based on people's unprobed—or even probed—ideas and beliefs such as racial and xenophobic bias may lead the empathizers to inaccurately understand certain situations.

However, as Hoffman claims, in order for the observer to properly use other-oriented perspective-taking, they need to have more information about another's past and future, the integrative life circumstance, than to use self-oriented perspective-taking.[82] Other-oriented perspective-taking, in this vein, requires much more information on the life experiences of the other than self-oriented perspective-taking. Without either self- or other-oriented perspective-taking, our empathic capacity will be far more limited than it is supposed to be, based on which Hoffman and Oxley suggest *dual perspective-taking*.[83] This concept will be useful to examine cases of communal empathy and how people come to build an empathic bond and engage with social activism for the example in the case of digital activism on behalf of sexual violence victim-survivors who are total strangers. In addition to these three forms of perspective-taking, I add *interdimensional*

---

82. Hoffman, *Empathy and Moral Development*, 54–58.

83. Oxley, *The Moral Dimensions of Empathy*, 22; Hoffman, *Empathy and Moral Development*, 58.

perspective-taking as a more mature form of perspective-taking in chapter 2 when I discuss features of mature empathy.

I have examined three important concepts, i.e., mimicry, emotional contagion and perspective-taking; and related debates in the field. This exploration will provide a useful lens to examine digital social activism for sexual violence victim-survivors in faith communities in order to witness how empathy plays out in communal responses. Now, I will turn to the work of Martin Hoffman to provide the theoretical foundation on empathy and its moral implication. In his theory of empathy, he shows the psychologically related emotions that motivate people to take certain actions as they engage with another which is applicable and useful as I construct my concept of mature communal empathy.

Martin Hoffman's Theory of Empathy in Moral Developmental Psychology

Developmental psychologist Martin L. Hoffman has been acknowledged as the most constructive theorist related to empathy. His account contributes the best understanding of the prosocial nature of empathy concerning morality, which includes his bystander model. His basic idea on empathy is that empathic distress aroused from five different modes generates empathic guilt and anger, sympathy, and the feeling of injustice, which may turn into moral motivation. Empathy and its related feelings, however, may or may not transform into actual moral actions. The transformation requires a proper course of empathic development with the help of cognitive interpretation and intervention and, as a result, sympathetic distress. In this section, Martin Hoffman's theory of empathy in regards to morality will be explored as a cornerstone of building communal empathy for social justice.

Five Modes of Empathic Arousal

Hoffman theorizes five distinctive modes from which empathy is aroused. The first three modes are identified as primitive modes of empathic arousal. They are mimicry, classical conditioning, and direct association. These three modes are automatic and involuntary. In other words, the reactive feelings aroused by these modes are not cognitively or knowingly generated. Each mode is used to arouse empathy depending on the types of stimuli, cognitive and perceptual involvement, and the types of previous experiences of the person. For example, if the only stimulus is a direct cue such as the other's voice, face, or body posture, empathy is aroused *through* mimicry, described above.[84]

If the only distress cues are situational, they are picked up through classical conditioning or direct association for empathic arousal. For example, Hoffman illustrates, when a mother is distressed and her body shows the signs of stress such as trembling, stiffness etc., the baby who is being held by the mother becomes distressed by association.[85] It is the same process from a positive perspective when the mother is happy with a smiling face, then the baby may also empathetically feel similarly.[86] Classical conditioning is important because this is applicable not just to the mother and the child but anyone in general. Moreover, this accompanies a certain degree of affect match—not to the full degree though; the full match happens only in mimicry as a direct response to the other's facial, vocal, and posture expression. Conditioning can be construed as a response to the other's situation.

Direct Association is a variant form out of the conditioning model. Direct association occurs when the cues from the other evokes the previous memory of experiences and feelings in the observer which arouse the feelings in the observer that fit the other's situation. Direct association in a child can occur when they see another child crying due to separation from the parent. The observing child, as a result, cries because of their own similar, past experience. The difference between conditioning and direct association is that the latter does *not* need the observer to have the same past experience of distress. It *only requires* that the observer has undergone *pain and distress in the past that can be evoked by the cues* from the other or their situation.

This mode of direct association has a very significant implication for moral use of empathy as it can be used to build solidarity based on the *shared* pain and emotions that humankind holds rather than on shared

---

84. The concept of mimicry is originally introduced by Lipps as he used it in the term "objective motor mimicry," which later is developed by Hoffman. Mimicry comes into action as the observer (1) automatically imitates another's expression such as facial expression, voice, and posture; and (2) those changes in the observer's face, voice, and posture trigger the "afferent feedback" in the observer. This generates the change of feelings accordingly in him/her and, hence, occurred the affect match between him/her and the other See Hoffman, *Empathy and Moral Development*, 37–45. As it is explained earlier with the related concept, emotional contagion, mimicry is seen in infant's reactive crying to the direct sound of another infant's cry on site.

85. Hoffman, *Empathy and Moral Development*, 45–47.

86. Hoffman, *Empathy and Moral Development*, 45–47.

events and *peculiar conditions* of life. This means that it is possible to build communal empathy among people regardless of their background, class, gender, race, and so on; suffering and pain are *the universal language of humankind* to varying degrees. Direct association can be applied to diverse empathic responses in a range of stressful experiences.[87]

Hoffman argues that these three primitive modes of empathic arousal are characterized by being preverbal, automatic, involuntary, fast-acting, and assisted by afferent feedback to various degrees. Thus, they have significant implications for empathic development and arousal. First of all, mimicry is particularly significant for infants since it produces the full affect match between the observer and the other even if the feelings that the observer has were not previously experienced. Second, empathic development may be facilitated by repeated empathic distress arousal that coincides with another's distress. This co-occurring emotional state between the observer and another is self-reinforcing through repeated experiences of empathic distress, and then relief as the observer takes action to improve another's welfare. This relief or empathic helping behavior is especially related to positive conditioning. Empathic relief can be experienced in the observer as she sees a smile in another's face as an expression of relief or appreciation of the observer's help. Third, these three modes are automatic and a quick-acting mechanisms that can encompass experiences across all life stages including infancy, childhood, and adulthood in order for individuals empathize with others.

If the observer is only exposed to a verbal expression of another's distress such as a written description of the distress, empathy is aroused through the other two modes of empathic arousal that are *verbal mediation* (or "mediated association") and *role-taking*.[88] These modes can synergize with the three primitive modes mentioned above when paired with immediate cues such as vocal, facial, and posture expressions. This allows the observer to empathically engage with the other in a more integrated manner.

According to Hoffman, *language* is the bridge between the other and the observer in verbal mediation, the fourth mode of empathic arousal. More precisely speaking, it is the *"semantic meanings"* that are "encoded"

---

87. Hoffman's theory of afferent feedback as component of mimicry, conditioning, and direct association is built based on the idea that all humans share (1) common experiences of distress (2) similar process for distress-relevant information due to the similar structure of humankind and (3) similar feelings about similar stressful situations. Hoffman, *Empathy and Moral Development*, 45–47.

88. Hoffman, *Empathy and Moral Development*, 49–59.

by the other.[89] The observer imagines another's feeling through identifying and categorizing the words, and then associating them with the observer's own experiences and existing conceptions of the words. Since this mode involves a decoding step, Hoffman states that the original semantic meanings might be lapsed or misled in the process. This error will likely be corrected if the other is on site, and thus provides the observer with immediate cues such as facial, vocal, and posture expressions. If the person is not on site, the observer's *knowledge* of the person helps to form a more congruent empathic response.

This fourth mode has some distinctive features compared to the primitive modes. First of all, the decoding process demands more of a *mental endeavor* to achieve empathic arousal. Secondly, it retains psychological distance between the observer and another because of the indirect cues, i.e., language. Overall, the fourth mode of empathic arousal has significant implications for the moral use of empathy. It signifies that direct and immediate cues from the other have a much stronger and more intense impact on empathic arousal than when only indirect verbal cues are available because direct cues are more "vivid" and "salient."[90] Second, when it comes to verbal mediation, a more intense mental endeavor is demanded of the observer in order to be empathetic. Third, the use of *imagery cues* facilitates association between the *observer's previous experiences* and the other's situational and affectionate state.[91]

The last mode of arousal is *role-taking*. I understand role-taking as Hoffman's term for perspective-taking, which was previously mentioned.[92] As I explained, in the process of self-focus role-taking, i.e., self-oriented perspective-taking, the intense and direct affect connection between another's current distress and the observer's past experiences creates vulnerability in the observer. This may expose the observer to overwhelming and

---

89. The observer "decodes" the message by reversing the sequence of the encode. Hoffman, *Empathy and Moral Development*, 49–52.

90. Hoffman, *Empathy and Moral Development*, 51.

91. These will be further engaged or applied in later chapters when we discuss the moral use of empathy and social activism in online social media settings.

92. As I explained earlier about perspective-taking, Hoffman makes important points that self-focus role-taking tends to generate more intense empathic arousal but less sustainable empathic response to another's distress than other-focus role-taking. It is because imagining the observer in another's position reminds the observers of their own associated struggles in the past, or, in Hoffman's terms, "observer's own need system." Hoffman, *Empathy and Moral Development*, 56.

immersive pain generated by their memories, severing the empathic connection with and focus on the other. Hoffman calls this phenomenon "egoistic drift."[93] Because of this vulnerability, an empathic response is likely to fade away and Hoffman no longer considers it empathy, even though the affect was triggered by another's situation of distress.[94] Hoffman suggests "combination" role-taking that brings together the intensity of the empathic emotion and a stable empathic response to the other, makes for a very powerful motivational source.[95]

I have explored Hoffman's five modes of empathic arousal which include mimicry, classical conditioning, direct association, verbal mediation (or "mediated association"), and role-taking. Each mode has its own features. When distress cues are direct and strong, empathic arousal may be fast and intense. When the cues are indirect such as verbal, the observer needs to rely on a mental endeavor by employing the semantic process. Through this process, the observer uses her own previous experience to arouse empathy. When empathic distress is overwhelming through role-taking, egoistic drift may occur. In that case, the observer may sever the empathic relationship with the other in order to avoid personal distress. All of the features of each mode have significance for the relationship between empathy and morality. Now, I turn to Hoffman's four empathy-based moral affects, which are generated as empathic reactions.

Four Empathy-Based Moral Affects

Hoffman's theory of empathic moral affect provides a profound theoretical basis for empathy as moral motivation and action. Specifically, as communal empathy involves varied social emotions such as anger, guilt, sympathy, just to mention a few, looking into empathy-based moral affects significantly contributes to the articulation of mature communal empathy. In specific, the four empathy-based emotions are applicable to analyzing empathy when actualized in communal and social justice cases. They are: sympathetic distress, empathic anger, empathy-based feeling of injustice, and empathy-based guilt. The observer's empathic distress transforms into these four affects based on the attribution that the observer makes about the cause of

---

93. Hoffman, *Empathy and Moral Development*, 56.
94. Hoffman, *Empathy and Moral Development*, 56–57.
95. This aspect of role-taking is also relevant to empathic over-arousal as a limitation of empathy for morality, which will be examined later in depth.

events in which the other experiences distress. Hoffman explains that depending on the type of attribution, the empathic distress of observers can be reduced, transformed, or neutralized into empathic moral affects.[96]

The first empathy-based moral affect is sympathetic distress. I briefly explored the difference between sympathy and empathy earlier. To simply put it, for Hoffman, sympathetic distress is a feeling of compassion.[97] Hoffman states an example of empathic/sympathetic distress: "I feel so much of your pain. It hurts me so much to see this happen to you."[98] In this "dual distress,"[99] an observer may help people to reduce their own distress because they feel concerned and sorry for the other. He argues that the element of sympathetic distress is children's "first truly prosocial motive."[100] An observer's empathic distress, however, may shift from empathic distress to sympathetic distress when the event is caused by a natural disaster or any event that is uncontrollable, and hence, beyond the observer's ability to help the other. This transformation also occurs when the cause of the event is unclear.

Empathic anger is the second empathy-based moral affect. When another's pain is caused by someone else, the attention of the observer may be redirected from the victim to the offender and generate empathic anger at the offender. The observer shares vicarious—sympathetic and/or empathic—feelings related to the attack with the victim-survivor. Either of these two affective states, empathic/sympathetic distress and empathic anger, may be alternatingly in play, or empathic anger may completely take over. Any change in information related to personal understandings of the cause and dynamics of the event, however, may result in decreasing empathic anger and distress. For instance, the observer later learns that the current offender was a victim attacked previously by the current victim. In that case, empathic/sympathetic affect and anger may be reduced or diverted from

---

96. Hoffman, *Empathy and Moral Development*, 93–94.

97. When children develop the self-other differentiation, they move from egocentric to quasi-egocentric empathy. In this developmental advance, children attain "a qualitative transformation of empathic into sympathetic distress" (Hoffman, *Empathy and Moral Development,* 88). According to Hoffman, in the final three developmental stages—quasi-egoistic, veridical, beyond the situation—the empathic distress always involves the element of sympathetic distress (Hoffman, *Empathy and Moral Development*, 89–90). I explore the developmental stages of empathic distress in the following section.

98. Hoffman, *Empathy and Moral Development*, 56.

99. Hoffman, *Empathy and Moral Development*, 56.

100. Hoffman, *Empathy and Moral Development*, 88.

the current offender to the other. Hoffman regrets that the domain of morality has neglected the value of empathic anger. He depicts empathic anger as "the guardian of justice," drawing on John Stuart Mill's statement.[101] A similar negligence exists in Christian traditions. For example, Christian ethicist Beverly Wildung Harrison shares similar concerns as Hoffman.[102] She suggest that Christian traditions downplay or even consider anger a sin without distinguishing how empathic anger can be a source for moral motivation or justice-seeking. I investigate this further in chapter 4.

According to Hoffman, there are two types of empathic anger: the first type is when the other *is* angry and the observer picks up the same feeling through the mechanisms of empathic arousal. The second shows partial discrepancy in the affect between the observer and the other. The observer may feel angry toward the offender, when the other does not feel angry but is in despair, pain, distress, and/or sadness. Hoffman identifies this second type as "an empathic duality."[103] In an empathic duality, the affect has both "an empathic-distress-for-victim component" and "empathy-based anger-at-aggressor component."[104] In this case, the observer's empathic anger at the abuser may help the victim-survivor to release "direct anger" by being reassured and validated by the empathizer's expression of empathic anger that reinforces the victim's right to be angry.

Hoffman argues that empathic anger has this "secondary prosocial motive function of empathic anger—secondary and subtle, but nevertheless prosocial."[105] Hoffman points out, however, that when aggressive behavior out of anger comes into play, it is oftentimes hard to distinguish between direct anger and empathic anger. Yet, a non-violent reaction is a distinctive manifestation of empathic anger. Hoffman brings up a case in which a bystander at a subway station held an attacker, who pushed someone onto the track, captive until police arrived. This does not involve any aggressive behavior but still expresses empathic anger toward the offender.

Empathic anger, however, does not require a particular abuser. When it comes to problematic cases in which one cannot identify a particular responsible person for the problem, one may still feel empathic anger. For example, social structural injustices such as extreme poverty, civil war, and

---

101. Hoffman, *Empathy and Moral Development*, 96.
102. Harrison, "The Power of Anger," 41–57.
103. Hoffman, *Empathy and Moral Development*, 98.
104. Hoffman, *Empathy and Moral Development*, 98.
105. Hoffman, *Empathy and Moral Development*, 99.

maltreatment of refugees continue, and politicians do not directly respond. One may feel empathic anger toward the politicians and be sympathetic at those dying from starvation. Another example can be found in Christian contexts. Some Christians may feel empathic anger towards Christian indoctrination by leaders who either neglect women's equality or reinforce practices of women congregants being told to be submissive to men. Empathic anger, then, might provoke activism to disrupt the unequal gendered culture in the Christian community.

This feature of empathic anger endows significant moral connotation in regards to empathy and its communal use for social justice. Empathic anger with or without a culprit can be a powerful emotion that may create dynamic moral motives of social justice activism. Employing John Stuart Mill's statement and a letter to New York Times, Hoffman signals the importance of empathic anger for justice movements: "Justice requires empathic anger."[106] Then, might we robustly say communal and social justice demands communal empathic anger to create communal social change?

The third empathy-based moral affect is *bystander guilt over inaction*. Empathic guilt may occur when an observer who notices others in need of help does not engage in a helpful action due to their egoistic motives competing with their empathic response. According to Hoffman, fear and avoiding involvement are the two primary examples of egoistic motives. When bystanders are scared of getting involved in a tragic situation or, in retrospect, feel they did not do enough, their empathic distress turns into a feeling of guilt.

Then, how does "guilt over inaction" transform into moral action? Hoffman carefully suggests that innocent bystanders' guilt may work as a prosocial motive. He maintains that people take moral actions by anticipating the fear of guilt that they may face in the future if they do not help others in distress. As a result, they take part in action in order to avoid *guilt over inaction*. This anticipation may be more likely to happen if one experienced guilt in the past; Hoffman calls this "anticipatory guilt over inaction."[107] Hoffman states:

> [T]he guilt that bystanders feel over hesitating, over failing in their efforts to help, and over not preventing the event in the first place may add to their motivation to help in similar situations in the

---

106. Hoffman, *Empathy and Moral Development*, 101.
107. Hoffman, *Empathy and Moral Development*, 105.

future. To this extent, guilt is self-reinforcing and contributes to the further "learning" of guilt as a prosocial motive.[108]

Empathy-based guilt is "cognitively demanding,"[109] since this process requires observers to analyze and evaluate the past, current, and future events for the sake of others' wellbeing.[110] Empathy-based guilt may function not only as a prosocial motive but also as a powerful *learning* emotion for moral deliberation. This aspect will be applied to what I describe as pedagogy for social cognition as I further develop the notion of mature communal empathy that is realized in a morally mature society.

One of the core questions that I pose in this book is what redirects an empathy-based affective and cognitive *reaction* to *both* near-and-dear *and* distant others in distress *towards* taking moral *action*. When empathy remains as a mere emotional and cognitive reaction to others' distress, the moral implication and significance is very limited. If, however, we can turn an empathic inner response to empathic moral action, empathy has limitless potential for moral deliberation and action for humanity. If Hoffman's claim is right, empathy-based guilt holds a powerful positive pressure and impact on the moral decision-making process and action related to future events. Thus, anticipatory future consequences affect current moral decisions; and a past decision impacts future moral deliberation and action. However, proactive responses do not reflect the cases in which, by blaming a victim, people deflect their emotions to avoid intense empathic distress and guilt over inaction. By doing this, they keep their psychological distance from the victim. Hence, they avoid intense personal distress such as guilt and empathic over-arousal.

The last empathy-based moral affect is the empathic feeling of injustice. Hoffman's empathic feeling of injustice directly relates to philosophical justice principles. Observers may have an empathic feeling of injustice when they think the other does not deserve to suffer based on the person's characteristics and/or deeds. The incongruity between another's deeds

---

108. Hoffman, *Empathy and Moral Development*, 104.

109. Hoffman, *Empathy and Moral Development*, 105.

110. Emergency situations, however, proceed with different processes. Because an immediate response is needed in an emergency, there is no time to process cognitive reflection and anticipatory guilt.

and what she[111] experiences is called "nonreciprocity."[112] Hoffman further explains that empathic or sympathetic distress may be transformed into an empathic feeling of injustice when the observer finds "the obvious lack of reciprocity between character and outcome."[113] An empathic feeling of injustice is yet another strong motive for prosocial action.

Thus far, I have examined Martin Hoffman's theory of four empathy-based affects. Hoffman's argument concerning the four empathy-based affects and its relation to morality suggests that empathy-based emotions such as anger, sympathy, guilt, and feeling of injustice arouse multiple moral motives in various circumstances. These four significant emotions are also great resources for arousing mature communal empathy. To support a balanced view of the moral implications of empathy, we also consider how empathy is prone to biases that might affect moral judgment. Before turning to empathy's limitations, I examine Hoffman's theory at a deeper level to understand what motivates people to make care-based empathic decisions and not to remain distant bystanders. Following this, I turn to exploring the role and importance of social cognitive intervention in the empathic process.

Five Developmental Stages of Empathic Distress

Hoffman categorizes empathic distress into five stages, which include (1) *reactive newborn cry*, (2) *egocentric empathic distress*, (3) *quasi-egocentric empathic distress*, (4) *veridical empathic distress*, and (5) *empathy for another's experience beyond the immediate situation*.[114] *Reactive newborn cry* is explained earlier related to the concept of emotional contagion that it is an automatic involuntary response to another baby's cry. The following stage generally begins in the later months of the first year of life. In this stage of *egocentric empathic distress*, the infant still does not have a concrete distinction between self and the other, so that when they respond to the other's distress they feel empathic distress as their own.

In the third stage, *quasi-egocentric empathic distress*, which starts around 13–15 months, babies have the cognitive ability to differentiate

---

111. Throughout this book, I use "she/her" as a pronoun of another who possibly gets empathy, just to avoid male-centered language.

112. Hoffman, *Empathy and Moral Development*, 107.

113. Hoffman, *Empathy and Moral Development*, 108.

114. Hoffman, *Empathy and Moral Development*, 6, 63–92.

between the self and the other. Since their psychological and cognitive abilities are still developing, they tend to try to help the other as they might help themselves. Their role-taking ability is not mature enough to read or acknowledge another's situation independent of their own. To different degrees, these first three stages of empathic distress are primarily limited to the three primitive preverbal modes of empathy.

In the fourth stage, *veridical empathic distress*, which begins later in a child's second year, they come to awareness of the other's independent psychological state as different from their own. This fourth stage is important for developing *mature* empathy. First of all, according to Hoffman, unlike the two previous stages, this stage develops throughout the life course. Also, it develops all the essential factors that mature empathy requires. The child grows out of an egoistic state of the self and develops into the "reflective self," which can experience "self-reflection" and "metacognition" during empathic distress. This reflective self enables the child to employ both types of the role-taking, since they are now able to recognize that they have the "inner experience" and an "external image" which is the "other side" of the inner experience. They also realize that others have the same. The development of empathic ability usually starts from a simple object. Later they can empathize with a broader range of people, situations, and experiences. Their cognitive process also develops as they now have metacognitive ability.[115]

Lastly, Hoffman names the final stage of empathic distress as *empathy for another's experience beyond the immediate situation*. The development of this stage has significant implications with regard to care ethics, especially to empathy's important prosocial role for distant others. As empathic distress develops, one can expand the empathic capacity from immediate individuals to a group of people or to individuals who are not physically present. The scope of empathic distress is expanded. This stage of *empathic distress beyond situation* broadens the cognitive spectrum to include social structures, concepts, and groups of underrepresented people based on their political, economic, racial, gender, ethnic, and social state. In this stage, the observer may generalize empathy for an individual to the group to which the individual belongs. However, as we think about Christian communities, which will be the part of the case study in chapter 3, Christian teachings often define certain groups as sinful impeding empathic responses of the church members for these groups. Such teachings or doctrines especially

115. Hoffman, *Empathy and Moral Development*, 72–74.

founded on heteropatriarchal norms and hierarchical practices hinder Christians' empathic ability to mature to this final stage. This is clearly the case for some congregation members when they respond to sexual violence victim-survivors. Some Christian teachings suggest victim-survivors are to blame for their sexual abuse because of false gendered theologies that view women as temptresses and sexual desire as uncontrollable. This kind of impediment in Christian context sometimes makes it harder for *devout* Christians to develop their empathic ability, which is paradoxical given Jesus's teachings on compassion, like "to let the oppressed go free."[116]

Nevertheless, this feature of empathic distress signifies a crucial ethical connotation. As the observer empathizes with a certain disadvantaged group, empathic distress may motivate the observer to lean toward political ideas and social practices, which can improve the distressed situation of the group.[117] This stage of empathic distress forms the most mature type of empathy, which I will explore in depth for the development of mature communal empathy in this book.[118] Now, I move on to see how Hoffman understands the role of cognition in empathy.

The Role of Cognition in Empathy

Cognitive ability is a significant factor not only in the process of developing mature empathy, but also for empathy's contribution to justice-seeking movements as well as morality more generally. Cognition is necessary when a baby starts differentiating the other from the self, from the mode of the *preverbal empathic arousal* to *veridical empathic distress* and *empathic distress beyond the situation*. Especially, in the stage of *empathic distress beyond the situation*, the range of cognitive ability is expanded to a social cognition of underrepresented groups of people and their plight.[119] This cognitive contribution to forming mature empathy enables human beings to care about and care for those who are not physically present. Or in other terms, distant others "need not be present for empathy to be aroused in observers."[120] Hoffman emphasizes:

---

116. Luke 4:18.
117. Hoffman, *Empathy and Moral Development*, 85.
118. Hoffman, *Empathy and Moral Development*, 85.
119. Hoffman, *Empathy and Moral Development*, 91–92.
120. Hoffman, *Empathy and Moral Development*, 91.

Empathy can thus be aroused when observers imagine victims: when they read about others' misfortunes, when they discuss or argue about economic or political issues . . .

In other words, cognitive development expands the bystander model to encompass an enormous variety of situations, limited not by the other's physical presence but only by the observer's imagination.[121]

Imagination based on social and moral cognitive ability is key to expanding the moral potentials of empathy. People can have morally-nuanced empathy for individuals' and represented groups' suffering by using their imagination with social cognition. If this is how empathy is carried out in society, which I strongly believe, the critique of care ethics on the problem of parochiality may be mitigated by empathy as it provides moral and prosocial motivations beyond one's immediate situations.[122] The capacity of empathy as a provision for the motives of caring for distant others is particularly noteworthy for us to explore empathy's moral value and its contribution to justice-seeking activity. Cognitive ability featured in empathy leads humankind to go beyond limited time and space to create the potential space of solidarity with others' sufferings, holding a range of emotions. Caring based on a morally-nuanced and psychologically mature form of empathy encompasses intersectional awareness which includes gender, race, and economic and social class as such. In order to comprehensively explore the potential of empathy in moral life, I look into the alleged weaknesses of empathy for moral use and their categories. This will help us to understand the basic psychological and ethical findings on the disposition of empathy in order to construct a better understanding of the possible pitfalls and benefits of empathy's moral use.

---

121. Hoffman, *Empathy and Moral Development*, 91.

122. Feminist scholars in the ethics of care have the ethical contemplation on the caring for the cared-for who does not share the direct relationship with the one-caring, so-called the distant other. Noddings brings up the controversial argument that in certain situations, we have more caring responsibility toward the present other—who has a direct relationship with the caretaker such as mother-child—from the distant other. Also, due to the nature of care, impartial ethicists criticize that when care comes into the first moral standard, the agent would make biased moral decisions for the sake of those who are proximate. This issue of the moral responsibility of the distant other and the present other is named as the problem of parochialism in care ethics. Larrabee, *An Ethic of Care*; Noddings, *Caring*.

Alleged Weaknesses of Empathy for Morality and Their Categories

Scholars take a careful stance when employing empathy for moral purposes. For example, Martin Hoffman states that he has considered the limitations of empathy seriously, though he still concludes that empathy is one of the essential moral motivational sources for humankind:

> I have long studied empathy's limitations (Hoffman, 1984, 2000), which I consider *serious*. To begin, it should be clear from the foregoing that empathy is limited by its fragility, by its being influenced and biased in favor of one's similarity to, familiarity with and relationship to victims, and by its dependence on the salience of distress cues. [italics added][123]

Like Hoffman, most proponents of empathy come to an agreement that empathy is not a panacea for unjust social issues or moral problems. This is because there are always risks lurking in using empathy for moral purposes especially when empathy is indiscreetly used. Thus, defining the moral weaknesses of empathy has been a core debate in the field.

In this section, after a brief introduction of the weaknesses of empathy, I categorize the possible weaknesses of empathy into three categories i.e. limits, risks, and dysfunctions of empathy, and then explore what each category implies for moral life. This learning process will help us to build balanced views on the moral implications of empathy and the ways in which we maturely actualize empathy, gaining the full moral benefit from it for integratively building a just and caring society.

Many scholars from different disciplines have tried to name the possible problems of empathy. Based on its multiple, divergent claims, I categorize them into four weaknesses of empathy. Empathic over-arousal as well as empathic preferential and selective biases are the most well-known weaknesses including familiarity bias and here-and-now bias.[124] In addition, empathic inaccuracy is an alleged weakness.[125] Also, manipulation out of empathy can occur.[126] These weaknesses are aroused due to three main factors, which determine the strength and shape of empathy:[127] The first

---

123. Hoffman, "Empathy, Justice, and Social Change," 93.
124. Hoffman, *Empathy and Moral Development*, 197–217.
125. Ickes, *Empathic Accuracy*.
126. Prinz, "Is Empathy Necessary," 211–29.
127. Hoffman summarizes the factors into two i.e. the intensity of distress cue and

factor is *the intensity* and *conspicuity* of the *distress cues* from another. The second factor is *the relationship* of the observer to another. In addition to these two factors, the observer's current psychological and circumstantial state also affects the degree of empathy. These factors contribute to molding one's empathic distress, which determines the consequential response. The stronger the factors, the more intense the empathic distress. When the distress is too strong to cope with, however, "empathic over-arousal"[128] occurs. When empathic over-arousal overwhelms the observer, they could completely shut down their empathic mode. In this case, the utilization of empathy for moral action becomes obstructed.

Bias is the second alleged weakness of empathy. Empathy involves two major types of bias, that is, "here-and-now bias" or "near-and-dear bias," and "familiarity bias," which is prone to "in-group," "friendship," and "similarity bias."[129] In other words, people tend to be more empathetic and caring for those whose issues of distress are similar to one's own or who are in-group members such as family and friends. In-group membership also involves race and ethnicity as well as immigration status and other factors as we think about how bias might function in various social contexts. Empathy tends to be aroused by those who are present (here-and-now bias)—this includes hearing a particular person's stories or directly witnessing a person or other people in need. These factors could limit or bias the intensity of empathic motivation and moral action. In addition, empathic inaccuracy is another alleged weakness.[130] When someone empathizes with another, the accuracy the observer can infer of the state of another's thoughts and feelings is questionable. In the case of an inaccuracy, the empathic response might be misguided.

However, I agree with Hoffman that each of these claimed limitations are "not fatal ones."[131] Alternatively, these vulnerabilities could promote people's prosocial motivations and moral actions. For example, *empathic*

---

the relationship between the observer and the other. However, he often notes that the observer's own situation also impacts on to what degree the observer empathizes with the other. See Hoffman, *Empathy and Moral Development*, 197–217.

128. Hoffman defines "empathic over-arousal" as "an involuntary process that occurs when an observer's empathic distress becomes so painful and intolerable that it is transformed into an intense feeling of personal distress, which may move the person out of the empathic mode entirely." Hoffman, *Empathy and Moral Development*, 198.

129. Hoffman, *Empathy and Moral Development*, 206–13.

130. See Ickes, *Empathic Accuracy*.

131. Hoffman, *Empathy and Moral Development*, 213.

over-arousal often cues people to psychological and social limits. Hoffman puts it this way: "if we empathized and tried to help everyone in distress . . . society might quickly come to a halt."[132] In addition, the state of empathic over-arousal could motivate the observer because they may try hard to relieve their empathic distress in particular situations rather than to turn their attention away from the scene.[133] Also, a person's empathy is mostly accurate *enough* to help others in distress. *Familiarity bias* could also help the observer to employ perspective-taking by applying the feelings from their own context to a complete stranger, resulting in imagining how the other's family would feel about the current unfortunate situation. In this case, familiarity bias rather facilitates empathetic moral intervention rather than frustrating it. *Here-and-now bias* can also be carried out differently depending on various circumstances. Here-and-now bias is not an absolute route to empathic arousal. It rather is a *possible* bias, which is not always the set outcome. In contemporary society, media is one of the variations that disrupt the here-and-now bias; media can draw our attention to a particular story or a person who is not usually physically present.[134] In sum, the alleged weaknesses of empathy are neither virulent nor an absolute problem; rather, under various situations, weaknesses often turn into strengths for moral motivation and action.

Despite the debate whether empathy is helpful or harmful for morality, deciding empathy's usefulness for morality in principle is not effective since empathy *per se* has both positive *and* negative impacts on morality. For a constructive discussion, I suggest that we focus on finding out *when* the manifestation of empathy plays positive or negative roles, and *how* we overcome limits, avoid potential risks, and prevent dysfunctions of empathy. This way, we can utilize empathy as a valuable human faculty for the sake of the vulnerable and oppressed in the society.

Depending on the *types of empathy* employed in a situation, the course of empathic reaction is determined. In other words, relying on the type of empathy the empathizers adopt in social interactions, empathy may

---

132. Hoffman, *Empathy and Moral Development*, 214–15.

133. Hoffman takes an example that especially when the observer is taking a helping role in a relationship, empathic over-arousal makes them try even harder to solve the problem for the one in need, rather than to avoid the situation. Hoffman, *Empathy and Moral Development*, 213.

134. Hoffman explores the function of media specifically in regard to here-and-now bias, drawing on several experimental examples in detail. For more information, see Hoffman, *Empathy and Moral Development*, 209–17.

play its role as a positive human faculty for morality or as a hindrance for creating social justice. After the inspection of the categories and their moral implications, I conclude that in order to facilitate just and caring social systems, we need to promote a psychologically mature and morally nuanced empathy for just and caring communities.

In the current scholarship of empathy, the term *limitations* of empathy has referred to limits, problems, harmfulness, and risks that the manifestations of empathy could possibly hold or cause. In this light, the term *limitations* of empathy needs to be challenged, since the term can cause confusion between its limits and potential harmfulness. I categorize these *weaknesses* of empathy into three categories that are *limits*, potential *risks*, and *dysfunctions*.

The *limits* of empathy imply that empathy cannot be a cure-all for moral issues. We have to admit that there are *limits* when empathy is morally used even with a mature form of empathy. *Limits* are what we need to be *aware of* and to find a way to overcome if possible. Potential *risks*, however, imply that empathy might be an actual threat to our moral life *at times*. These risks may or may not be actualized depending on the adopted type of empathy and the involved context. *Dysfunctions* of empathy means that empathy can be abused or misused against others' will and well-being, and/or against social justice. This abused or manipulated empathy is *pseudo-empathy* because it lacks a core element of empathy, which may result in sustaining or even promoting unjust social systems.

It is important to be aware of empathy's *limits* as we utilize empathy in our everyday moral life and judgment. However, I do not believe that the limits in and of themselves are much of a threat for morality. For example, regarding the problem of empathic accuracy, we cannot accurately understand someone in extreme hunger unless we directly experience the exact same situation. There is an existing *epistemological limit* to the degree that we cannot hold completely accurate empathy for them, i.e., empathic inaccuracy. However, this does not mean that empathy cannot play a role in making a moral judgement and action. We can use our *good enough* imagination and understanding in the empathic process regarding how hard it would be to starve or watch her children starve to death, which may motivate the observers to take a moral action to relieve the distress. Even if our understanding of the suffering is not completely correct, we can be empathetic *enough* to be motivated to take moral action.

Another example of the limits of empathy, which is related to near-and-dear bias, can be found in the work of Nel Noddings[135] who claims that it is hard to care for distant others as much as we care for in-group people like our own child. We have various responsibilities and emotional attachment with people. For example, we cannot give the same attention to anonymous children on the opposite side of the globe while we watch our own kid starving. We have epistemological and emotional *limits* to empathize with those who are distant from us.

Unlike the limits of empathy, potential risks of empathy, however, might or might not be put in place. Using empathy as a sole reference to decision-making can be risky at times especially when the person is employing a form of immature empathy. I already included two earlier examples of the mother of a rapist who only empathizes with her own child and tries to hide evidence for the crime he committed; or the wife that protects her husband, a minister, who is a sexual abuser. These risks are harmful for our society, which need to be avoided by *educating* our children and community to develop a mature form of empathy. The risks include some cases of here-and-now, near-and-dear, and familiarity bias when the empathizers take actions to give benefits to those in the empathic relationship with them, e.g., significant others. And, *indiscreetly used* empathy without integrative social consciousness can result in harming innocent and distant others. However, it is highly possible to avoid these risks. What type of empathy is actualized is the important factor. If it is a morally, socio-culturally, and psychologically mature empathy, we can avoid the potential risks of immoral judgment and actions.

Critics of empathy such as Jesse Prinz, an ethicist, who argues that empathy is not necessary, not good enough, or worse, harmful for moral judgments, oversimplify the concerns.[136] Not everyone makes the same decision in the same situation based on their empathy, because the course in which empathy is manifested can be determined by the empathizer's personality, ethics, philosophy, emotional and cognitive propensity, context, education, and so on. For example, in the cases of extreme poverty or domestic abuse, not all mothers take the same actions towards their children. In extreme cases, there are some mothers who kill their children out of their immature empathy and twisted love so as to *save* their children from

---

135. Noddings, *Caring*.

136. Prinz, "Is Empathy Necessary," 211–29; Prinz, "Against Empathy"; Bloom, *Against Empathy*.

the suffering they face.[137] Filicide based on immature empathy is a horrific and rare example for the argument that empathy can be harmful for morality. In an exact same situation, some mothers might leave the abusive partner in order to save the children and be even more motivated to challenge themselves to overcome their traumatized mental state, which is extremely difficult.[138] One cannot dismiss the role of empathy based on outlier cases.

So, is empathy *per se* good or bad for our individual *and* communal morality? We cannot state in principle one way or the other because the empathic process is manifold; it really depends on the type of empathy employed, and the involved context along with many other factors such as the observer's educational background, the degree of social cognition, psychological maturity level, and so on. When she comes to a point where she makes a final moral decision through the complicated empathizing process, she is asked to determine if she would choose to help significant others over the distant others due to her personal relationship; or to help distant others because of multiple combinations of attributions of the situations. If the moral agent chooses 'what is morally right' over 'who is personally more important to her,' her empathic ability is helpful for our moral life. If it were the other way around, her immature empathic state would be harmful for society.

Meghan Masto, a feminist philosopher of psychology who holds a pro-empathy position, points out an important aspect of empathy: that empathy is *"sometimes* epistemologically necessary" for engaging right action and *"sometimes* necessary" for being motivated to take right action [italics added].[139] She further explains that empathy's moral role is more remarkable in more *nuanced* and complicated contexts such as those we face in our daily life than "homogenous action-types" such as genocide, in which it is easy to judge what is right or wrong. She states:

> What should I say to a friend who has just lost her spouse? Can I bail on my sister whom I was supposed to meet at the movies tomorrow? Is it okay to throw out my 5-year-old's artwork? . . . Should I

137. See Adams, *Mad Mothers, Bad Mothers*; Schwartz and Isser, *Endangered Children*.

138. I am not attributing the abusive environment for children to mothers here. For domestic violence and poverty, there is a range of factors in play such as social structure, social welfare system, gender inequality, women's vulnerability, racial and other intersectional factors, and so on. The example is only to show different reactive decisions using empathy. Motherhood is an extremely complicated subject to discuss.

139. Masto, "Empathy and Its Role," 74.

The Power of Mature Empathy

give up my career to take care of my terminally ill child? In many cases, what makes these decisions so difficult is that it is unclear how those involved will be affected by our choices. But empathizing with others can help us be more informed and thus, in cases in which we want to do the right thing, make it more likely that we will do the right thing.[140]

In order for us to use empathy morally in our everyday life, what we need is *mature* empathy which involves good enough accuracy, well-developed perspective-taking, and many other features, rather than completely eradicating empathy from moral discourse in a sweeping effort to avoid the potential risks. Then, questions arise as to the ways in which we distinguish mature empathy from an immature expression and develop it for promoting the common good in ways that define well-developed perspective-takings. I will investigate this question in later chapters.

The last category of the weaknesses are *dysfunctions* of empathy. The dysfunction of empathy means empathy's authentic function is hindered by unhealthy and unjust factors such as heteropatriarchal social structure, cultural taboos, psychological manipulation, and so on. As a result, the realization of empathy plays a role against the well-being of another—the core element of genuine empathy[141]—or even against the well-being of the empathizer with or without recognition. It may also sustain, induce, or even promote social injustice. The type of empathy that is adopted here is pseudo-empathy. The prototype of dysfunctional or pseudo-empathy is a manipulated one. As Prinz exemplifies,[142] one of the examples is in a trial setting when the jury empathizes with either the victim or the offender heavily according to the intensity of their distress cues. Then, the jury's judgment on the sentence might change. In this case, empathy is manipulated by distress cues and biases.

Another dysfunction of empathy can be found when an offender manipulates the involved community to empathize with him and hold position against the victims. This often happens in cases of sexual harassment perpetrated by religious leaders. As a religious leader, the abuser might argue that the younger girl was seducing him or it was his caring act that was misunderstood by her. Even farther, he might argue that his sexual desire was too strong to control. This manipulation is based on misogynistic

---

140. Masto, "Empathy and Its Role," 83.
141. For its definition, see n50 above.
142. Prinz, "Is Empathy Necessary."

stereotypes of seductive and sexualized images of women or on the myth that men's sexual desire is by nature uncontrollable. Due to his social position and power, and unjust socio-cultural belief systems, the congregation may listen to him more than to the victim-survivor. These excuses represent underlying unjust cultural, social, and legal systems, by which empathy is manipulated.

Behind these cases of dysfunctional empathy, heteropatriarchal, hierarchical social structures and cultural taboos are often the underlying factors that enable offenders to manipulate people and victims. If that is the case, we should advocate for our community to *maturely* empathize with the victim-survivors as a way of resistance against the unjust social systems, heteropatriarchally biased traditions, and pseudo-empathy. Through mature empathy, people bring in social cognition, moral principles, and developed perspective-takings of the victim-survivors in order to challenge pseudo-empathy.

I have explored three different categories of the weaknesses of empathy in this section, which include limits, potential risks, and dysfunctions of empathy. Each category has a different nature, contexts, and causes. *Limits* of empathy are induced from the human ability to empathize with another. The limits of accurately reading, understanding, and imagining another's experience are the most common examples.

Potential risks are mainly caused by the biased tendencies to lean more towards those who are in-group members, here-and-now significant and others, and respond to intense distress cues. To prevent these risks, we need to find ways to form and educate the members of society to develop mature empathy. With mature empathy, we as human beings will know the possible consequences of our empathic reactions that can impact everyone that is involved in the situation rather than focusing only on the person that one cares about. This will be explored in the following chapter.

Dysfunctions of empathy are manifested against the other's or the involved community's well-being as well as against genuine empathy's core nature and function. I call this type of empathy pseudo-empathy.[143] The most keen social awareness and attention are essential to prevent the dysfunctions of empathy, because dysfunctions of empathy occur through

---

143. There is also dysfunctional empathy that is realized at person-to-person level, the example of which is an offender at a trial setting who manipulates the jurors by expressing his own distress cues. In this case, mature empathy needs to be encouraged through an educational and social consciousness-raising process, so the observers would avoid being manipulated. See Prinz, "Is Empathy Necessary."

unhealthy socio-cultural power structures and psychological manipulation along with other unjust systems. Educating the members of society to establish a socio-ethical consciousness and intercultural perspectives on various social issues is one of the key strategies to prevent empathy from being manipulated and misused. As a result of the underlying social, institutionally unjust systems and practices, pseudo-empathy may contribute to sustaining or even promoting social injustice. We as moral agents need to stay vigilant against actualized pseudo-empathy in society and try our best to resist it, as we strive to practice social justice. These three categories help to explore the ways in which we can fully benefit from empathy as a moral resource, while avoiding or overcoming the actualization of the weaknesses of empathy in our daily moral life.

I concluded that empathy *per se* cannot be determined to be morally helpful or harmful due to its manifold factors that are put into play when empathy is employed. I emphasized that, rather than questioning whether empathy is good or bad for morality, we need to ask *when* empathy plays negative or positive roles and *how* we can avoid or overcome the weaknesses, or even, transform them into strengths. According to the nature and cause of empathy's weaknesses, I contended that we need various strategies so that empathy's prosocial and moral benefits would be maximized in our moral life, one of which is establishing mature empathy.

Conclusion

I have selectively introduced and explored significant aspects and concepts of empathy in the interdisciplinary scholarship, which will help me to conceptualize mature communal empathy. Among varied definitions of empathy, I have described empathy as *an observer's or observers'—as a community—cognitive and affective inner process and response to another or others in various negative and positive circumstances, which leads the observer(s) to feel congruent and oftentimes matching feelings with the other(s) through mimicry, perspective-taking, imagination, and/or simulation.* There are significant features of empathy that I want to stress from this definition. *First,* the aspects of genuine empathy[144] should involve *inner engagement and interaction* with the person based on the intention for the person's welfare. Empathic response should not be against the other's will or "cognitive

---

144. Refer to n50 above for its definition.

content."[145] All of the empathic responses and actions must be for the sake of the well-being and will of the other. If any cognitive and affective empathic response does not meet these conditions such as that of sadists or torturers who are aware of the other's pain but go against the well-being of the person, it is pseudo-empathy.[146] I do not consider this a form of empathy. *Second,* empathy involves a range of emotions; I called the emotions aroused out of empathy *branches of empathic affect* such as *empathic* anger, disgust, hate, sympathy, and compassion, etc. *Third,* empathy by itself does not guarantee moral action as an outcome. However, when empathy, which is an affective *and* cognitive inner response, is transformed into an action for reducing the distress of the other, this action is called empathic action. Empathic action, then, can form social solidarity. This transformation of empathy into an empathic action creates "transitional space"[147] as it builds reciprocity through intersubjective space with others, forming solidarity. *Finally,* empathy has various forms ranging from immature to mature, and genuine and pseudo-empathy along with affective and cognitive empathy. When a mature form of empathy is realized, it involves morally-nuanced social cognition and a psychologically developed structure as well as a healthy boundary between the self and others through metacognition. I will investigate the features of mature empathy in the following chapter.

In the second section, I introduced the notions of mimicry, emotional contagion, and perspective-taking. As I stated earlier, I understand mimicry as a crude but a very powerful form of empathy. It is subconsciously—or involuntarily—communicative and interactive with the other, which can be developed into a mature form through integration of cognitive empathy. Emotional contagion is a closely related concept with mimicry. When people mimic others' immediate expressions or see their happy or sad face, the emotion of the other is transmitted to the observer. This involuntary empathy shows how humankind is neurologically designed to live together with present *and* distant others. Also, emotional contagion through seeing other's facial expressions on a computer screen signifies the potentials of empathy to be aroused through digital space. For perspective-taking, I concluded that we need dual perspective-taking

---

145. Oxley, *The Moral Dimensions of Empathy,* 25.

146. See the examples of sadists and torturers in the section of "Definitions of Empathy" of this chapter.

147. As I mentioned earlier, I will explain this concept in relation to empathy in chapter 4.

for building a mature form of empathy. Dual perspective-taking can overcome the limits and strengths of self-oriented perspective-taking and other-oriented perspective-taking. In addition to dual perspective-taking, I move one step further to suggest a more developed form of perspective-taking in chapter 2, i.e., *interdimensional perspective-taking,* as one of the significant features of mature empathy. These various types of perspective-takings will be helpful when we explore communal empathy evident in digital activism such as the #MeToo Movement.

In the third section, I explored Hoffman's concepts and theory that are significant to build a theory of communal empathy. I first explored Hoffman's five modes of empathic arousal. The last two modes provide special insights for care ethics and communal empathy. In the fourth mode, verbal mediation, language is the main tool through which empathy is aroused. In this mode, the observer's previous experiences come into play, as their knowledge helps to form a more congruent empathic response to the other. When this indirect cue is combined with vivid direct cues from the other, empathy is aroused with more intense feelings and distress. The important feature of the fourth mode, role-taking, is that if the empathic distress is too overwhelming due to various factors, the observer may sever their empathic connection to the other, the phenomenon of which is called "egoistic drift." If this happens, empathic response is overruled by egoistic drift, and the affective state is no longer considered empathy. This might be one of the pitfalls of empathy when it is realized in moral deliberation and action.

I also introduced Hoffman's four empathy-based moral affects, which included sympathetic distress, empathic anger, bystander guilt over inaction, and feeling of injustice. All these emotions aroused from empathic processes can generate multiple moral motives in various circumstances. These are also great affective resources to arouse communal empathy along with other emotions such as shame and disgust.

Empathic distress develops through five stages; among them, the last two stages provide significant implications for care ethics and the realization of communal empathy in justice-seeking movements. The fourth stage, veridical empathic distress, is important due to its life-long development. Also, at this stage, the observer's self develops into the reflective self, which has self-reflection and metacognitive ability. According to Hoffman, this reflective self and metacognitive ability are the basic components of mature empathy. This fourth stage can maximize the moral power of empathy when it is combined with the final stage, empathy for another's experience beyond the immediate situation. In this final stage of development, the observer may expand empathy from an individual to the group to which the person belongs. The observer also can come up with political ideas to improve the well-being of the distressed others beyond an immediate situation. Care ethicists can apply insights from this process for the difficulties faced by limitations in caring for distant others as well as the parochiality of care ethics. This stage of empathic distress forms the most mature empathy.

In the final section, I examined possible moral weaknesses that empathy might involve by introducing a brief summary of the alleged weaknesses of empathy and their categories, which are limits, risks, and dysfunctions. By scrutinizing the possible problems and dangers of empathy as a moral reference, I tried to offer possible ways of preventing and overcoming each weakness to be actualized in our moral life.

Overall, this chapter was dedicated to presenting a comprehensive view and development of the scholarship of empathy in relation to morality, and to show the possible ways in which empathy might work for or against morality. Now, I turn to explore what kind of moral society is envisioned from a care ethics perspective. This exploration of a social imaginary is an attempt to clarify what I mean by a just and caring moral society, so we can construct a concept of mature empathy that contributes to it. After proposing the kind of a moral society that we should pursue, I will illuminate the features of mature empathy.

2

Mature Empathy and Its Moral Implications

THE SCHOLARSHIP ON EMPATHY has been presented primarily from the psychological and moral perspectives in chapter 1. Reviewing the significance and weaknesses of empathy as a source of moral motivations in human interactions, I conclude that in order to construct and promote socio-political and cultural systems for a moral society, it is important to conceptualize *mature* empathy. Rather than debating whether empathy *per se* is helpful or harmful, I suggest we focus on the moral implications of empathy's role and value in our lives as it heavily depends on *contextuality* and *the form* of applied empathy. In this chapter, I contend, when mature empathy is well established among members of society, it contributes to building *a morally mature society* that compositionally involves the visions of mature empathy, justice, and care.

Studying the possible moral implications of empathy is foundational work for three reasons in order to conceptualize communal empathy and empathy's ethical and psychological significance for justice-seeking movements. First, we can glimpse how the range of caring practices can be expanded from a parochial relational network to that of distant others by employing mature empathy. Second, studying the moral implications of empathy guides us to envision a moral society, in which mature empathy can play a significant role. Lastly, understanding empathy's moral implication underlies the way in which we can construct a notion of mature communal empathy. In this chapter, the moral implications of empathy are explored primarily from the perspectives of feminist care ethics in conversation with the moral psychology approach presented in chapter 1.

Accordingly, this chapter seeks to answer a few primary questions: Before exploring what it means to use empathy for building a moral society, what do we mean by a *moral society*? In other words, how do we envisage a moral society that we want to pursue? How do we conceptualize mature empathy in order to utilize it as a moral motivation, a reference for moral judgment, and a facilitator to transform moral thoughts into moral action? These are some primary questions to think about as I envision a moral society and explore the moral implications of empathy, especially the mature form.

My underlying intention here is not to suggest a new theoretical framework out of which abstract and definitive *principles* on moral use of empathy are offered. Rather, it is to offer possible ways to describe an *empathic thinking process,* through which we can conduct moral practices in our daily life. The way we employ empathy in our thinking process is extremely complex, intermingled with a range of experiential factors and circumstances, tailored to each different moral context, and learned knowledge and internalization of our experiences. There is no way to define if one's realization of empathy is moral or immoral. When someone attempts to give a definite answer to that, they are either too naive or too ignorant to see our intricately entangled moral contextuality and human nature. The moral questions that we are facing in our everyday life are much more nuanced than what the dominant moral theories on justice offer. Practical and real moral judgments are a very complicated process for which empathic ability is foundationally required. If it is our intention to build a moral society, we need to focus on the *complexity* that mature empathy enables us to grasp related to a range of contextual moral inquiries in our thinking process.

In order to explore the moral implications of empathy, this chapter is composed of two main sections. The first section, 'envisioning a moral society,' offers a vision of a moral society that requires a community to pursue. The moral society is *a mature society,* in which the spirits of empathy, justice, and care complement each other in a balanced way. This section draws on the discipline of feminist care ethics in order to envisage the moral society that we need to seek. For that, I first examine the normative nature of *maturity* and *mature empathy.* Then, I move on to explore the contributions of feminist care ethics to envision a moral society in which our daily life is appreciated as a moral practice. In the last subsection, drawing on feminist care ethics, I suggest why and how justice and care should complement each other, as they are needed to build a morally mature society.

The second section, 'features of mature empathy,' offers the characters of mature empathy that can contribute to the building of a mature society, which we envisioned in the first section. There are three primary features of mature empathy I creatively offer, drawing on feminist care ethics and moral psychology. I also recount a few other features that scholars in the field suggest related to mature empathy. I finish the chapter by restating the implications of mature empathy and its contributions to building a mature society, which foundationally involves the vision of empathy, justice, and care.

Envisioning a Moral Society

As a continuation of the main suggestion in the previous chapter, it is important to explore *how* we as moral agents can enhance our human faculties to attain full maturity, moral nuance, and psychological balance so as to promote social justice through perspective takings with those who have been marginalized, silenced, and invisible. Questioning whether empathy is helpful or harmful for morality is beneficial only to the extent that it allows us a space to think about the nature and the possible use of empathy in relation to morality. However, attempting to seek a fixed answer to this question is rather consuming, for empathy *per se* sometimes is or sometimes is not helpful for composing our moral life as I demonstrated earlier. Rather, it is a *mature* type of empathy that conveys moral significance to just moral actions. In this light, I contemplate the features of mature empathy, and what they imply for morality in our daily individual *and* communal life. We need to mull over two things in this section: First, how do we understand *maturity* and *mature* empathy in terms of morality? Second, what is the vision of a moral society and justice to which mature empathy can contribute?

Maturity signifies the apex of a development, which guides us in what we should seek after and defines what kind of person we should become. Thus, it has morally normative implications. Also, one's understanding of morality and a moral society impacts one's conception of what is mature and what mature empathy is. Therefore, envisioning a moral society and clarifying the meaning of justice helps us to conceptualize mature empathy which we can make use of for building a moral society that we want to pursue. To answer these questions about a moral society and the normative implication of mature empathy, I draw on the work of care ethicists such as Virginia Held, Elena Pulcini, and Carol Gilligan in this section. Particularly, Virginia Held provides fascinating work on feminist moral theory and an integrative view on care and justice. Based on the vision of a moral society, I offer the features of mature empathy in the following section.

Understanding Mature Empathy as a Normative Moral Faculty

First, how do we understand *being mature* and *mature empathy*? The word *mature* originated from the Latin word, *maturus*, which stands for being ripe or fully developed. According to the *Oxford English Dictionary*, when it comes to a person or thought, mature implies that she is "capable of a balanced judgement or response as a result of experience," and the thought is "suitably prolonged and careful," based on sufficient deliberation.[1] In this light, mature empathy can be understood as the most developed form of empathy, which is accompanied by sufficient deliberation and balanced perspectives. Roughly saying, a mature empathizer is one who can make *a balanced judgement* out of her adequate deliberation, experiences, and empathic process through her mature perspective-taking, imagination, and simulation as she interacts with another and responds accordingly for the well-being of the other as well as the community. Mature empathy should thus be something that contributes to building a moral society, enacted through an agent's balanced judgment as a moral practice. Those with mature empathy cannot promote or tolerate social injustice by any means. It will be an oxymoron to say that it was injustice done by mature empathizers. I will suggest a deeper exploration of mature empathy by proposing its features later in this chapter.

Since the word mature connotes a normative nuance, being morally and mentally mature is what we *pursue* as it implies a paramount mental state of a person. Therefore, identifying the psychologically and morally mature state of an individual implies the developmental *direction* that we are constantly seeking after. This state is what we are developing into so as to be personally, morally, socially, and communally a *better* person, a *better* moral agent. In this vein, *mature* empathy involves a normative disposition as it constantly guides us to who we *ought to* be and what we ought to do.

1. Oxford English Dictionary, Online, s.v., "mature."

Maturity, then, involves *perspectives* and *embeddedness* since it refers us to what is better and what is right in and for the society. Thus, the society or a shared notion of the common good guides us and shapes how we identify what maturity is. On the other hand, we as members of society can also construct the mature society and community as we *imagine* morality and endeavor to realize it. So, we need to ask: How do we envision a moral society that we want to pursue? What is our primary moral vision to compose a moral society? How do one's social constructions of race and gender, or one's nationality and (im)migrant/citizenship status affect our moral vision for society? How do religious communities, e.g., Christian communities, contribute to or detract from the moral vision? In this chapter, I build the framework through which I test whether the suggested moral vision is reinforced or hindered within the case studies in later chapters. These questions offer *directions* to a clearer view of the features of mature empathy. In order to explore this assertion, I need to address the theoretical background that I draw on to undergird the vision of a moral society.

Contributions from Feminist Care Ethics to the Vision of a Moral Society

Without concrete lived experience, theorizing ethics and morality is a vain endeavor, for ethics should offer the world what we ought to do, being aware of *contextuality*. Therefore, I pay tribute to the rich scholarship of care ethics for its special attention given to morality out of *the particular* as well as its integrative view on justice and care. Despite the significant emphasis on emotions and their moral value, specific discussions on empathy within the discipline are limited. Even so, they still provide essential directions for the study of empathy and its moral implication. Therefore, I first examine the contribution of care ethics to challenging dominant moral theories and develop integrative concepts of morality and moral epistemology, in which emotions are valued and human interdependency is acknowledged. Then, I turn to conceptualize a moral society and build an integrative view on justice and care.

Among a range of theories on moral and psychological development, the quarrel, beginning in 1982, between Carol Gilligan and Lawrence Kohlberg is well-known. They debate findings related to human developmental stages of morality in light of gender differences. Gilligan, however, has also been critiqued for her lack of an intersectional viewpoint and racial diversity in her experimental data, and for promoting gender essentialism in her work. Despite these critiques, she greatly contributed to the scholarship of care ethics by raising a very significant objection to the male-centered norms and research standards in the field of moral psychology. Due to Kohlberg's the proposed *different* tendencies of women's and men's morality, he considered women to be morally "either deviant or deficient" in the male dominant society.[2] According to Gilligan, women's moral vision tends to be grounded on relationships, sensitivity to others, and a caring responsibility to "alleviate the 'real and recognizable trouble' of this world."[3] Men's moral judgments are more often based on "rights and rules," whose moral context is more hypothetical and abstract. For Gilligan, women's moral language is *caring*, while men's is *justice*. "Attachment and connectedness" are the main motif for women, with "individuation and separateness" for men.[4] For women, it is the *ethic of care*, for men, the *ethic of justice*.[5]

Gilligan's groundbreaking critique of the male-dominant moral norms offers us a space to think about the need for *different* moral theories, reconceptualizing caring as a moral *practice* in our daily life as well as exploring the tension between the moral principles of justice and care. Thus, I am not arguing for gender essentialism here, for I believe what we perceive as women and men or women's and men's moralities are social constructions to a great extent.[6] Moreover, neither is it the case that all women are care- and relationship-oriented, nor that all men are individualized and abide by the principle of justice and "rights and rules." The factors are manifold that explain the root causes of why reason, politics, the public, and the workplace have been considered men's domain, while emotion, the personal, the private, and caring work are women's.[7] As we contemplate on the moral roles of mature empathy, Gilligan's question lays a basic ground for how we see and build a moral society and community, for it invites us into questioning dominant and rationalistic understandings of morality.

The tension between self and other, and between attachment and separation is a significant subject with a long history in psychology, ethics,

---

2. Gilligan, "In a Different Voice," 278.
3. Gilligan, *In a Different Voice*, 72–73, 100.
4. Walsh, *The Psychology of Women*, 274.
5. Gilligan, *In a Different Voice*, 62–63; Gilligan, "In a Different Voice," 278–320.
6. Held, *Feminist Morality*, 17.
7. I do not discuss this further here. However, Nancy Chodorow's feminist psychoanalytic and sociological view on this problem provides an important answer as well as that of Held. See Chodorow, *The Reproduction of Mothering*; Held, *The Ethics of Care*.

and philosophy. Individuation and separation have been considered more mature and developed states. On the contrary, relationship and care-oriented tendencies have been deemed as less mature stages especially in western countries. Theorists in deontological moral traditions argue that a caring-based morality is dangerous and not well-equipped due to its biased tendency toward in-group caring circles.[8] Whereas care ethicists contend that the most foundational aspect of human morality is always built upon caring practices such as mothering and caring for elderly or ill, i.e., the rudimentary practice for human survival. Despite its essential moral role, caring has been neglected and devalued in rationalistic moral theories.

Care ethics is not without its problems just as all other moral theories have their own problems. As Maurice Hamington points out, "there is no issue more important to care ethicists than how to expand the circle of caring inclusion."[9] Care ethics should constantly strive to bring attention to caring practice exhibited to and for distant others. I believe mature communal empathy can contribute to this endeavor. The problematic exclusion of distant others in a caring circle is significant especially in our current global age. Despite its weaknesses, care ethics has contributed to lifting up the voices of the unheard and brought attention to *real* life problems that we face in our daily lives.

Within the discipline of care ethics, feminist care ethicists have made compelling contributions to ethics by bringing attention to the moral importance of relationship, emotions, the personal, and particularities arising from intersectional contextuality that has been neglected in legal, social, political, and economic institutions and systems, and existing dominant moral theories. At the same time, they put a great deal of effort into constructing an integrative moral view between principles and particularities and between subjectivity and objectivity.[10]

Virginia Held, a prominent feminist care ethicist upon whom I heavily rely, emphasizes the importance of care as she states that care is a "truly universal experience" of human beings since "every human being has been cared for as a child or would not be alive."[11] For Held, care is "the most

---

8. Held, *The Ethics of Care.*

9. Hamington, "Empathy and Care Ethics," 265.

10. Held, *Feminist Morality,* 17, 35.

11. Held, *The Ethics of Care,* 3. As I already stated in chapter 1, humankind is hard to survive as a baby without empathy as well. There is then a significant question raised here: what is the relation of empathy to care? Despite the significance of the question, however, I would not explore the question here due to its irrelevance to the book. For

basic moral value" and "both a practice, or cluster of practices, and a value, or cluster of values." Her care ethic is a moral theory that shares common ground with virtue ethics but is distinct from it.[12] Since caring always requires both parties, including but not limited to, the "one-caring" and the "cared-for,"[13] it cannot be realized without relationship in either narrow or broad ways.[14]

Held and other care ethicists try to find a way to challenge the dominant moral theories and their methodologies including expanding the significance of care as a moral *practice* and value as well as emasculating the dichotomic worldview between justice and care, the public and the private, the political and the personal, reason and emotion, and men and women. Held argues that moral values of caring, emotions including empathy, the private, and the personal should be as important as and equal to the moral values of justice, reason, the public, and the political.[15] As she conceptualizes "feminist moral epistemology,"[16] she demands an epistemological change for the notion of morality.

> To speak of moral epistemology may suggest that morality is primarily a matter of knowledge, as science is usually thought to be. In contrast, most feminists see morality as a matter of practice and art as well as of knowledge. Practice is involved both in understanding what we ought to do and in carrying out the norms of morality . . . To engage in the development of feminist morality is to seek to improve practices in which knowedge is only one component, though an important one.[17]

For Held, morality is the integration of knowledge, practice, and an art of living. It requires a dialectic ongoing process of moral discourse in which moral theory needs to be constantly challenged and adjusted in relation to concrete lived experiences. Held continues to address the importance of practice in morality.

---

more information, see Held, *The Ethics of Care*.

12. Held, *The Ethics of Care*, 4, 9.

13. Noddings, *Caring*. There are many critiques of this dyadic view of the caring relationship. I explore this later in this chapter.

14. Held, *The Ethics of Care*, 4.

15. Held, *The Ethics of Care*. There is still the need to re-conceptualize what is private, public, personal, and political, which is what feminist moral theorists have tried to propose.

16. Held, *Feminist Morality*, 22.

17. Held, *Feminist Morality*, 22.

> Moral theories ... should give us guidance in confronting the problems of actual life in the highly imperfect societies in which we live. We need moral theories about what to do and what to accept here and now. Ideal theories of perfect justice or purely rational theories for ideal societies leave the problems of what to do here and now unsolved, even unaddressed ... In my view, not only must moral theories be applicable to actual problems, they must in some way be "tested" in actual experience ... Otherwise they are intellectual exercises that may be intriguing and impressively coherent, but they are not adequate as *moral theories*.[18]

Held offers a compelling challenge to the *purely rational* moral theories that are founded on the fictional belief of autonomous, independent, and rational moral agents living in an *ideal society*. Her argument further suggests that moral theories also need to be contextually *tested* in order to reflect real lived experience.

Building on Held's and Joan Tronto's work, Elena Pulcini also critiques "the abstractness" and the elusive image of autonomous and independent moral agents in the dominant moral theories, while emphasizing the significance of contextuality for verifying the usefulness of moral theory. These wrongful assumptions about the character of moral agents make the theories too abstract to solve the "complexity of the present" moral problems.[19] Dominant moral theories that are exclusively grounded on reason and impartiality fail to answer—or even address—the issues of "here and now" that are outside of their own criteria with which the marginalized and the oppressed are most likely dealing.

The ethical problems coming out of the private sector are largely ignored or difficult to remedy based on the existing ethical tradition and legal system. Heidi Maibom calls this neglected part of morality: *private morality*.[20] The paradigmatic examples include domestic violence and sexual abuse. I will return to this point in the next chapter. The *impartial* ethical tradition that rejects the moral value of emotions, embodied experiences, intersectional contextuality, and human relationships ironically offers moral theories only to the *partial* problems that are solvable by using reason and principles. The tradition of care ethics suggests more integrative moral theories in which holistic human faculties and propensities are appreciated bridging the gap between emotion *and* reason, practice *and* principle, and

18. Held, *Feminist Morality*, 23.
19. Pulcini, *Care of the World*, 225–26.
20. Maibom, *Empathy and Morality*, 39.

relationality *and* individuality. Feminist care ethics re-envisions morality and moral theory by re-evaluating particularity and emotion as significant moral elements.

Another distinctive contribution to the field by feminist care ethicists is reconceptualizing the self as a being in relationship with *particular* others. The traditional dominant moral theories conceptualize self as an individual and egoistic being, which Held calls "the liberal individualist conception,"[21] whereas care ethics provides a representation of the self that is molded by relationships with particular others rather than hypothetical anonymous others or abstract universal others.[22] Care ethics understands human beings as "relational and interdependent, morally and epistemologically."[23] As I mentioned earlier, every human being needs care to survive. With that being said, we are born into a caring relationship to survive. Thus, relationship[24] is an essential element of composing who we are rather than being a source of biased moral judgments.

Held distinguishes care ethics from the dominant moral theories. She asserts that the ethics of care acknowledges human being's *constitutive dependency* and *interdependency*, and facilitates human emotions as a valuable moral faculty. The "constitutive dependence" and "interdependence" of human beings[25] motivate humans to take moral action based on certain "*moral emotions*" such as "empathy, sensitivity, and responsiveness."[26] These moral emotions guide rather than hinder human beings as to what is morally right and wrong.[27] What Held emphasizes regarding the moral value of emotions is not merely grounded on the vision of care itself, but an *ethics* of care, which morally scrutinizes and evaluates the morality of emotions so as to prevent them from being misguided.[28] While arguing that care is "the most basic of moral values," Held stresses the need for a

---

21. Held, *The Ethics of Care*, 14.
22. Held, *The Ethics of Care*, 11–15.
23. Held, *The Ethics of Care*, 13.
24. Feminist care ethicists emphasize the importance of rejecting oppressive and self-sacrificing relationships. This is a significant subject in the discipline, while I cannot explore this deeper in this book. See Held, *The Ethics of Care*; Kittay, *Love's Labor*.
25. Pulcini, *Care of the World*, 226.
26. Held, *The Ethics of Care*, 10; Pulcini, *Care of the World*, 226.
27. Held, *The Ethics of Care*, 10.
28. Held, *The Ethics of Care*, 11.

new relationship between justice and care, for which we need to refuse "the impulse toward reductionism."[29]

In line with Held, understanding mature empathy from a perspective of care ethics as a normative moral theory requires a very cautious and nuanced approach. Kohlberg's male-centered perception of moral developmental stages excludes women's ways of living and considers them morally immature in comparison to men's ways. In an attempt to construct a notion of mature communal empathy, the moral theories that I employ have to include an integrative perspective of human faculties and reject "the impulse toward reductionism"[30] so as to not repeat the same biases and omissions that Kohlberg and other scholars made. Feminist care ethics will not and should not be criticized for "merely rushing after 'phallic power,'" as Julia Kristeva once ruthlessly stated.[31] Instead, Eva Feder Kittay states that "it has become increasingly clear that a simple opposition between care and justice is inadequate to the needs of our moral and political lives."[32] What we need in the asymmetric power structure is an integrative view of care *and* justice, and a vision of inclusive morality rather than attempting to replace justice with care, merely rushing after another version of phallic power. Partial benefit from either care or justice will not be enough for us to make an inclusive mature society.

I contend that feminist moral theories should neither solely rely on the subjective nor the particular. Moral theories should be able to respond to moral inquiries out of concrete lived experiences at both macro- and micro-level. As Held emphasizes, normative morality is "not merely expressions of subjective" perspectives[33]; rather, the subjective perspectives should be cross-checked with others' experiences. She states that: "Normative moral theory is the most general theory, aspiring to provide guidance for what we should value and how we should act as human beings in any domain of activity from the personal to the political, from worker

---

29. Held, *The Ethics of Care*, 73.

30. Held, *Feminist Morality*, 73.

31. Kelly Oliver expatiates that what Kristeva meant for feminism is "a feminism that merely wants to make women's difference central and move everything traditionally central to the margins." However, Oliver argues, there are feminism*s*, among which there are those who object to that kind of feminist thoughts. I share the same regret with Oliver that Kristeva should have taken more attention to the diversity within the scholarships of feminism. Oliver, *Reading Kristeva*, 2.

32. Kittay, *Love's Labor*, 19.

33. Held, *The Ethics of Care*, 17.

in healthcare to judge in a courtroom, from parent with a difficult child to friend in a dangerous situation. It aims to be *comprehensive*."[34] Moral theory should be something that is able to offer integrated moral guidance in a range of nuanced situations from workplace to home or from the lives of citizens to refugees. We need to acknowledge the limits of the particular while not losing its important epistemological richness. This is where perspective-taking of mature empathy can play an important role. Therefore, when conceptualizing mature empathy and its normative nature, I make an effort to present a balanced view of the particular and the general and of contextuality and principles based on the *ethics* of care as Held emphasizes.

A Suggestion for a Complementary View on Justice and Care

In rationalistic dominant moral theories and heteropatriarchal white-supremacist societies, the concept of empathy as well as other affects have been privatized and gendered as feminine and personal. Emotions have been considered inappropriate for moral use due to their allegedly biased tendencies. Hence, there has been a tendency for empathy to be deemed a valuable emotional asset only in person-to-person relationships but not proper, or worse, dangerous for the political, legal, and economic sphere. This limited biased concept of empathy denies the enriching and beneficial moral resources that empathy can produce.

I ask: What does a moral society and social justice that we try to construct look like? To what kind of a moral society does *mature* empathy contribute? What insights and challenges can mature communal empathy bring in when evaluating religious doctrinal teachings, e.g., Christianity? After reflecting on these questions as an attempt to construct a new complementary relationship between justice and care, the features of mature empathy will be clearer. These features contribute to the society at a both personal *and* communal level.

Justice and care share an ambivalent relationship in moral theories. Virginia Held, however, makes it clear in her article that justice and care, or the ethics of justice and the ethics of care have their own distinctive roles in different social institutions such as legal, political, economic systems, and family.[35] However, she also strongly emphasizes that justice needs help

---

34. Held, "Care and Justice, Still," 23; italics added.

35. This is a very significant insight that Held provides. See Held, "Care and Justice, Still."

from care, even though justice has its own strengths in certain fields such as the legal system.[36] I agree that there are eminent distinctions between the roles and natures of justice and care in morality. Care, I think, is a much more foundational and essential element of what we perceive as justice and other moral norms and values. Justice without care produces moral theory that is unembedded in the world, which makes the oppressed and marginalized even more vulnerable to asymmetrical power structures in a heteropatriarchal and racism-ridden society. Justice and care should not be put into a conflictual relationship.

Held and other scholars such as Pulcini argue that justice and care should "necessarily complement each other" to build a better moral society.[37] Current concepts of justice and care in traditional dominant moral theories should be expanded and complemented so the two can benefit from each other, while their distinctive moral value and vision are conceptually separated.[38]

Then, what is the notion of justice and that of care that I am trying to elaborate here? From whose perspectives do principles of justice get defined? And what does a moral society look like, which involves both visions of justice and care?[39] I offer that an achievable form of care is *just* caring—when an ethic of care gets helpful assistance from an ethic of justice. Just caring invites distant others into the circle of caring of moral agents who are aware of the fact that they are inherently interdependent. I think this is a basic intention that most care ethicists hold as they consider care as a moral

---

36. Held emphasizes, "While legal and political institutions ought themselves to be more caring than they have been, they should still, I think, give priority to justice. But while legal and political institutions should look for moral guidance primarily to moral theories of justice, institutions and persons in the wider domain should look primarily, I think, to the ethics of care." Held, "Care and Justice, Still," 27. There are more discussions needed regarding this argument, which I do not press further here.

37. Pulcini, *Care of the World*, 222.

38. Pulcini provides a great comparison on several scholars' thoughts on the issue of combining the two concepts versus keeping the two separate while maximizing each moral value. See Pulcini, *Care of the World*, chapter 10.

39. These questions can also be applied to the domain of theology. When we think about the justice of God, from whose perspective is God's justice defined? In whose narrative is it justice? The narrative of the powerful or that of the lowly, the abject? Justice with a distorted interpretation may even be used against justice for the socially and politically marginalized people. For this discussion is not directly related to the book, I do not explore this further.

practice. On the other hand, when we think about an ethic of justice being complemented with an ethics of care, there is significantly more to address.

When we adopt the complemented forms of justice and care, one of the essential compositions of an envisioned moral society is social consent among moral agents to include the vision of care as a fundamental consideration of justice, while nurturing a vision of care that remains distinctive. In this kind of moral society, people would be mindful of caring for those who are vulnerable and marginalized in the current system and, hence, there is an underlying and proactive motivation to change and challenge the unjust systems which perpetuate inequality, ostracizing certain groups of people in order to maintain the status quo. Rather than understanding care in terms of a private and gendered practice, caring becomes a personal *and* political exercise fundamental in social discourse. The unaddressed moral problems of "private morality"[40] or perpetuated inequality of unjust social systems become actively discussed in the public discourse on the basis of justice charged with the vision of care.

In social interactions, caring is a moral practice for both significant and distant others. Since human beings as *constitutively dependent and interdependent*,[41] we are subject to care and to be cared for. We can neither survive nor nurture ourselves and non-human living beings without caring. Hence, *justice* in our heteropatriarchal and hierarchical society, which is far from a moral society, should cultivate the ways in which solidarity and inclusiveness become vital values of the society.[42] This justice should be grounded on care for those who are the abject;[43] for those who are de-

---

40. Maibom, *Empathy and Morality*, 39.

41. Pulcini, *Care of the World*, 226.

42. Inclusiveness as an aspect of care here is a counterpart of "fairness" that the ethic of justice mainly focuses on. See Kittay, *Love's Labor*, 19.

43. This term is borrowed from Julia Kristeva's notion of abjection and the abject as she illustrates maternity from a psychoanalytic philosophical view. I use this term politically referring to those who are considered as the abject and pushed out from the binary and traditional, or even symbolic society, as the counterpart of semiotic. Because of the unfitted state to the binary heteropatriarchal power structure, the existence or their subjectivity is a threat or even arouses a sense of horror and disgust to the conventional autonomous and independent subject of the society. The abject is "ambiguous" and "disgusting" to the eyes of the orderly society because the abject is the "unruly border" who is "in-between." Oliver, *Reading Kristeva*, 56–57. Abjection, a sense of ambivalence between negation and identification, being attracted and repelled, and the desire for separation and impossibility of doing so, is not something caused by a "lack of cleanliness" but caused by "what *disturbs* identity, system, order."[italics added] Kristeva, *Powers of Horror*, 4. The abject, however, "never entirely recedes . . . with the potential to

prived of one's legal, political, and economic rights and opportunities; for those who are exposed to unfair treatments due to their appearance, physical and mental conditions, skin color, (im)migration/citizenship status, nationality, language, culture, religion, gender, and any kind of factors that physically, mentally, religiously, and socially contain the person; and because of that unfairness and marginalization, those who need to try harder to make their voices heard. This view of justice is shared by segments of believers in the major world religions. In Christian traditions, this moral vision of just caring/caring justice is often seen in the practices and teachings of Jesus found in the Gospels. This will be discussed in further detail in chapters 3 and 4.

The *unresolved* or even oftentimes *unaddressed* moral inquiries in dominant moral theories burden and cause more suffering to *the abject,* the *other* who is objectified and ostracized by the *I,* the *subjects* of the mainstream society. The current society is governed by a belief in "elusive equality"[44]—or even *illusive.* Autonomous moral agents who are not aware of such foundational interdependency of human beings and other living things cannot bring about justice for all. Unaddressed ethical problems are *urgent* and *real* out of concrete lived experiences. This is why an ethic of justice needs to attain a great deal of help from an ethics of care. When justice is charged with a caring vision, which centers epistemological insights from *the others,* its perspectives will guide the direction of the ethics of justice. The current principles of justice founded on rationalism and impartialism have little space for those who are excluded from the discourse.

With this expanded perception of justice, care should not be put into a conflictual position with justice since this notion of justice *is* what an ethic of care stands for. In a moral society, caring cannot be shunned in the moral dialogue because without the vision of care true justice cannot be accomplished. I name this kind of justice as *caring justice,* when enacted our society becomes *a just caring society* rather than a society built only upon rational and disembedded principles of justice. In the envisioned moral society equipped with this extended concept of caring justice, empathy—especially mature empathy—motivates people/community to nurture *the*

---

unravel the confines that have been constructed." Rodgers, "Maternal Abject (Kristeva)." Also see Kristeva, *The Powers of Horror.* Kristeva's position against feminism and her understanding of difference might not be comfortable to some feminists. Her *ambivalent* relationship with feminism renders us a significant political issue that we as feminists need to discuss from within and without.

44. Kittay, *Love's Labor,* x–xi, 2.

others as interdependent beings. It prevents people from objectifying and treating as abject, the other. Rather, the others' perspectives are revealed to the subject through the process of mature empathy. In the following section, I explore the features of mature empathy, which contribute to building a mature society, *an empathic just caring society*.

Features of Mature Empathy

I have suggested a morally mature society is *an empathic just caring society*, in which moral agents make moral deliberation and judgment based on *caring justice*, i.e. justice attaining epistemological insights from the vision of care, and *just caring*, i.e. an *ethic* of care, in which distant others are invited to the caring circles of moral agents. Then, what is the relation between the complementary understanding of justice and care and empathy?

Empathy takes a more important role especially when it comes to the *integrative* moral understanding of justice and care for moral motivation and action. This is because empathy involves both cognition and affect as the primary compositions. As he compares and tries to integrate Kohlberg's and Hoffman's theory, John Gibbs, developmental moral psychologist, argues that justice and affective empathy—por cognition and affect—are "equally primary and mutually irreducible sources of moral motivation."[45] In chapter 1, I illustrated empathy *an observer's or observers'—as a community—cognitive and affective inner process and response to another or others in various negative and positive circumstances, which leads the observer(s) to feel congruent and oftentimes matching feelings with the other(s) through mimicry, perspective-taking, imagination, and/or simulation*. As an integrative inner process of both cognition and affect, empathy confers rich moral resources that can bridge the gap between the principle of justice and care. It helps moral agents to form a balanced moral judgment out of nuanced moral contexts. Since empathy within itself involves both elements of justice and care, it offers the ways in which *caring justice* and *just caring* can be actualized in our moral life. Then, the question of *how* needs to be asked. How can empathy contribute to building a moral society that is more caring and more just for the marginalized? What part of the nature of empathy should we focus on in order to strengthen its potential moral benefits, as we employ empathy as a way of moral practice? These questions will be explored by scrutinizing the features of mature empathy in this section.

45. Gibbs, "Toward an Integration," 97.

Then, what are the features of mature empathy that can motivate people to build a just caring society? I examine moral implications and features of mature empathy, and how mature empathy can contribute to building a just caring society and community. I suggest six primary features of mature empathy based on works from the psychology of empathy and the ethics of care. After I offer this characterization of mature empathy, I will conclude that a mature society, an empathic just caring one, is a vision that we can pursue as a moral society. Hence, the current social and educational systems need to be challenged to educate and nurture members of society as moral agents, who flexibly utilize mature empathy in their moral thinking process and practice. In a mature society, the constructed systems of society and communities should be able to offer and encourage moral agents to use integrative human faculties from reason to empathy-induced emotions to make moral judgments and take moral action even in very complicated and nuanced contexts. Through the mature-empathy-driven moral deliberation, the social discourses and thinking processes of a society may be enriched, dynamic, and intersubjective through *interdimensional perspective-taking*.[46]

Mature empathy is the most developed form of empathy, and resultantly contributes to the composition of a moral society. It involves balanced, integrative, and intersubjective views from psychological, cultural, social, political, ethical, (inter)religious, and communal perspectives. Unlike theories based on decontextualized social norms and principles, mature empathy is *not* fixed in nature; rather, it is resilient and flexible, vulnerable and communicative, and open-minded as it faces challenges from various complicated and intersectional contextualities. Most importantly, mature empathy is intrinsically caring since genuine empathy[47] carries an intentional stance that corresponds to the *well-being* of the other(s) *and* the community beyond the immediate situation.

In scrutinizing the relationship between the ethics of empathy and ethics of care, Jolanda van Dijke et al. summarize empathy's normative moral functions:[48] First, empathy can inform us as to what is at stake and when to engage with others as moral responses. Second, empathy can guide us to understand and expect the moral consequences out of our empathic

---

46. The concept of interdimensional perspective-taking is explored later in this section.

47. For its definition, see note 50 in chapter 1.

48. Van Dijke et al., "Care Ethics?"

response. Third, it extends our range of understanding to distant others. Most importantly, when we make a moral judgment, empathy advises us to reflect on whether in hindsight the judgment and action in the past were morally right. Jolanda van Dijke et al. use Michael Slote's work, to explain that "mature or genuine empathy can thus function as a *moral compass*."[49] Despite that there are things that need to be discussed more in these arguments, these suggested normative moral functions of empathy provide basic ideas of empathy's prosocial roles.

In this section, I argue that empathy has a rich potential for enhancing our moral practice in terms of its relational, intersubjective, and caring nature. Furthermore, I challenge the dyadic understanding of empathy in the current scholarship to expand the notion from dyadic and unilateral understandings to a multidimensional understanding that includes social, political, institutional, and communal levels.

Drawing on the work of Martin Hoffman and of care ethicists such as Virginia Held, Jolanda van Dijke, and Inge van Nistelrooij in this section, I attempt to reconceptualize the notion and moral potential of mature empathy. Six features of *mature* empathy are suggested here, including but are not limited to, (1) *inter*subjective understanding of self, others, and the community, (2) *inter*dimensional perspective-taking, (3) ability to make a strong partnership with justice and care principles, (4) metacognitive ability and self-reflexivity, (5) willingness to make emotional, cognitive, and behavioral effort on behalf of both significant and distant others, and (6) active and heightened ability of empathic affects that concur with didactic moral principles. My exploration primarily focuses on the first three features in which I attempt to engage the scholarship of empathy with that of care ethics. The later set of three is briefly explained since I either previously mentioned them or the features have been thoroughly investigated by other scholars.

Intersubjective Understanding of Self, Others, and the Community

An intersubjective understanding of self is a significant feature of mature empathy. In the state of mature empathy, one is voluntarily immersed in another's existence and proactively engages with them. As I stated earlier, empathy is the significant prosocial and altruistic asset for humankind that allows people to temporarily put their own interests aside and take others'

---

49. Van Dijke et al., "Care Ethics?" 5.

as a priority. Inge van Nistelrooij, a care ethicist, makes an impressive remark, drawing on Emmanuel Housset:

> As Housset stresses, the meeting with the suffering other breaks open the subject enclosed in itself. Pity is the experience of a community, for, in the encounter with the suffering other, the other gives him- or herself indisputably as my neighbor. The horizon of the self is *broken open* by the other evoking pity. And, as Housset argues, it is not possible in the event of pity to divide what comes from me and what comes from the other, but rather pity reveals the 'ourness'(nostrité) that is a community.[50]

Seeing the self as radically intertwined with the other and the community, Van Nistelrooij offers a radicalized notion of self and identity. She highlights the notion of self-sacrifice in an ethics of care. Reviewing the insufficiency of care ethics' exploration of human passivity, she presses her argument about the self as a ceaselessly molded intersubjective and interdependent being. Van Nistelrooij proposes a "de-centered" self, which to a great extent depends on passivity, or what is given in the surroundings or the contextuality that existed even before the self existed. It is impossible to distinguish between my own and the other's because of its intersubjective existence and dependency on that which is already given.

Through empathy, the two existences become entangled and *inter*subjectively encounter each other. Through this intersubjective understanding of self, I see a mature empathizer as one who *voluntarily* gets immersed with the suffering of others and puts aside her own egoistic interest based on the foundational belief that the self is not detached from the world; rather the world, the community, and others intersubjectively contribute to forming who she is.

My argument here should be taken with caution. I am not arguing that to be maturely empathetic, one has to *abandon* the self, at least in the light of traditional understanding or Christian notion of self-sacrifice especially how the self-sacrifice of Jesus on the cross has been theologized as a central virtue in Christianity. The traditional male-centered belief of self-sacrifice—as exemplified by the Christian doctrine of self-sacrifice as a virtue or a caring obligation—sustains and promotes the marginalization of the other. Tronto cautions against this as well: "[s]ome people make greater sacrifices of themselves than do other people; some will even sacrifice too much. Part of this moral problem is exacerbated by the fact that those who

---

50. Nistelrooij, *Sacrifice*, 234; italics added.

are most likely to be too self-sacrificing are likely to be the relatively powerless[51] in society."[52] The attempt to balance between self-care and other-care, and the relational balance between the one-caring and the cared-for is always challenging to care-givers who are oftentimes marginalized in society.[53] When we explore the moral value of self-sacrifice related to caring practices, it reveals a complicated social structure.

Therefore, what I am trying to say here is the opposite of abandoning self. What I postulate here is about *acknowledging* the understanding and the composition of the self as intersubjective. To *acknowledge* the fundamental influence of another's existence to the composition of the self as intersubjective is a significant awareness of the mature empathizer. Van Nistelrooij states that "One's identity has come about through others, through the relations that have been given and discovered when the self develops, that have grown over time, forming the self and being inexorably part of the self's identity."[54] I agree with this argument. The self is being formed and constantly changing and challenged by one's contextuality, relationships, and what is given such as time, place, body, events, and so on. No one can be completely unembedded in the world. As Tronto states, this world and our community are "comprised of people enmeshed within networks of care."[55] The dualistic thinking structure of I and the other as completely separate subjects cannot be sustained in a mature form of empathy as the mature empathizer *voluntarily* comes forward to be vulnerable and be "broken open by the other." In this vein, again, I see mature empathizers as ones who become voluntarily immersed with the suffering of others and they temporarily put aside their own egoistic desire based on the foundational belief that the self is intersubjectively formed as well as a care-recipient in the world.

---

51. Even though Tronto uses a word "powerless," I want to point out that we need to be careful when we define those who are vulnerable in society due to the oppressive social environment as powerless. Those whose power and agency are constantly threatened to be taken away in society still resist the socially given identity as "powerless," and claim their own power and agency, becoming a *survivor* as opposed to only remaining as the victim or the powerless. This is my practice to claim their/our agency, resisting the "powerlessness" that the unjust power structure ceaselessly implies to the vulnerable.

52. Tronto, *Moral Boundaries*, 141.

53. Tronto, *Moral Boundaries*, 141; Van Nistelrooij, *Sacrifice*, 56.

54. Van Nistelrooij, *Sacrifice*, 223.

55. Tronto, "Democracy Becomes Care," 37.

Understanding the self as an intersubjectively-formed-being allows us to consider ourselves also as a care-recipient, not only a caregiver, since a self cannot exist or be formed without receiving care from the outside world, the community. This kind of intersubjective notion of the self breaks the asymmetric power structure between the empathizer and empathized. It also prevents us from conceptualizing of the caregiver as autonomously and independently sacrificing herself purely for the sake of the other. The dualistic dynamic of self and the other, or the subject and the objectified subject loses its standing. Tronto argues that when all the members of society view themselves as care recipients, the view of the care receiver as the other can be disrupted. Tronto maintains that: "Once people can begin to make judgments about these "others" as if they were making judgments about themselves, a different social psychological process of more genuine empathy will be necessary. That people can exercise such empathy is well established, though its scope is limited. Changing our understanding of care allows the scope of empathy to be expanded."[56] This way of thinking stops people from understanding others as detached and objectified; rather, it enables people to develop a genuine empathy[57] as they now begin to view themselves also as a care recipient.

Then, what does this intersubjective understanding mean when we think about self-other differentiation? Self-other differentiation does not mean that the self objectifies the other. It is an ability to *distinguish* me and not-me, while understanding me as a being always in relation with others and the world. It acknowledges the separate being of the not-me, which I cannot and should not violently or forcefully control in my own omnipotent illusion.[58]

As I explained earlier, self-other differentiation takes on an important role in the developmental course of children's empathic ability. The significant implications of self-other differentiation in terms of mature empathy are twofold. First, developmentally, this self-other differentiation takes an important role as it guides children to move from egocentric to quasi-egocentric empathy as I explained in chapter 1. From this point of development, Hoffman argues, children involve sympathetic dimension in empathy, which develops into sympathetic distress. Sympathetic distress, a feeling of compassion or *fellow-feeling* as compared to a vicarious feeling,

---

56. Tronto, *Caring Democracy*, 151.
57. For its definition, see n50 in chapter 1.
58. Winnicott, *Playing and Reality*.

is a component of the later three mature stages of empathic development—quasi-egoistic, veridical, and beyond the situation stages. The dual mode of empathic and sympathetic distress allows the empathizer to transform their egoistic motivation to a "truly prosocial motive"[59] when they help the distressed person. In other words, the action of helping or caring for people in order to reduce their own empathic distress becomes transformed to the dimension where one takes empathic action truly out of compassion for the sake of the distressed other. The *limits* of empathic motivation that could not move beyond egoistic motivation resolves and the range of caring moral action extends to the point where empathizers take action to genuinely help others, not to reduce their empathic distress.

Second, as Amy Coplan and others point out, failing self-other differentiation makes empathizers build a fused relationship with others, which may end up causing empathic over-arousal. The empathizer's empathic distress may increase because the other's distress may involuntarily become her own. Also, it can be hard for some people to employ dual perspective-taking, which combines self-oriented and other-oriented perspective-taking. This hinders the empathizer's ability to build an integrative perspective on the distressed other and their situation. When this happens, immature empathy may be engendered and thus it maximizes the weaknesses of empathy.

In order to overcome this potential risk, we can consult with Hoffman's fourth stage of empathic distress, which was explained in the previous chapter. In this stage, the self develops veridical empathy, in which the self develops a reflective self that has an ability for self-reflexivity and metacognition. The range of empathizing ability in this stage broadens from themselves to people, situations, and experiences in the empathic circle. This developed form of empathy enables the empathizer to view others' situations through integrative analysis and take proper action in the midst of empathic distress. This reflective self with veridical empathy enables the empathizer to employ both types of the perspective-takings as well as continuing the self-other differentiation.[60]

Self-other differentiation guides the self to respect the not-me as one who has her own psychological and physical preferences, characteristics, and faculties. The differentiation socio-politically aids the vulnerable,[61] e.g., women, and caregivers to be more aware of socially imposed

---

59. Hoffman, *Empathy and Moral Development*, 88.
60. Maibom, *Empathy and Morality*, 75–79.
61. "[T]he relatively powerless" in Tronto's term.

self-sacrifice and to resist the imbalanced caring practices between self-care and other-care. Without a concrete sense of differentiation, society could force and reproduce the marginalization and vulnerability of caregivers.

The intersubjective understanding of the self when based on the ability of self-other differentiation is a starting point for building mature empathy. Mature empathizers are those who are *voluntarily broken open* by the voices of suffering others. They come forward to voluntarily participate in the vulnerability of others, as they recognize and accept their intersubjectivity and vulnerability shared with the others. Thus, they are vulnerable human beings affected by various surroundings and circumstances. They embrace and respect the care recipients as a whole human being who is *different* from me in terms of identity, living conditions, preferences, thoughts, feelings, and behavioral patterns. The intersubjective empathizers consider themselves also as a care recipient in the relational network of the world.

Interdimensional Perspective-taking

I already explored self-oriented, other-oriented, and dual perspective-taking drawing on Martin Hoffman, Julinna Oxley and other scholars in the previous chapter. Now, I want to suggest an extended and more complex form of perspective-taking, i.e, *interdimensional perspective-taking*. Dual perspective-taking is a useful way of perceiving and imagining others' thinking and feeling process. What Oxley, Maibom, and Hoffman suggest is composed of dyadic perspectives between the observer and the one observed. This way of thinking generates a two-fold problem limiting perspective-taking to only two subjects' standpoints. First of all, in this dyadic presupposition, empathic deliberation and empathic action out of caring are limited to two parties between the empathizer—the one who actively engages—and the emphasized—the one who passively receives. This may create an asymmetric and hierarchical power structure within the empathic relationship. The one who observes holds the power and the other passively receives the empathy. Second, this cannot include an intersectional standpoint between race, gender, nationality, (im)migrant/citizenship status, religion, class, and so on as much. Moreover, this dyadic mechanism may promote familiarity bias and near-and-dear bias as it makes it harder for the observer to empathize with someone from a different racial group or any other background than her own. These two problems can be resolved with interdimensional perspective-taking. Let me explain in detail here.

Joan Tronto strongly refuses the dyadic understanding of caring, criticizing Nel Noddings' notion of care in the dyadic relationship between the one-caring and the cared-for. Tronto maintains that understanding care as dyadic is not only inaccurate but it also generates "asymmetries of care."[62] She states that, "the problem with this model is that it begins to import into the very nature of care its inequality. From the standpoint of democratic societies, such inequality can serve as a justification for continuing to exclude and not think about care receivers and their close caregivers as full, participating citizens . . . an important part of democratic caring concerns the breaking down of hierarchical relationships. One starting point for doing so is to undermine the logic of care as dyadic."[63] For Tronto, caring is not and should not be restricted to two parties, giving vs. receiving, which promotes hierarchical relationships. Caring in this case is perceived as "naturally individualistic."[64] The caring should rather involve political, social, and cultural aspects.[65] Inge van Nistelrooij also agrees with Tronto's rejection of care as a dyad practice, emphasizing the importance of extending the notion of care to social, political, and communal levels.[66]

The same critique and the need for reconceptualization should be applied also to the ethic of empathy. Understanding empathy in a dyad relationship is not comprehensive and could promote *dysfunctions* and *risks* of empathy. Dyadic understandings of empathic relationships cause a misunderstanding of the nature of empathy as a one-way communication from the empathizer to the empathized. The empathizer holds all the initiative and power, and the other passively awaits to receive empathy. An empathic relationship is not one-way, nor is the process unilateral. Rather, it is *inter*-actional. Empathy is a *dynamically moving and forming* interaction that is influenced by all the involved people or non-human beings in one's or communities' life course. Also, empathic perspective-taking limited to two may imply that empathy is employed by a detached independent individual. This is not an accurate understanding of the nature of empathy and the empathizer, for the self is inherently an intersubjective being. The empathizer is antecedently a recipient of empathy as a social, political, and intersubjective being in the world.

62. Tronto, *Caring Democracy*, 152.
63. Tronto, *Caring Democracy*, 153.
64. Tronto, *Moral Boundaries*, 103.
65. Tronto, *Moral Boundaries*, 103.
66. Van Nistelrooij, *Sacrifice*, 51–64.

Second, mature empathy cannot be formed by one's or two people's perspectives, which calls for the necessity of reconceptualization of empathic perspective-taking. The mature perspective-taking of the observer is neither solely self-oriented/other-oriented nor dual perspective-taking. While these distinctions of the types of perspective-taking are helpful to understand the significant natures of empathy, the human mind and psychological analytic process is not that simple. It cannot be grounded on a dualistic mindset of "if I were in your position" or "I know you, thus I imagine how it would feel to you from your perspective."

Interdimensional perspective-taking is three-fold: self-oriented perspective-taking, other-oriented perspective-taking, and *supplementary perspective-taking*. Unlike the first two perspective-takings, *supplementary perspective-taking* can take multiple perspectives from and beyond one's direct relational network. Anyone in or beyond one's relational network can become the source of the supplementary perspective-taking. The supplementary perspective-taking can come from multiple sources when the empathizer goes through an empathic process. The sources beyond one's relational network can be, but are not limited to, public figures, a person from a story in a news article, and even something from nature as long as the empathizer has a deep understanding of the source.

For example, my sister-in-law who is a white-Hispanic American saw an Asian elderly couple physically and verbally being mocked by white supremacists in a grocery parking lot in the midst of the Covid-19 pandemic. The white supremacists swore at them and called them cancerous beings and the source of the dirty coronavirus. My sister-in-law was processing and analyzing the situation. She started the process of perspective-taking. First, if she were in their shoes (self-oriented perspective-taking), she would be angry and embarrassed, and desperate for help from other bystanders. Second, if she were an Asian American who is old and could not speak English fluently—collecting information from their responses in their own language mixed with broken English and they were frozen (other-oriented perspective-taking), she would feel humiliated and frustrated that she was not able to express her opinion fluently, and also be scared of being physically attacked.

What she did here is dual perspective-taking as she utilizes both perspective-takings, even though she had limited access to the personal information of the couple. However, perspective-taking goes one step further: Third, she thinks, "the Asian couple reminds me of my sister-in-law(*supplementary perspective-taking* from the third person), who is a Korean immigrant, who is also vulnerable like them in this kind of challenging time, and this could happen to her, too. And I remember that she mentioned the fear and anxiety of being attacked like this during this pandemic. What would *she* (my sister-in-law) feel in this kind of situation as an Asian immigrant like them (this move uses the familiarity bias of empathy as a supportive mechanism to better understand the strangers' situation)?" Then, her reference of perspective-taking comes from with-in herself, the others, and an extended relational network, *beyond the dyadic structure*. Her white-Hispanic identity is intersubjectively interconnected with other racial, immigration statuses, national, ethnic, and gender groups. Any experience of rigid identity is broken by her empathic inner response, expanding the caring network outside of her own identity groups. This is a prime example of interdimensional perspective-taking as the empathizer wittingly and unwittingly embraces the fact that the self always exists within a wide relational network and robustly uses her intersubjective experiences for her perspective-taking.

Unlike the illusion of an independent and detached moral agent, we as socially intersubjective beings can take interdimensional perspective-takings when we witness or hear distressed stories of others regardless of whether they are significant others or distant others, or they were physically present or absent. As an intersubjective self, one can be advised from the direct and indirect experiences of one's entire life network and can attain much more comprehensive perspectives than those from the dyadic system. Especially in the digital era, the range of experience and cognitive capacity of distant others' life narratives are eminently extended. When one begins perspective-taking, even a news article about a victim-survivor's story of a hate crime and racism against Asians in New York City during the Covid-19 pandemic can provide the person the third, supplementary perspective to take. The scope of empathic resources becomes expanded from person-to-person to beyond personal interactions.

This interdimensional perspective-taking benefits us in at least two significant ways. First, through referencing multiple perspectives, one can more effectively and easily take an intersectional approach to the moral context. One of the main critiques of empathy was that due to human's limited cognitive ability, empathizers might only be able to imagine situations and states that are relevant to what they have already personally gone through. However, through interdimensional perspective-taking, one's reference now is not limited to one's own race, gender, religion, nationality, class, citizenship/immigration status, and any other social identity components. It helps the observer to build a morally-nuanced social cognition, which may direct an empathizer towards more balanced moral deliberation and action.

This also helps to avoid the *dysfunctions* of empathy to some degree. The dysfunction of empathy, as I described, means empathy's authentic function is impeded due to outside unjust and unsound factors such as psychological manipulation, white-supremacist socio-politico-cultural settings, and heteropatriarchal/hierarchical social systems. As a result of the dysfunctional empathy, the realization of empathy works against the well-being of another and the community. Interdimensional perspectives push bystanders to stay away from one-sided or only two-folded perspectives as they are advised by multiple and intersectional references.

Second, it allows them to flip their familiarity or near-and-dear bias into strengths. The strong empathy that was formed toward significant or present others or others that share similar experiences and backgrounds with the empathizer such as race can now be redirected to distant others. In the example of Asian racism, the sister-in-law's strong empathy with her family member was diverted to the Asian-American older couple, who were complete strangers to her. Now, she becomes *engaged* and *interconnected* through empathic interaction with them, where *solidarity* may be formed. It is more likely that bystanders will execute their empathic action when they have a morally nuanced social cognition followed by engagement and interaction with others.

As I argued in chapter 1, when empathy is transformed into an *engaging* action, i.e. *empathic action*, in order to seek the welfare of the other, it may form solidarity and intersubjectivity; or, maybe, mature empathy forms solidarity through engagement first, then it motivates empathizers to take empathic action. The intersubjective understanding of the self through interdimensional perspective-taking now expands empathy's scope to the one with an intersubjective relational and caring network for distant others. One's empathic capacity becomes broadened from a personal level to a communal level as the empathizer embraces personal, societal, political, and cultural references in the process of interdimensional perspective-taking.

Empathy goes far beyond the dyadic system because our life itself is not and cannot be confined to a dyadic environment; rather, it is more complexly intertwined at every possible level beyond our imagination. Moral motivation and action that start from perspective-taking and imagination are referenced by numerous relational resources from our personal relational webs to the narratives of distant others whether in face-to-face encounters, indirect interactions, and/or virtual formats. Empathy is formed at a more communal level than we regularly imagine, considering our being itself is intersubjectively and communally formed in the world.

People with mature empathy consider all the factors as they commit to perspective-taking. It is an ability to comprehensively collect, analyze, and utilize all their integrative knowledge through the process to create a new integrative perspective that the self is going to adopt. For example, the mature empathizer might ask: What would this distressed event mean to the stranger? What would my mom think if she were here to see this elderly woman suffering from this distress? What would I think and feel in that situation? What would my child think and feel while watching this scene? All the possibilities of her relational and experiential network come to her as multiangular references. These extremely inextricable perspectives from with-in and with-out the self advise her or the community to take an integrative analysis and perspective on the situation and toward others. This allows her to affectively and cognitively decide *in what ways* she or the community would empathize with the distant others, and *how deeply* she/they would engage with them as an empathic action. Interdimensional perspective-taking, then, helps moral agents or the community to overcome or avoid the moral *risks* and *dysfunctions* of empathy such as familiarity bias and near-and-dear bias.[67] This form of mature empathy may overcome the limits of the empathic scope bound by time, space, and direct relationships. Through this perspective-taking, some concerns about the moral use of empathy may be resolved and the model of a mature society, an empathic just caring one, realized.

---

67. Hoffman also suggests a concept of "multiple empathizing" process to avoid and overcome the biases. The multiple empathizing is empathizing process with multiple people in a situation. It is a much more complex empathizing process than empathy with one person. The empathizer takes into consideration multiple people's perspectives or of how they would be affected by her decision based on empathy. This is a similar concept with the interdimensional perspective-taking. However, I think the multiple-empathizing process is a broader concept than perspective-taking and has a different nature. For more information, see Hoffman, "Empathy, Social Cognition."

The Strong Partnership with Justice and Care

The third feature of mature empathy is the ability of empathy to enhance justice and care principles. Mature empathizers have an ability to integrate empathic affect with moral principles. Hoffman thoroughly scrutinizes how empathy plays a significant role in morality and how one's social cognition works with empathic affects for moral judgment. He argues that empathic affects such as sympathetic distress, empathic anger, guilt, and feelings of injustice are mostly congruent with two major moral principles, i.e. *caring* and *justice*. Hoffman asserts that the relation of empathy to the caring moral principle is "obvious and direct" because empathic affects and the caring principle both share "a feeling of concern" and its inherent tendency to act on behalf of the distressed other.[68]

On the other hand, the relation of empathy and the justice principle is "less obvious"[69] but holds a very significant implication in my view. In an attempt to explain the relation, Hoffman proposes three principles that distributive justice may be based upon; they are need-, equality-, and equity-based distributive justice. Each principle is built based on the belief that the resources of society should be allocated based on the need (need-based), or on one's productivity, effort, and contribution (equity-based), or equally (equality). He further explains that non-empathic people would lean toward moral judgment based on their own state. This means that those from the privileged class may have tendency to support an equity-based principle. On the contrary, people equipped with an empathic moral tendency would take others' distressed situation into consideration, imagining what the consequences of their moral judgment would do to others. This might lead them to support a need or equality-based principle even if it does not benefit their personal state. At the least, if the person is more egocentric but empathic to some degree, they might choose equity supervised by the other two principles so "no one is extremely deprived (need) and vast discrepancies in wealth cannot occur (equality)."[70] Empathy, therefore, takes an important role in creating a just caring society, cooperating with both caring and justice moral principles.

Hoffman's assertion implies that a moral agent equipped with empathic ability has a potential to make a more balanced- and nuanced-moral

---

68. Hoffman, "Empathy, Social Cognition," 290.
69. Hoffman, "Empathy, Social Cognition," 290.
70. Hoffman, "Empathy, Social Cognition," 293.

Mature Empathy and Its Moral Implications

judgment and action, even if the moral decision does not coincide with one's own interest. In other words, mature empathy's moral value is significant to both caring and justice. Moreover, empathy can be a bridge to integrate the two principles and motivate people to think and imagine *intersectionally*, overcoming the egoistic epistemological limit of one's own group based on nation, race, gender, religion, class, culture, nationality, citizenship/(im)migration status, and economy. In my view, this aspect of empathy is most likely activated when it is in a mature form, since egocentric or primitive empathy would not be strong enough to triumph over one's biased empathy and to reduce egoistic desires. I agree with Hoffman and Gibbs, stating that "[e]mpathy and justice have a deep partnership," if they keep being "co-primary or mutual." Moreover, when empathy works with justice, justice becomes more integrative and builds a more caring society with balanced and nuanced morality.[71]

Other Features of Mature Empathy

Mature empathy also has other features. I explore a few non-sequential features briefly, for some of them are already explored in chapter 1 and they are mostly grounded on the existing work of Hoffman along with other scholars. However, the features of mature empathy are not limited to the list I offer here.

First, mature empathy has *metacognitive ability* and *self-reflexivity* as I briefly explained earlier.[72] This means the empathizers know the self as only one member of the entire web of the world and others as an entity who have their own identities, lifestyles, worldviews, personal histories, and, most importantly, "lives beyond the immediate situation."[73] Moreover, they have the cognitive ability to find the nature of events and what caused the event.[74] They acknowledge that there are diverse standpoints and emotional structures, as many as there are members of the world, including human and non-human beings; hence, they understand that their epistemological capacity and cognitive/affective standpoints are limited. Nevertheless, mature empathizers have a sense, to some degree, about how most people would feel in certain situations and an ability to imagine how I

---

71. Gibbs and Hoffman, "In Defense of Empathy."
72. Hoffman, *Empathy and Moral Development*, 63–64, 74–75.
73. Hoffman, *Empathy and Moral Development*, 63–64.
74. Hoffman, *Empathy and Moral Development*, 74.

would feel in such situations. This metacognitive and self-reflective self is a starting point to utilize interdimensional perspective-taking, as the self has an ability to think beyond the immediate situation and understand the underlying social structures and even political dynamics of the others' plight.

Second, mature empathizers are the ones who are willing to make emotional, cognitive, and behavioral extra effort. Doing so, they can employ interdimensional perspective-taking as well as relieve the unjust distress even for the sake of distant others. In other words, the mature empathizer holds a strong intentional stance to make things better for the others.

The last feature is an active and heightened ability of empathic affects such as sympathetic distress, empathic anger, empathy-based guilt, and feelings of injustice as I explained in chapter 1 drawing on Hoffman's theory. These empathic affects can be a very strong motivational resource for an observer to take an empathic action. In addition, when they are combined with properly related social cognition, it generates "hot cognition," i.e., "the affectively charged moral principles," which can be encoded in one's mind.[75] When people go through the empathizing process in moral encounters in their lives, they can bring back this hot cognition and use it to assess the situation or figure out possible empathic actions.

Hoffman explains that one's empathic response can be brought up not only due to distress cues—"the stimulus-driven component"—from the other; but also due to "the category-driven component"—in other words, "affectively charged moral principles"—that are *activated by the cues*.[76] The stimulus-driven component alone might be too weak to overcome one's own egoistic motives. On the other hand, the category-driven component alone or in combination with the former can generate a powerful motivation to transform empathy into empathic action.[77] When a moral principle is learned in "a *cool* didactic context," it becomes more powerful when combined with affective components to fight against social injustice.[78]

In this vein, another feature of mature empathy is the ability to use the internalized moral principles charged with affective components in a morally challenged context. This is because egoistic immature empathy cannot

---

75. For more information, see Hoffman, "The Contribution of Empathy," 18–57; Also see Hoffman, "Empathy, Social Cognition," 293–95.

76. Hoffman, "The Contribution of Empathy," 185–87.

77. Hoffman, "The Contribution of Empathy," 71–73.

78. Hoffman, "The Contribution of Empathy," 71–73; Hoffman, "Empathy, Social Cognition," 293–95. For more information on the concept of hot cognition, see Hoffman, "The Contribution of Empathy," 71–73.

overrule the egoistic motive and transform empathy into empathic action unlike the form of empathy composed of social cognition charged with affective components.

In sum, other features of mature empathy include the following: First, metacognitive ability and self-reflexivity, which enable empathizers to know the distinction between the feeling of others and their own feeling as a response to the other's. Second, it involves an empathizers' willingness to take on emotional, cognitive, and behavioral effort that is required in order to generate interdimensional perspective-taking as well as to relieve the unjust distress even on behalf of distant others. Lastly, it is the active and heightened ability of empathic affects as well as the ability to use the internalized moral principles charged with affective components in a morally challenged context, since immature empathy alone may be too weak to override the egoistic motive and transform empathy into empathic action.

Establishing the Moral Implications of Empathy

I have explored six significant features of mature empathy in relation to morality. Three primary features include (1) the intersubjective view on the self, others, and the world; (2) interdimensional perspective-taking; (3) and the ability to make a strong partnership between caring and justice principles along with three other features.

Understanding the self, others, and the world through an intersubjective and interdimensional frame means we open up ourselves to not only significant others but also the distant ones that we have never met before. It allows us to voluntarily share the vulnerability of others. Moreover, the metacognitive ability to take interdimensional perspective-taking enables moral agents to make a comprehensive and balanced moral judgement. This helps the agents to avoid the biased forms of empathy. Through this intersubjective and interdimensional empathizing process, the range of empathic moral action is extended and mature empathizers will be more likely to contribute to building a mature society, an empathic just caring one. Furthermore, *how* we obtain knowledge, interpretation, and internalization of the obtained knowledge would also be different through mature empathy since multiple people's perspectives come into the process. As well, others are not complete strangers anymore in the intersubjective world.

Empathy, particularly mature empathy, as a complex internal process where emotion and cognition make a strong partnership has significant

The Power of Mature Empathy

epistemological, social, and *moral* implications. *Epistemologically,* emotion and cognition together contribute to forming and interpreting knowledge—a knowledge that is not limited to cognitive knowledge, rather, it is an integrative form of cognition and emotion. Alison Jaggar also emphasizes the interrelation of the two to form knowledge as she criticizes a positivistic approach to gaining knowledge. She explores the epistemic potential of emotion and the interrelation between emotion and knowledge: "Just as appropriate emotions may contribute to the development of knowledge, so the growth of knowledge may contribute to the development of appropriate emotions. For instance, the powerful insights of feminist theory often stimulate new emotional responses to past and present situations."[79] Emotion affects what we cognitively know and what we cognitively know affects our emotions.[80] Emotions without a proper cognitive process and cognition without affective reflection can never form an integrative knowledge. Without this balance, we are filled with unembedded abstract knowledge or with a blinded and lopsided cluster of feelings. Hence, through the empathizing process, especially a mature one, we are able to attain comprehensive knowledge about the others that those without empathy cannot attain.

Metacognitive ability enables us to think about the person's life beyond the immediate situation; the unjust social system that is the probable cause of the plight; and interdimensional perspectives crossing boundaries of race, gender, religion, nationality, citizenship/immigration status, culture, class, etc. The mature empathizer listens to the particularity out of the context as well as interpreting the particularity with comprehensive emotional and cognitive frames that she has built through her previous experiences, cross-passed narratives, education, and moral philosophy. Our knowledge is enriched by the moral principle of caring justice and just caring going beyond immediate situations and the life of the other, and beyond our own experiences, narratives, and education, recognizing the foundational mutuality of our existences.

Morally, moral agents utilizing mature empathy may make their balanced moral judgment in nuanced moral encounters as they consider what is the most just caring way for everyone involved as they imagine multilayered, possible consequences of their action. Hoffman emphasizes that, "mature, morally internalized individuals have empathy-charged caring and justice principles in their motive system. They should therefore be

---

79. Jaggar, "Love and Knowledge," 498.
80. See Jaggar, "Love and Knowledge," 497–98.

sensitive to both caring and justice perspectives, and vulnerable to empathic distress, anticipatory guilt, and other empathic emotions associated with multiple claimant and caring-justice dilemmas . . . sensitive to both caring and justice"[81] Through a mature empathizing process, the moral agent voluntarily posits themselves in the vulnerable position, challenging the unjust social system, as the empathic/sympathetic distress leads them to the experience of "ourness," i.e., solidarity. They embrace the empathic affects as they share others' burdens imposed by the system. "The experience of a community" through the encounter of *the suffering other*[82] opens their eyes to the uncovered knowledge of others that they have not seen before. Then, building a mature community, i.e. an empathic just caring community, may be possible with the help of their expanded knowledge and the process of moral deliberation and action grounded on mature empathy.

Socially, mature empathy's intersectional and interdimensional perspective-taking guides and motivates us to socially engage with participation and justice-seeking action for distant others based on our extended knowledge through mature empathy. Social awareness may be promoted as well. Empathy with significant others is redirected towards the suffering distant others through interdimensional perspective-taking. With the empathically charged moral motivation, empathy may be transformed to empathic action accompanied with social interaction, engagement, and solidarity. This mature empathy with social cognition is a powerful motivational source for social justice and building an empathic just caring society.

I have explored the possible moral implications of empathy in this chapter. Based on the findings from chapter 1, I concluded that we need to ask *how* to enhance empathy to be more *mature* and morally-nuanced so we can promote social justice. Examining the features of mature empathy, therefore, is a meaningful exercise to propose *a way* in which we get closer to building a mature society.

In the first section, I tried to depict the social imaginary pursued from a care ethics perspective. An empathic just caring society as a mature society is a proposed model to which our mature empathy can contribute. The moral society equipped with the complementary principles of justice and care where empathy can play a significant moral role prevents people from objectifying and abjecting the other. Other fellow human and nonhuman beings' perspectives can then be revealed to moral agents in moral

---

81. Hoffman, *Empathy and Moral Development*, 21.
82. Van Nistelrooij, *Sacrifice*, 234.

encounters through the mature empathizing process. The moral agents make moral deliberation based on caring justice and just caring in this society, where human and nonhuman beings are considered constitutively dependent and interdependent as well as listening to the voice of particularity while keeping a balance between particularity and generality.

In the following section, the possible features of mature empathy were proposed. Along with other features, I suggested three primary features that are: intersubjective understanding of self, others and the world; inter-dimensional perspective-taking; and the ability to make strong partnership with caring and justice principles. This intersubjective and interdimensional framework allows us to be voluntarily vulnerable to empathic affect that can motivate us to transform our empathy to empathic moral actions with social cognition. I suggested that mature empathy can be a starting point toward a just caring society, for it expands our epistemological ability, guides our moral deliberation, and motivates us to participate in social change.

In the next chapter, I look into digital activism against sexual violence, e.g., the #MeToo Movement and the #ChurchToo Movement. I uncover how empathy is actualized in the digital movement as a caring practice for distant others. Since empathy has been accused of having a biased tendency toward significant or here-and-now others, I attempt to discover how *mature* empathy can be helpful in a caring practice for distant others. I scrutinize two cases of the #MeToo Movement as a rich example of the realization of communal empathy, both of which happen within a Christian context. In exploring the movement, it illustrates how empathy can be realized in the communal sphere as a moral motivational source on behalf of known and unknown victim-survivors. The examination of the cases of the #MeToo movement related to the #ChurchToo movement aids not only to develop the idea of communal empathy but to obtain a perspective on how members of a Christian community can engage in the ethical healing process of care with empathy. The case study specifically in Christian communities will help us see the complicated dynamics of factors such as religion, gender, transnationality, ideologies, misogynistic norms and practices, the manifestations of systemic evil, and, most importantly, pseudo-empathy and mature communal empathy.

3

Case Study
Sexual Violence in Faith Communities and the Role of Empathy in Digital Activism

IN AN ATTEMPT TO integratively explore the nature and context of sexual violence against women and its impact on victim-survivors, driving questions need to be asked: How does sexual violence happen and why is it overwhelmingly prevalent? How does the traumatic event affect victim-survivors, and why is it so hard for them to share, sometimes taking years to break their silence? Why do so many families and faith communities encourage or demand silence about this kind of victimization? As one tries to answer these questions, she finds primary factors entangled together, forming complex dynamics within the nature of sexual violence against women. Thus, attempting to answer these questions requires a similarly attentive approach to complexity.

Every individual's identity forms at the intersection of various components. These components come together and interweave with each other, and hence create a unique form of identity. This identity is thus an outcome of various factors such as emotional and cognitive states of mind, behavioral tendencies, and the power related to the social status of each component that is directly affected by the *dynamic* socio-historical context. These intersectional components may include but are not limited to race, gender, nationality, social and economic class, (dis)ability, citizenship/immigration status, sexuality, religion, familial and communal culture, and institutional and social affiliation, just to name a few. These components foundationally influence people as they form their own unique perspectives, personal ethic and rationale for their behaviors, and a set of belief systems. Therefore, understanding each other's various standpoints can be especially hard if two individuals come from very different backgrounds, or, even worse, from contrasting social and religious belief-systems.

Keeping this complexity in mind, I aim to see how we can facilitate just and caring responses to sexual violence victim-survivors with a focus on faith-based communities. This will be explored by observing how empathy functions in the process of promoting those responses. Through the findings, my ultimate purpose of this chapter is to offer a particular space that demonstrates how we all can participate in promoting just and caring communities through mature communal empathy. If we can find a way in which mature empathy promotes a just caring society and communities, the study may help us to find a way to transform bystanders from passive to active moral agents through mature empathy. Also, the examples suggests people can emotionally and cognitively move beyond their own standpoint and circle of care, and to be intersubjectively and voluntarily broken open to the agonies of *distant others*.

As a method to analyze the *responses* to victim-survivors from faith-based and secular communities, I closely investigate the two social media examples from the #MeToo movement as an umbrella movement. Also, I will use a narrative methodology throughout the chapter, probing the questions of how empathy is actualized and what the potential moral implications of empathy are in justice-seeking movements. In the journey of seeking answers to the questions, I also give attention to the voices of marginalized groups—especially those stories that involve (im)migration/citizenship status issues, transnational settings, and cross-cultural particularities—to see if those from racial and (im)migrant minority groups tend to be left out or included in the #MeToo movement and how the movement affects minority victim-survivors.

For the stated research purpose, I reflect on the nature and context of sexual violence in the first section asking the four driving questions that were introduced earlier. After looking into the questions, I make an appraisal of dominant responses from church communities to sexual violence and its victim-survivors. In the process of appraisal, I investigate the implications of dominant responses from the community.

Case Study

In the third section, I turn to analyze the responses in digital spaces with the aid of a feminist digital humanities perspective, trying to explore the unique nature of digital spaces and the negative and positive outcomes of it through the #MeToo movement. Furthermore, the role of virtual communities will be explored. When people construct responses to sexual violence and victim-survivors, virtual communities are created in the digital space, whose roles are worth being investigated. In the final section, based on the appraisals of the responses from church communities and in digital spaces, I offer a meta-synthesis of both cases in order to reappraise what the findings imply in terms of empathy's moral and political aspects and how we can promote bystanders' use of empathy in just and caring responses for victim-survivors. I will finally come to a conclusion that delineates how mature empathy has a rich potential to dismantle unjust power structures, form solidarity, and contribute to a just caring community. Mature empathy is an affective and cognitive tool for communal resistance to re-create a community that restores the "fractured communal tie"[1] experienced by victim-survivors.

The Nature and Context of Sexual Violence

> But that night, Jiyoung got an earful from her father. "Why is your cram school so far away? Why do you talk to strangers? Why is your skirt so short?" Jiyoung grew up being told to be cautious, to dress conservatively, to be "ladylike." That it's your job to avoid dangerous places, times of day and people. It's your fault for not noticing and not avoiding.
>
> —Cho, Nam-Joo, *Kim Jiyoung, Born 1982*

According to the Centers for Disease Control (CDC), in the United States, more than 1 in 3 women have experienced any form of sexual violence in their lifetime and approximately 1 in 5 women have experienced attempted or completed rape in their lifetime.[2] Unfortunately, despite the current high rates of sexual violence, it is highly possible that the actual percentages

---

1. West, *Wounds of the Spirit*, 57.
2. For men, nearly 1 in 4 people experienced some form of sexual violence, and 1 in 38 men experienced attempted or completed rape in their lifetime. For more data, see Smith et al., "The National Intimate Partner."

are much higher than the reported numbers due to the reluctance of the victim-survivors to come forth. As stated earlier, I investigate three driving questions on sexual violence throughout this section. First, what are the significant factors that contribute to the prevalence of sexual violence? Second, how do they affect the victim-survivors? Lastly, why is it so hard for them to break their silence in the aftermath? There is a range of great scholarly work answering these questions.[3] Here, I limit my exploration regarding these questions to a few significant factors that are most helpful for studying empathy's moral and communal role in justice-seeking actions.

The first factor that needs to be explored is intersectionality. Perpetrators of sexual violence exploit intersectional social components that are convolutedly intertwined. When one lives a life at the intersection of multiple marginalized identities and statuses, the marginalized components of her identity increase her vulnerability to being a target of sexual violence. We can find an example of this in an article by Julie Goldscheid and Richard Caldarone, in which they share Aura's story of seeking asylum.[4] Aura, who fled for her life from dangerous domestic violence in Guatemala, was seeking asylum with her nephew in the US. Unlike her hope and expectation, however, what she faced was another form of violence, sexual harassment and rape. A border patrol agent swore at her, insulted her about her body and forced her to have an alone time with him, threatening her that he will not release her nephew from custody. When she was alone with him, he raped her.[5] Despite the short elaboration of the sexual violence Aura experienced, it does not require much effort from us to imagine the event. It is a new story about a distant other, but, sadly, the nature of the story does not surprise us in our immoral society.

Looking into Aura's case, we find the intersectional components of race, gender, citizenship/immigration status, nationality, and economic and social class that are working *against* her. The offender knows that Aura has little power to protect herself as a woman asylum seeker with a dependent, hence he will face no consequence for the sexual crime he commits.[6] Sexual violence is not merely a violence against a certain gender and/or sexuality. In Aura's story, injustice is exacerbated through the various forms

---

3. For example, see Fortune, *Sexual Violence*; West, *Wounds of the Spirit*; Herman, *Trauma and Recovery*; and Taylor, *Sexual Violence and Humiliation*.

4. Goldscheid and Caldarone, "#MeToo and Sexual Assault of Immigrants."

5. Goldscheid and Caldarone, "#MeToo and Sexual Assault of Immigrants."

6. Goldscheid and Caldarone, "#MeToo and Sexual Assault of Immigrants."

of violence including racism, sexism, and xenophobia; this is systemic evil carried out through legal institutions by state officials. If one's identity is formed at the intersection of multiple oppressed social components such as a person of color from a low socio-economic class with undocumented status, they become more vulnerable to the violence. Furthermore, the degree and length of the exposure to the violence will likely be worse than those who are from a relatively socially privileged background. Example cases can be easily found. Among those women who flee from Central America, *80 percent* of them experience sexual assault *on their way* to seeking asylum in the United States.[7] Also, another study reports that young immigrant women experience sexual violence double the rate of their non-immigrant counterparts that are staying in their own country.[8] The international and domestic power dynamics surrounding victim-survivors directly affect one's vulnerability at the intersection of geopolitics, economic and social status, race, gender, ethnicity, religion, nationality, and (im)migrant/citizenship status. These factors are so intricately and particularly interwoven that they create a unique impact on each victim-survivor by being manifested in distinct manners.

The second factor that we need to pay special attention to is systemic evil in sexual violence. Systemic evil denotes immorality or sinfulness that is caused, sanctioned, promoted, and perpetuated by marginalizing socio-cultural and economic *attitudes* and systems as well as institutional practices. In terms of Christian institutional settings, this evil can take the form of spiritual abuse through preaching: preaching as a manifestation of hypocrisy of clergy abusers who publicly uphold values of justice. Through the use of preaching, the focus of the community's interpretational lens can be manipulated and shifted against victim-survivors. Systemic evil also included sanctioned indifference to systemic forms of harm, mostly targeting subjugated vulnerable groups of people. Systemic evil perpetuates a power structure that maintains consistent categories of dominance and subordination. Even though there are differences between personal wrongdoing and systemic evil, personal action and the deliberation process is directly influenced by socio-cultural systems as human beings shape and are shaped by religion, culture, society, and community. Systemic evil creates different forms of violence, one of which is sexual violence.

---

7. Hallett, "Immigrant Women," 61.

8. Recited from Hallett, "Immigrant Women," 61–62. For the original data, see Decker et al., "Sexual Violence against Adolescent Girls," 498, 503.

The severity of and sustained practice of sexual violence in detention centers is a bold example of how *scrupulously* and *orderly* systemic evil is carried out as a form of sexual violence. According to Community Initiatives for Visiting Immigrants in Confinement (CIVIC) in a letter of civil rights complaint filed in 2017 to the U.S. Immigration and Customs Enforcement (ICE) in the Department of Homeland Security (DHS), 33,126 complaints of sexual and/or physical assaults had been filed against agencies under DHS. Yet, according to the letter, only 0.07 percent (247 cases) out of the complaints were taken into open *investigation* by the Office of Inspector General, which rarely results in charging the offenders for sexual crimes.[9] Considering the fact that it is extremely difficult for the detainees to file a legal complaint against the officers, we can easily imagine how rare it is for the cases to be heard and justice rendered.

According to CIVIC, the top five immigration detention centers with the highest number of sexual assault complaints are privately operated facilities; and three out of the five facilities are run by the GEO group, which has earned an astronomical amount of profits over decades.[10] Due to such high and severe rates of assaults of officers against inmates and detainees in for-profit prisons and facilities, the U.S. Department of Justice and Homeland Security Advisory Council made a decision that the DHS should rectify the high rates of assaults in prisons and facilities operated by private companies by "phasing them out" under the Obama administration in 2016.[11] Unfortunately, GEO group and CoreCivic, another major detention center company, seem to be actively involved with political campaigns by contributing significant amounts of money. For an example, according to The Center for American Progress, "an independent, nonpartisan policy institute," these two companies donated $250,000 to the Trump presidential campaign fund in 2016 in addition to many other political involvements.[12] When President Donald Trump took office in January 2017, the profits of the two companies had become upsized, which was a direct reversal of initiatives made under the Obama administration. GEO Group won a $110 million contract to build a new detention center in April 2017 rather than being *phased out*, soon after the new administration came into office. As of

---

9. See the letter of complaint for more detailed data: Merton and Fialho, "Civil Rights Complaint, RE: Sexual Abuse."
10. Merton and Fialho, "Civil Rights Complaint, RE: Sexual Abuse."
11. Ahmed, "How Private Prisons Are Profiting."
12. Ahmed, "How Private Prisons Are Profiting."

2019, over $480 million to GEO and over $331 million to CoreCivic have been awarded by the ICE since the Trump administration started.[13]

What we see here is that the sexual violence that happened in the for-profit detention centers is not just neglected but, worse, it is *systematically sanctioned* by political and justice institutions due to intricately intertwined financial and political benefits. Sexual violence in detention centers in the United States is the epitome of systemic injustice perpetuated by the governmental system and capitalist free market values which elevate profit motives in a misogynistic society. It is a complete delusion that sexual violence is merely a matter of an individual violation against another individual. The complicatedly intermingled systems enable sexual offenders to commit such violence by taking advantage of marginalized people; unequivocally this represents how sexual crimes are not limited to a person-to-person event, but are systemically sanctioned by economic, political, and legal institutional practices in this case. The dominant or marginalizing systems that constitute systemic evil directly impact the dynamics of how sexual violence happens and how it affects victim-survivors, and why it is so hard for them to come forth to break their silence and to share what happened.

On top of these two factors, we need to pay attention misogynistic beliefs and norms from culture, society, and community that reinforce systemic evil. These norms and beliefs are not only one of the *causations* to the prevalence of sexual violence but also, they affect victim-survivors of sexual violence in the *aftermath* of the abuse. In a carefully argued book,[14] a feminist moral philosopher Kate Manne thoroughly illuminates the implications of misogyny. She starts her conversation with criticism of the largely believed "naive" definition[15] of misogyny, which is "too narrow" and "not focused enough."[16] She then suggests a very well-articulated definition. For Manne, misogyny should be perceived as: "the system that operates within a patriarchal social order to police and enforce women's subordination, and to uphold male dominance... in which women will tend to face hostility of

13. Ahmed, "How Private Prisons Are Profiting."
14. Manne, *Down Girl*.
15. Manne, *Down Girl*, 32. Manne points out the problem of the common understanding of misogyny: "According to a common, dictionary definition-style understanding of the notion, which I call the naive conception, misogyny is primarily a property of individual agents (typically, although not necessarily, men) who are prone to feel hatred, hostility, or other similar emotions toward any and every women, or at least women generally, *simply because they are women*."
16. Manne, *Down Girl*, 33.

various kinds *because they are women in a man's world* (i.e., a patriarchy), who are held to be failing to live up to patriarchal standard . . . Because of this, misogynist hostilities will often target women quite selectively, rather than targeting women across the board."[17] Let me echo with her definition. Misogyny is not merely about certain hostile *emotions* "toward any and every woman."[18] Rather, it is a system that is a part of larger systems, which *police and enforce* selected women who do not conform to the gendered and oppressive norms in order to perpetuate *man's world*. In this sense, within the system of misogyny, victim-blaming and victim-shaming cultures function alongside of and fuel attitudes about a lack of credibility for women. These cultures are prevalent especially in cases of sexual violence. I now delve into victim-blaming and—shaming cultures in relation to misogynistic society.

In a renowned award-winning novel, *Kim Jiyoung, Born 1982*, the main character Kim Jiyoung,[19] an ordinary South Korean woman, was followed and threatened by a strange man at night when she was in high school, on the way home from a private academic institution, known as *hakwon*, a cram school, that most Korean students attend after regular school hours.[20] Jiyoung texted her father to meet her at the bus station for her safety as the guy was following her in the bus. When the father arrived at the bus station, the guy had already left after insulting Jiyoung, thanks to another woman's intervention. The father was scared and terrified by what might have happened to his daughter if not for the woman bystander's help. "But that night, Jiyoung got an earful from her father. "Why is your cram school so far away? Why do you talk to strangers? Why is your skirt so short?" Jiyoung grew up being told to be cautious, to dress conservatively, to be "ladylike." That it's your job to avoid dangerous places, times of day and people. It's your fault for not noticing and not avoiding."[21] Even though this story is a fiction, this kind of incident and similar stories in different rhetoric and versions are something that any woman in South Korea—and probably many other countries all around the world—might have heard

---

17. Manne, *Down Girl*, 33–34.
18. Manne, *Down Girl*, 32.
19. Cho, Nam-Joo and Kim, Jiyoung's last names are put first as a way to respect the intention of the author of the novel as well as the cultural practice in East Asian countries, which is different from the Western cultures.
20. Cho, *Kim Jiyoung, Born 1982*.
21. Cho, *Kim Jiyoung, Born 1982*.

CASE STUDY

or experienced at least once in their lifetime. It enables us to understand the dynamics of not only the experience of sexual abuse but also the *reactions* of people to the abuse that impact victim-survivors, which reinforce a victim-blaming and—shaming culture.

Katlynn Mendes et al. from a feminist socio-cultural and educational perspective define victim-blaming myths as a statement that "women provoked rape through their dress and behavior, and biologically determinist views that constructed an aggressive male sexuality as erotic, healthy, desirable, and inevitable."[22] The belief that men's sexual desire is strong, healthy, instinctual, and natural contributes to the perspective that the woman victim-survivor is responsible for the violence and any related outcomes. This misogynistic understanding of men's sexuality fuels the beliefs that victim-survivors should have been more careful in how to dress, where to be, who to talk to, and watching every move and action in order to prevent such an unfortunate tragedy. In this rationale of victim-blaming myths, there is an underlying assumption that sexual abuse can be prevented *by regulating women's* behavior, attitudes, and daily life activities. This is a quintessential example of misogyny that those women who do not conform to *women's subordination* and not *uphold male dominance* are to be condemned and punished. The hostility toward women victim-survivors is not only from male misogynists, but also from those women who conform to the gendered roles and rules in the society.[23]

This predominant belief system causes victim-blaming,—shaming, and –guilt culture. It suggests it was the woman victim-survivor who was not careful enough to prevent the event. Therefore, shame culture is prevalent in the aftermath of sexual violence and serves as another factor that contributes to aggravating victim-survivors' distress and suffering. Shame as a social emotion is often called a "master emotion" due to its powerful social and self-related impact on the individual in relation to society and community, and its broad involvement of other emotions such as guilt, humiliation, embarrassment, and mortification, just to name a few.[24] Shame along with guilt is also believed to be major "motivators and instruments

---

22. Mendes, Ringrose, and Keller, *Digital Feminist Activism*, 6.

23. Manne, *Down Girl*, 72.

24. Even though there is a keen debate on how to define the relationship between shame and guilt, I agree with the assertion that guilt, closely related to the shame matrix, is developed later than shame in developmental psychology and psychoanalysis. As Morrison answers the question of the relationship of shame to guilt: Morrison, *Shame*, 10–11. Also see Poulson, *Shame: The Master Emotion?*; Nathanson, *The Many Faces of Shame*.

of social control."25 Under this shame-controlling society and culture, shame can cause fear of abandonment, social isolation, and public ridicule from the community. Even worse, it often mars the victim-survivor's relationship with herself. Even though shame and guilt can also be used for positive moral functions, which are to prevent possible immoral actions or thoughts due to the fear of shame and guilt, the dysfunctions tend to disproportionately impact society's marginalized people and hence make them more vulnerable.26

Among various relevant affects, humiliation is a very closely related affect to shame. Most importantly, it has significant implications for exploring how sexual violence affects victim-survivors. One of the features of humiliation that is distinct from shame is that humiliation always requires a humiliator(s). Andrew P. Morrison, psychiatrist from a psychoanalytic tradition, understands humiliation that "specifically reflects the social, interpersonal manifestation of shame or internalized representation of the 'humiliator.'"27 In the process of humiliation, the humiliator considers and treats the targeted person as either nonhuman or subhuman, one who does not deserve full respect not only from another human being but also from oneself. Humiliation hence involves human objectification and dehumanization.28 A political philosopher Lisa Guenther posits that humiliation in this objectifying and dehumanizing process, "severs relations between one person or group and a larger community."29 The dehumanized person is "singled out" by the humiliator as nothing (an object) or no one (sub- or non-human), and exposed to the gaze of "real or imagined others."30 Guenther continues: "Humiliation works by singling out this or that person as deviant, out of place, abnormal, or bad, and displaying them before real or

---

25. Morrison, *Shame*, 187.

26. I will look into this further in chapter 4. In this section the focus will be limited to sexual humiliation in regard to sexual violence as a distinctive affect but still overlaps with broad shame spectrum.

27. Morrison, *Shame*, 15. Scholars on the scholarship of shame have long discussed the relationship between shame and humiliation. Some try to differentiate the two, while others think humiliation is an intense form of shame. I stand with the former as humiliation certainly has distinctive features compared to shame, whereas I do see the overlapping aspects of the two in many ways. See Morrison, *Shame*; Taylor, "Humiliation as a Harm of Sexual Violence"; Margalit, *The Decent Society*; Guenther, "Resisting Agamben."

28. Guenther, "Resisting Agamben," 61; Taylor, "Sexual Violence and Humiliation," 35–39; Taylor, "Humiliation as a Harm of Sexual Violence, 439.

29. Guenther, "Resisting Agamben," 61.

30. Guenther, "Resisting Agamben," 61.

CASE STUDY

imagined others. Humiliation individuates; it isolates someone from all the others, not as a subject with agency and voice but as an object of security, scorn and possible violence ... It marks one as that which does not belong, as that which must be expelled in order for the community to feel better."[31] Experiencing humiliation is, as Guenther illustrates, an experience of feeling rejected (from being fully human), disconnected from and abandoned by the society and community. Among those who are humiliated, when the experience of being objectified is intense enough, individuals not only experience the negation and rejection by the humiliator, but also internalize the humiliating gaze or action to themselves and now see themselves as the ones who were identified by the humiliator.[32] This marred self-image brought about by internalized humiliation changes self-relation as well as the other- and community-relations.[33] In this sense, the nature and the process of humiliation deeply involves socio-cultural and communal components, since one's understanding of another is deeply affected by social and cultural norms.[34]

One significant aspect of the brutality in the experience of sexual violence can be that it humiliates the victim-survivor in every possible way—bodily, emotionally, cognitively, and spiritually. Through sexual humiliation, she experiences being treated as if she is an object or not fully human; as if her body is some*thing* that can be violated and ruined; her emotions are not worthy to be heard; her autonomy is nothing to be respected; and she is not worthy to be loved due to her condemned sinful spiritual self. On top of possible internalized self-abhorrence, the social norms and cultural belief lead others to blame her based on misogynistic victim-blaming myths that the sexual violence was her fault, that she was failing herself, her significant others, and her community.

In addition to these socio-cultural oppressions against women victim-survivors, stereotypes of women as weak, non-reliable, hysterical, sexually seducing, and emotionally driven—that is, irrational—further weaken the credibility of women. This allows offenders to count on "cultural sanctioning"[35] of sexual violence, which makes it even more difficult

---

31. Guenther, "Resisting Agamben," 61.
32. Taylor, "Humiliation as a Harm of Sexual Violence," 439.
33. Taylor, "Humiliation as a Harm of Sexual Violence," 440.
34. Taylor, "Humiliation as a Harm of Sexual Violence," 440.
35. West, *Wounds of the Spirit*, 123.

for the victim-survivors to speak out about what happened to them.[36] The community and social institutions ignore or distort women's testimony against their abusers.[37] Such a process in the aftermath of sexual violence makes the victim-survivor feel abject, abandoned, and rejected by her community.[38] Sexual violence causes the victim-survivor to have a sense of severely "fractured community ties."[39] The state of being rejected by the community makes women feel sexual assault as an overwhelming communal-attack on her. However, this misogynistic communal-attack is rooted in collective negligence, ignorance, and unjust justifications that are fueled and perpetuated by marginalized social location and systemic evil.

In this section, I have explored three primary factors in relation to sexual violence, i.e. the dynamics of intersectional factors, systemic evil, and misogynistic norms and beliefs, which convolutedly intermingle with each other to exacerbate and perpetuate the prevalence of sexual violence and women victim-survivors' suffering. Based on this exploration, now I provide a case study example of what this looks like through a careful appraisal of church communities' dominant responses to sexual violence victim-survivors in the following section.

A Careful Appraisal of Dominant Responses in Church communities

> Many Christians hold the opinion that the sin of sexual violence is the victim's, not the rapist's.
>
> —MARIE FORTUNE, *SEXUAL VIOLENCE: THE SIN REVISITED*

Disturbingly, dominant responses from church communities to sexual violence have been filled with attitudes of avoidance, passivity, denial, and victim-blaming. Even though there are innumerable stories that demonstrate these disturbing dominant responses, here, I only share two selective stories that show two different types of responses from church communities.[40] The

---

36. I will not explore further the ethical problems of stereotypes of women and their socially given credibility here. For more information, see West, *Wounds of the Spirit*.
37. West, *Wounds of the Spirit*, 110–137.
38. Also see Herman, *Trauma and Recovery*.
39. West, *Wounds of the Spirit*, 57–59.
40. There are numerous literatures on this topic. For recent books on sexual

Case Study

first story is primarily to show how the church community *re-victimizes* victim-survivors, and the second how it *supports the offenders* in its typical responses. After sharing the two stories, I analyze the two cases through societal and cultural prisms resonating with the three factors that I explored in the previous section—intersectionality, systemic evil, and misogynistic norms. This analysis will be reappraised through the lens of empathy in the final section of this chapter.

People were shocked when Kim broke her silence in 2018 in South Korea about the sexual assault that she had to keep to herself for seven years. In 2011, when she was on a voluntary mission trip to build a school and medical clinics in South Sudan, a Catholic priest, Han, who was very renowned for his dedicated missionary work in Sudan sexually abused her and tried to rape her many times throughout the trip. Repugnantly, Han was also a steering committee member for the Catholic Priests' Association for Justice (CPAJ). One time, Kim states, he broke into her room, held her down and said that "I can't control my body. So please understand me."[41]

Kim could not scream for help because she was worried if she screamed for help, a Sudanese watchman would come and witness the scene of sexual abuse. If that happened, the whole mission might have been destroyed. The enormous amount of people's commitment of money, time, effort, prayers, and sacrifice to the mission might end up being jeopardized because of this incident. In the very first attempted rape, Han locked the cafeteria, held her wrist, and tried to rape her. The abuse finally came to an end when she grabbed something that could be used as a weapon. The next day, she told other junior priests about what happened. Unlike Kim's expectation, nothing changed, since Han was in charge of everything there. Thanks to the silence, avoidance, and ignorance of other priests, Han kept on trying to rape her throughout her stay. "I felt the atmosphere was like it would be peaceful if I only kept silent, and like everyone was struggling because of me . . . I was frightened to speak up. My legs were shaking. I was scared to be blamed. I couldn't imagine what was going to happen next. I have tried very hard to forget about Sudan since then. But I haven't been able to control my anger, have suffered from helplessness and depression, wondering what was causing all these. Every time, I ended up thinking about

---

violence and church community's response, see DeMuth, *We Too*; Everhart, *The #MeToo Reckoning*.

41. Ryu et al., "Cheonjoogyodo 'MeToo.'"

[what happened in] Sudan."[42] After those painful seven years, when Kim finally told others that she would go public with her experience of sexual abuse, people around her worried about the possible damage to the Korean church community, such as discontinued donations or possible closure of the mission in Sudan. She states "I do not want the missionary work to be shut down . . . I love my religion . . . I really do wish that the church will be a better one through my testimony."[43]

After seven years of suffering, she said it was the #MeToo movement that motivated her to come forward and break her silence as she saw women reporters join #MeToo, speaking up about sexual violence within their news company. Otherwise, Kim said, she would have remained silent for the rest of her life.[44] This is one of countless stories that women victim-survivors undergo in the aftermath of sexual abuse in the church community. With many other women's testimonies in the post #MeToo era, it is clear that sexual violence perpetrated by church leaders is not only the problem of the Catholic Church but all faith-based communities including Protestants.

With such emphasis on love and care, why is it that Christian communities not only adopt misogynistic and oppressive norms but also create their own unique ways of oppressing and spiritually harming victim-survivors? Why is it that too many Christian communities predominantly choose to sacrifice victim-survivors over fighting for them? Why do they choose to implicitly and explicitly pressure victim-survivors to forget and forgive over identifying the root causes and holding the offenders accountable? Many scholars find various reasons given as answers to these questions such as the misconception of sin, a distorted theology of atonement, and the virtuousness of self-sacrifice and forgiveness.[45] Oftentimes, women and marginalized groups are the most vulnerable people but also those regularly forced to remain silent, forget and move on, forgive, and sacrifice for the sake of the community and *sacred* purposes, which are deemed to be a greater good.[46] In addition to these problems rightfully claimed by feminist and womanist theologians, I add the distorted and biased, yet unaddressed

---

42. Ryu et al., "*Cheonjoogyodo* 'MeToo.'"

43. Ryu et al., "*Cheonjoogyodo* 'MeToo.'"

44. Ryu et al., "*Cheonjoogyodo* 'MeToo'"; AFP, "South Korea Catholic Church."

45. See Cooper-White, *The Cry of Tamar*; Brock and Parker, *Proverbs of Ashes*; Everhart, *The #MeToo Reckoning*; West, *Wounds of the Spirit*.

46. See Cooper-White, *The Cry of Tamar*; Brock and Parker, *Proverbs of Ashes*; Everhart, *The #MeToo Reckoning*; West, *Wounds of the Spirit*.

empathy at the root of the unjust rhetoric, which is explored in the final section of this chapter.

In Kim's story, there are a few noteworthy points in relation to the previous section. First, the socially and culturally supported myth that men's sexual desire is too strong to be controlled is obvious in the offender's mindset, given his saying that "I can't control my body. So please understand me." Hence, it should be Kim, according to his logic, who is expected to care and be *understanding* for his *uncontrollable* sexual urge. The problem is that Han's logic that is not solely created from his individual reasoning. Rather, behind it, there is the vastly accepted misogynistic myth in heteropatriarchal society supporting his excuse, not to mention two thousand years of accumulated sexual ethics in church history, which considered male sexual desire as something uncontrollable.[47]

The second problem is that the wrong question is asked. Asking victim-survivors 'why did you not leave?' or 'why did you not scream?' moves the focus of attention from accusing offenders to shaming and blaming victim-survivors. Traci West points out that such a wrongful and accusatory question for victim-survivors from the society and community "epitomizes their misplaced blame of women."[48] This locates the need for answers with the victim-survivors' *reactions* to the violence, instead of asking the abuser "how could you think that you are entitled to sexually abuse a woman?" The wrongfully directed questions also contribute to lessening women's credibility and testimony.

Third, the socially reproduced role of women as a mothering, caring, and sacrificial member of the community in heteropatriarchal culture is reinforced by silencing victim-survivors. When Kim tried to go public, the atmospheric pressure from her surroundings reinforced her silence and her feeling of responsibility as a member of the community. In this, Kim was expected to put others and the greater good of the mission and church first by sacrificing herself. The feeling of abandonment by her beloved faith community made her feel severed from her community as she was *singled out* and being exposed to the gaze of *real and/or imagined others*.

---

47. Ruether, "Sexual Ethics"; Also, there is a scholarly attempt to *integratively* understand sexual abuse especially in church context. Keenan is one of the first scholars who sparked this debate to understand and analyze abuse in its individual *and* systemic dimensions, and to offer a perspective that combines both individual and systemic aspect of sexual abuse. See Keenan, "The institution and the individual," 38; Keenan, *Child Sexual Abuse*.

48. West, *Wounds of the Spirit*, 156.

In addition to these three socially constructed types of reasoning against women victim-survivors, the church community re-harmed her in several other ways. The junior priests with whom Kim shared about the assault right after Han's first attempted rape were complicit in the on-going abuse by not doing anything, looking away from the violence, and implicitly forcing her to be silent. Their complicity with the assault represents the community's misogynist logic of rape culture where the interests of the rapist become the only interests of the community that are valued. In this misogynist culture, Kim disappears as a member of the community and is considered a communal enemy whose interests are not part of the community. Also, the communal complicity connotes an underlying belief that the importance of communal interest—or, in other terms, *loving* the community—outweighs personal wants and needs—*loving* oneself. In this case, the communal interest is to keep the peace (without justice) in Sudan at the cost of Kim's agency and dignity. This same unethical belief manifested again when Kim told other community members that she had decided to go public. When this order of priority in the community is compromised, the community tends to blame the person who refuses to remain silent and sacrifice herself, and thus who *hurts* their faith community. This kind of *indoctrinated communal thinking process* is based on the idea that women's agency is something that can be renounced and sacrificed. Kim's spiritual commitment as a believer is exploited and manipulated by the community. The worries that her community imposed on Kim made her feel guilty as if she was the one who was *sinful* for considering an action that might possibly hurt the community's sanctity. Kim is unjustly expected to be less than human, to suffer through objectification and dehumanization, so the community can continue to remain at peace *without* justice at the cost of her *being fully human*.

This is a *communal violence* that has been so prevalently done to victim-survivors of sexual violence in the name of *love* within Christian communities. Traci West points out abusers' manipulation of victim-survivors, using "the language of love" in Christian belief. West emphasizes Christianity's self-conflictual understanding and use of love-language:

> The moral implications of Christian use of language of love demands particular attention in the context of dismantling support for gender violence. Christian religious gender and sexuality values crudely reinforce forbearance with heteropatriarchal gender values embedded in Christianity and gender violence, even as

CASE STUDY

Christians call for the perpetual, salvific Christian work of love as a response to violence. An understanding of harm-free Christian love as the most authentic representation of Christianity denies the prevalent, authentic reality of the Christian gender-based violence and spiritual abuse interwoven throughout Christian practices of love.[49]

Founded on this double-standard of Christian love and its denial of facing the reality of gender-based violence, the dominant communal responses to victim-survivors have been re-harming victim-survivors—rather than "harm-free." By accusing them for not bearing the cross of love, not forgiving, and, for causing troubles in the community, they repeatedly re-harm the victim-survivors and wittingly and unwittingly remain blinded to the "authentic reality" of the violence in the community.

We also need to pay attention to the ways in which intersectionality impacts the story. Korean Christianity has been notorious for its heteropatriarchal worldviews and authoritative culture—primarily thanks to a charismatic-hierarchical leadership model—in the faith communities. Also, *some* communities' active—or aggressive—missionary works have been criticized for its colonial approaches in developing countries as *some* of the missionaries try to assimilate the unique native culture and language into Korean culture. This type of colonial approach often accompanies the dualistic misperception of the nature of relationship between the missionaries and the indigenous people as giver and receiver. This kind of hierarchical and dualistic understanding and attitude creates an asymmetry in power dynamics—hence "asymmetries of care"[50]—which affect everyone involved in the caring network.

Due to these sets of values and culture, in the particular context of being on the mission trip in Sudan, the double-layered oppressive systems were at play against Kim. Koreans tend to be educated to be complicit with authority. In Kim's case, that was the male priests. Kim was dedicated enough to be on a voluntary missionary work assignment, taking an assisting role for the priests as a layperson. Considering the cultural impact,

---

49. West, *Solidarity and Defiant Spirituality*, 237–38.

50. Tronto, *Moral Boundaries*, 152. I have explored this concept in the previous chapter in conversation Joan Tronto. See the section of Interdimensional Perspective-taking in chapter 2.

her Korean upbringing probably imposed pressure on her to put her communal dedication above her personal safety and well-being.[51]

Furthermore, the dualistic understanding of mission team as a caregiver and the people in Sudan as care receiver probably made it harder for her to take action to protect herself at the cost of possibly hurting the missionary work and the care receiver. This way of understanding the caring relationship contrasts with that of the missionary work as a reciprocally learning experience from each other in a caring network. Understanding the mission work as a one-way giving generates "asymmetries of care," which promotes hierarchical relationships. In this type of relationship, as a woman lay participant, Kim is in a double-bind through the socially perpetuated forms of oppressions against women, i.e., self-sacrifice and obedience. She was in a position where she was asked to play the socially trained role of mothering[52] as a caregiver for Sudanese converts and to be submissive to the authority of the priests. When Kim was considering screaming in response to the attempted rape, Kim was forced to choose between keeping the missionary work intact by preventing the Sudanese watchman from seeing the scene or protecting herself. Because of this understanding of Sudanese as a pure care-recipient and her communal dedication, she chose the former.

---

51. Regarding missionary and its dynamics with other social components, see Kwok, "Unbinding Our Feet," 62–81; Kwok, "The Image of the 'White Lady,'" 250–58. Kwok articulates the ways in which race, gender, and colonialism are carried out in the missionary works for women missionaries well in her works especially from an Asian feminist perspective.

52. Nancy Chodorow elaborated how women have been socially reproduced to be a mother and asked to be a caregiver. A woman-mother is socially expected to be selflessly sacrificing for her own children and is believed to love them no matter what, and to be held responsible for the result of how she raised her children. This socio-cultural expectation is applied to the context outside of the mother-child dyad. The long-established social equation of women as mothers has asked women to be a good and sacrificial caregiver who is primarily responsible to take care of people around her. Women in this socio-cultural environment thus tend to be trained to deny or ignore their own needs and wants when their own needs are conflicted with others'. Regarding the socially reproduced role of mothering for women, see Chodorow, *The Reproduction of Mothering*. Also, on women-mothers' ambivalent feelings and struggles, see Parker, *Mother Love/Mother Hate*.

CASE STUDY

As Tronto emphasizes, those who are socially vulnerable and marginalized[53] tend to be "too self-sacrificing."[54] These people disproportionately include but are not limited to women and people of color. The problem of building proper boundaries between self-care and other-care is complex in nature. However, when it comes to the particular context in which women who are from a very conservative hierarchical and heteropatriarchal culture are asked to choose between other-care and self-care, it is much more complex and hard not to be *too self-sacrificing*.[55] Even worse, when the decision involves their own *faith* community, it is more complicated since it now has a spiritual dimension.

Stories of sexual violence victim-survivors should be heard with the ears of the mature empathizer, who has an ability to pay attention to the complexities, which are brought by the varied socio-politico-cultural and spiritual particularities and contextualities. The intersectional particularities of social, cultural, political, spiritual, and religious norms and contextualities create complicated dynamics in which victim-survivors often become more vulnerable and re-victimized. Keeping this complexity in mind, let us move to the second story.

When church communities respond to sexual violence and especially to offenders who are clergy, they tend to defend or stand by offenders rather than victim-survivors. The second story is an example primarily but not exclusively to show how church communities not only *re-harm* victim-survivors, but also *support* the offenders in the aftermath of the violence. Under the title, "I was Assaulted. He was applauded," The New York Times interviewed Jules Woodson who is a victim-survivor of a sexual assault by her former youth group pastor Andy Savage at the age of seventeen. I now depict the assault in detail by using Jules's narrative provided through various platforms such as news articles and blogs in order to gain a victim-survivor centered view of the assault and church response.

---

53. As I pointed it out earlier, even though Tronto uses a word "powerless," I try to avoid using the word "powerless" as much as possible as an acknowledging gesture of those who survived, claiming their own agency and power by resisting the socially defined identity as "powerless." For more information, see chapter 2 note 51 of this book. Tronto, *Moral Boundaries*, 141.

54. Tronto, *Moral Boundaries*, 141.

55. Self-sacrifice is often understood as the epitome of virtuousness for followers of Jesus in Christian tradition. Such understanding should be challenged. I will revisit the concept in chapter 4 to re-conceptualize sacrifice from the perspectives of mature communal empathy and care ethics.

According to Jules Woodson, in 1998, Andy offered her a ride home from church. Jules, then 17 years old, got her mom's permission for the ride. Andy, however, had a different plan in his mind. He passed the turn to her home and pulled the car over on a dirt road, and asked her to unbutton her shirt, and to perform oral sex after he unzipped his pants. Jules continues to describe: "I looked up to him. I trusted him. So when he asked me to do that, I thought, this must mean he loves me. This is a man of God I look up to. What happened was a crime. This is not something that the church should handle internally."[56] After the assault, Andy ran out of the truck and begged her not to tell anyone about it, saying "You have to take this to the grave with you."[57] When Jules reported the assault to the associate pastor Larry Cotton, he asked her a question, "So you're telling me you participated?"[58] Jules continues to describe her feelings of shame, guilt, and embarrassment:

> I remember feeling like my heart had just sunk to the floor. What was he asking? More importantly, what was he trying to imply? This wave of shame came over me, greater than I had ever felt before. I had just gotten done telling him everything that Andy, my youth pastor, asked me to do . . . Every ounce of courage I had gathered, to walk in there and tell Larry the truth about what had happened to me . . . Not only did I suddenly feel this immense guilt for doing what Andy had asked me to do but I also started to feel that this was my fault somehow because I didn't stop him.[59]

When she asked about the follow-up process, Larry told her that the church would handle it and asked her to "not mention anything . . . to anyone else."[60] Andy was still teaching and ironically even leading a two-day event at the church about sexual purity and the importance of abstinence. "Yet, here I was sinking deeper and deeper into this pit of depression. I had nowhere to go, no one to talk to. After all, I was given one job by the person I had sought help from (Larry), and that was to keep my mouth shut."[61] After some time passed without any reaction from the church leadership, in an "all female discipleship group," Jules took her "final breath of courage"

---

56. Smith, "Silent No More."
57. Smith, "Silent No More."
58. Smith, "Silent No More."
59. Smith, "Silent No More."
60. Smith, "Silent No More."
61. Smith, "Silent No More."

CASE STUDY

and told the group about what had happened.[62] "Looking back now, I know without a doubt, it was a cry for help. Tears ran down my cheeks. I remember feeling a slight sense of relief as this was no longer just a secret between myself, Andy, Larry and Steve [the senior pastor] . . . I knew I had broken the rules of silence and that there would be consequences to my actions."[63] When Jules talked to more people about the assault, the church leadership finally let go of Andy. But they also threw a farewell party for him. Because people did not know the severity of the assault, Jules did not feel much empathy from the community. Rather, she noticed people showing love and affection to Andy. Jules narrates: "Andy was allowed to go before the church and basically say that he had made a mistake and that it was time for him to move on. I did not attend that service, nor did I attend the going-away party that they had for him afterwards. People were celebrating him, and showering him with love, and telling him how much they'll miss him. And here I am struggling."[64] After two decades passed, encouraged by the surge of #MeToo along with #ChurchToo and #SilenceIsNotSpiritual, in 2018, Jules sent an email to Andy about the assault. With no response from Andy, she came forward and shared her story to a blog for sexual abuse victim-survivors.[65]

In 2018 at Highpoint Church (HC), a megachurch in Memphis, the lead pastor Chris Conlee called Andy Savage, a teaching pastor at HC, to the pulpit. Conlee with a soft and placid tone begins to talk while ambient background music is playing: "I want you to know that we love you [pause] in an incredible way. And we are sincerely [pause] sorry for any dishonor . . . Only love covers a multitude of sins. Andy is going to come and share with us at this time. [As Andy Savage was walking out toward him, Chris slightly tapped his shoulder and said] 'Love you.'"[66] Chris as the lead pastor apparently intends to build a very emotional and empathic/sympathetic atmosphere, using Christian virtuous and biblical language such as love, sins, pray, and sincerely sorry. His saying that "Only love covers a multitude of sins" implies the Christian responsibility of loving and forgiving others. To be a good Christian, the congregation needs to hold love that "covers" sins. Given the authority Chris had as the lead pastor, it will be reasonable

62. Smith, "Silent No More."
63. Smith, "Silent No More."
64. *The New York Times*, "I Was Assaulted." The transcript is embedded in the video.
65. *The New York Times*, "I Was Assaulted"; Smith, "Silent No More."
66. *The New York Times*, "I Was Assaulted."

to assume that his introduction had a strong impact to form a certain atmosphere within the community as the congregation was reminded of the importance of Christian virtues such as love, sincere repentance, embrace, and forgiveness.

Andy came forward, admitted, and apologized about the "sexual incident" that he mentions many times was "more than 20 years ago."[67] He also emphasized the Christian terms of repentance, sin, and forgiveness as he puts it: "Until now, I did not know there was unfinished business with Jules. So today, I say, Jules, I am deeply sorry for my actions 20 years ago . . . My repentance over this sin 20 years ago was done believing that God's forgiveness is greater than any sin. And I still believe that. (congregation) Amen."[68] When his confession was over, the congregation gave him a standing ovation for about twenty seconds for his courage and his repentance as if they were offering him forgiveness. Jules was still in so much pain and got personal attacks through various ways after the church's service.[69] Her personal information was shared and people blamed her and hurt her dignity via online platforms. There are multiple points that need to be explored in this second story from a perspective of empathy: how empathy was actualized in the story and whether the ways in which empathy was manifested were moral or immoral. We will revisit this in the following section.

Through the two different stories of sexual violence in two different countries, we can see the similarities in the disturbing communal responses from the churches. The victim-blaming and -shaming attitude is found through Larry's statement in a questioning form to Jules, by asking "so you're telling me you participated?" Despite the fact that Andy was the youth group pastor who was supposed to protect the teenage students, the church's senior level pastor seems to diminish the severity of the abuse due to Jules's *participation*, hence, to imply that it is partially Jules' fault. The absence of caring and protective actions for victim-survivors in church communities is neither new nor surprising. This type of response to the victim-survivors was also shown through the story of Kim.

While the faith communities showed blaming and shaming reactions to the survivors, the reaction to the clergy offenders were different. When it

---

67. *The New York Times*, "I Was Assaulted."
68. *The New York Times*, "I Was Assaulted."
69. *The New York Times*, "I Was Assaulted"; Haag, "Memphis Pastor Admits 'Sexual Incident.'"

comes to clergy offenders, the caring and loving action toward them from the community comes to the center, often carrying an obligatory sense of understanding, loving, and embracing the sinner, thus saying a line such as "Only love covers a multitude of sins." The leadership reminds the congregations of the *good Christian* virtue of forgiveness and repentance.

This double-standard for victim-survivors and sexual offenders is exacerbated within church communities especially when they talk about biblical virtues and responsibility such as love, care, repentance of sins, and forgiveness as God "forgive[s] us our debts, as we also have forgiven our debtors."[70] *Victim-survivors* then become the *sinners* who make trouble and cannot forgive people even though their greater debts were forgiven by God. Reversing their position from the victim-survivor to a sinner may lead people to the victim-blaming questions such as "What did you wear?" or "Why did you stay with him late at night?" and, even worse, to asking them to repent for "having lost her virginity."

Jules's story also raises the ways in which the intersectional complexity takes part. In her narrative, we can find the community of conservative evangelical churches in the southern part of the U.S. and purity culture at play exacerbating heteropatriarchal church structures for a white teenage girl like Jules. Elizabeth Gish, feminist philosopher, in her intriguing article thoroughly demonstrates the terrain of purity culture and how "the harm and damage rhetoric" affects teenage—predominantly white—girls in conversation with feminist theological scholars.[71] The purity movement is primarily developed by white conservative Christian communities. In the movement, according to Gish, the frequently used objects of analogy are dirty tape, a half-eaten candy bar, and a damaged *trashable* Styrofoam cup that analogically represent the white young girls who had any sexual interaction before their heterosexual marriage.[72] Who would want the dirty tape pieces that lost their function, a disgusting half-eaten candy bar, or a trashable and damaged Styrofoam cup? Girls' worthiness is judged through a rhetoric of innocent and praised purity, regardless of whether their experiences of sexual intercourse are voluntary or involuntary. If their *purity* is compromised, they are not only unworthy and unwanted, but also spiritually sinful because the purity that God gave them is ruined.

---

70. Matt 6:12.
71. Gish, "Are You a 'Trashable' Styrofoam Cup?"
72. Gish, "Are You a 'Trashable' Styrofoam Cup?"

This binary purity rhetoric categorizes girls into either sexually pure or sexually impure, spiritually innocent or spiritually ashamed, and worthy or unworthy. Victim-survivors' sufferings in conservative Christian communities are exacerbated at the intersection of socially given victim-blaming/shaming culture and the sexual violence with the emphasis on sexual not on violence. Furthermore, they are perceived as the one who is unworthy, unwanted, and even sinful. The reaction from the pastors and church community that Jules had to face, as she already described in her own voice, had reassured her that she was the one who needed to be ashamed. Linda Kane Klein, an activist against gender/sexual abuse in faith-based communities, points out that the purity movement understands sexual violence as something that they need to hide or silence, and as "sex" rather than "violence."[73] Due to this objectifying indoctrination, she argues, a sexual violence victim-survivor is considered not as *a survivor*, but as *a sinner*.[74] This argument explains how Andy was still able to lead the special purity movement event after he assaulted Jules. In this heteropatriarchal white supremacist point of view, the purity movement allows men to make excuses for their supposed 'legitimate' sexual desire, while it endorses white girls "as the ideal embodiment of sexual purity,"[75] the idea of which "shames consensual sexual activity and silences non-consensual sexual activity"[76] for women.

The absence of just love and just caring found in the blaming and shaming responses of church communities to victim-survivors is appalling. Even worse, the distorted theology of forgiveness and love that are so generously applied on behalf of sexual offenders are formidably unjust and worrisome as they destroy the be-all and end-all of the existence of Christianity, i.e. just caring out of just love.

Through the cases of Kim and Jules Woodson, I have explored socially constructed oppressive norms such as misogynistic norms, victim-blaming/shaming culture, and intersectional factors. I also investigated the ways in which these norms intermingle with heteropatriarchal culture and belief systems of church communities, which re-harm victim-survivors and support clergy offenders, and, even worse, convert victim-survivors into the position of sinners. The heteropatriarchal social norms, double-standards,

---

73. Klein, *Pure*, 91.
74. Klein, *Pure*, 91. Also, see Fortune, *Sexual Violence*.
75. Gish, "Are You a 'Trashable' Styrofoam Cup?" 6.
76. Klein, *Pure*, 233.

and *deceptive*[77] church values interweave each other and resultingly feed into dynamically powerful forms of oppression against targeted groups, in this case women victim-survivors of sexual violence.[78] Traci West sharply points out this immoral partnership of the heteropatriarchal oppressive values of churches and society. She argues, "[t]his merger can create forceful cultural sanctions that enable intimate abuse and violence to proliferate, at great cost to victim-survivors, especially socially marginal ones."[79]

However, Christianity also has violence-countering values as West also suggests.[80] These values certainly call for *moral imagination*,[81] which will possibly defeat the churches' own immoral functions that undergird contextualized oppressions and subjugations.[82] In the same vein, I invited readers in the previous chapter into imagining *a mature society* that is equipped with the complementary principles of justice and care where empathy can play a significant moral role, and that can prevent people from objectifying and abjecting the other. I accentuated that other fellow human and nonhuman beings' perspectives can then be revealed to moral agents in moral encounters through the simulating and imagining process of mature empathy. If we can find a way in which a moral imagination of Christian values is carried out through mature empathy, we then might be able to find *a* way to fight against the deceptive double-standard oppressive values that heteropatriarchal society and church communities have utilized to sustain immoral systems of abuse.

I will thoroughly scrutinize *how* we can actualize this *moral imagination* in chapter 4 in addition to the question of *why* Christian communities carry out such unjust double-standards which will be discussed in the final section of this chapter. On the way toward the imagined mature society through mature empathy, now I turn to explore communal responses in digital spaces to sexual violence victim-survivors, which will eventually help me to envision the idea of communal empathy in digital communities.

---

77. West, "Ending Gender Violence," 199.
78. West, "Ending Gender Violence," 199–203.
79. West, "Ending Gender Violence," 200.
80. West, "Ending Gender Violence," 199–203.
81. West, "Ending Gender Violence," 199–203.
82. West, "Ending Gender Violence," 199–203.

A Careful Appraisal of the Responses in Digital Spaces

Digital spaces have been given a growing attention by the studies of humanities in recent decades. The ethical appraisals of digital platforms, however, have been controversial in the discipline of digital humanities. This section has a methodological significance to carefully examine the ways in which people in digital space actualize their empathy and/or develop any type of communal empathy in response to sexual violence victim-survivors. My intention here is to evaluate and examine people's responses in digital spaces with integrative perspectives, avoiding a dichotomic appraisal that is either helpful or harmful. To do that, I aim to investigate the strengths and weaknesses of #MeToo and #ChurchToo as an example of empathy-based resistance to heteropatriarchal oppressive culture and systems against sexual violence victim-survivors. This section is designed to be descriptive rather than prescriptive as I plan to analyze the implications of the phenomena of the movements in terms of mature empathy in the following section.

For this, I employ micro, meso, and macro approaches. In other words, I will explore the implications from a personal, a communal, and a systemic perspective. At the micro- or personal level, I explore what kind of role #MeToo and/or #ChurchToo played in the cases of Kim and Jules Woodson, and its advantages and disadvantages for their healing processes. For this, I will introduce and analyze how both Kim and Jules were influenced by the feminist hashtag movements and how people reacted to them through posts and comments on social media. At the meso- or communal level, I also compare the two extremely different groups of reactions that criticize or support Kim and Jules to inspect the phenomena through the perspective of empathy. At the macro- or systemic level, strengths and weaknesses of the movements will be explored primarily from an intersectional perspective in order to see if there are groups of people that are still left out of the movement and how this digital justice movement can be more just, caring, and inclusive. Overall, this section will discuss what is advantageous and disadvantageous about #MeToo and #ChurchToo, and what we find in peoples' responses to victim-survivors in digital platforms specifically in terms of the realization of empathy. The findings in this section will be analyzed at a deeper level in the following section as I offer a meta-synthesis of the responses in church communities and digital spaces through the lens of empathy.

Case Study

#MeToo has invoked the political and social upheaval that accompanies gender justice movements. Through #MeToo and #ChurchToo, individuals and groups of women victim-survivors across the world have been coming forward with sexual assault allegations that were silenced for decades. This truth-telling activism[83] has formed solidarity across race, nationality, and other intersectional factors through various feminist hashtag movements provoked by #MeToo. Solidarity and empowerment have been so powerful that victim-survivors are given courage to come forth together. However, it is controversial if #MeToo and/or its derivative movements such as #ChurchToo are helpful for victim-survivors' healing process. I look into the two previous cases of Kim and Jules Woodson in relation to these feminist hashtag movements; examining the role of social media and #MeToo in the two stories, and the limitations of and potential for mature empathy in the movement. Even though there are limitations of social media, in this section I pay more attention to its potential and strengths to amplify the ways it promotes a just and caring society and communities through empathy.

At an individual level, there is no doubt that Kim's biggest motivation to speak up about the assault was from #MeToo as she stated that "I would have kept this secret had I not known about the #MeToo movement . . . I just didn't want other victims like me . . . to spend the rest of their lives blaming themselves like I did."[84] Until the surge of #MeToo in South Korea, Kim was suffering from depression and a range of emotional distresses. Then, as she heard about others like her, she attained courage to speak the truth. Nevertheless, we have to stay vigilant to not romanticize networked digital space. Before moving to its helpful role for Kim and Jules Woodson, I first explore the weaknesses of social media for victim-survivors at a micro level.

The repercussions from her truth-telling were harsh for Kim. Soon after she broke the silence, various forms of re-victimization took place by priests and community members, while many also supported her, admired her courage, and called for justice-seeking action that was never realized for sexual violence victim-survivors in their own community. Massive insults and blame were leveled at Kim and untruthful rumors were created through online platforms at lightning speed. Most of the accusations were about Kim hurting the community, being harsh to Han the priest offender, and untruthful stories of her having a personal relationship with Han even

83. Collins, "Truth-Telling and Intellectual Activism."
84. *Agence France-Presse*, "South Korea Catholic."

after the assault happened. One of the most significant and critical rumors was created by Kim You-Jung, a priest and the president of Daejun Catholic University. According to a news article by Pen and Mike, the priest Kim You-Jung in his posting on Facebook implies as if there is a politically hidden intention by the news media through sharing the news about Han's assault. Then, he continues to share that he heard from *someone* that it *seemed like* Han had tried to apologize to Kim for seven years but the apology had never been accepted, which was completely untrue according to Kim and her therapist. You-Jung carried on his justification for Han's abusive behavior, stating that the reason why Han sacrificed himself so much for socially marginalized people and social justice was possibly because he wanted to do penance for his sin which was made seven years ago.[85]

Since priest Kim You-Jung's Facebook posting was published, there have been unimaginable condemnations of Kim arguing that Kim did not forgive the repenting priest. Her therapist advocated for Kim by making an official statement on Twitter with the consent from Kim, demanding a stop to the revictimization of Kim, clarifying the rumors are not true, and appealing that Kim is re-victimized by the groundless rumors and condemnations.[86] After her therapist tweeted the statement, the hostile public sentiment changed and more people poured out encouraging and empowering words in support of her, withdrawing their manipulated empathy for Han.[87]

Jules Woodson's case also exhibits similar phenomena. After twenty years of silence, encouraged by #MeToo, Jules truthfully spoke out, which later made her an iconic figure in the #ChurchToo movement. After Jules's public sharing, the reaction splintered into two extreme voices. Most of the replies on Twitter stood on her side and supported her. *Church Silence is Violence*, a Twitter account that advocates for sexual violence victim-survivors in churches, initiated a petition on *Change.org* under the title, "Force Andy Savage to resign from Highpoint Church," which gathered around 7,500 signatures.[88]

85. Yang, "*Daejeon Catholic-dae*"

86. *Maumjari* [@mirboristar]. Tweet.

87. After this changed public sentiment, Han received a range of blaming, without the presence of mature empathy, i.e. caring justice, for him. This is another issue that needs our attention in terms of mature empathy for abusers. However, I do not explore this issue as it might distract the attention to victim-survivors. Mature empathy or caring justice for offenders will be a significant research subject for future studies.

88. *Silence is Violence*, "Sign the Petition."

CASE STUDY

Yet, Jules also encountered heavy personal attacks through online platforms including slut shaming,[89] sexual insults, claims of her voluntariness in the *incident*, doubting her credibility and accusations that she had hidden intentions to hurt the Highpoint Church, and so on. In the meantime, Andy Savage's supporters worked on a petition titled "Support Andy Savage!" on *Change.org* to the lead pastor Chris Conlee and High Point Church, which collected 3,000 signatures.[90] Andy, about 19 months after his resignation from High Point Church, started a church named Grace Valley Church. He chose this name for the church saying in his own words, "If we are going to experience the grace of God in our lives we have to recognize him in our valleys, in our struggles, in our difficulties."[91] He is now serving as a Lead Pastor of the church.

As we can see, #MeToo and other forms of feminist digital activism are not a panacea for social injustice or victim-survivors' healing journeys. The re-victimization after their sharing was traumatic for them. They had to suffer from insults and personal attacks made by anonymous people who support their offenders. They became easy targets for the misogynistic culture and beliefs by anonymous multitudes. This suffering of victim-survivors should not be dealt with lightly.

We, however, should also pay attention to the possibilities of #MeToo and digital activism via social media. One of the uniqueness of social media is its networked nature along with spreadability and searchability. Activism in the pre-digital era has been reshaped. The scope of participants in social discourses through social media are unimaginably extensive across the globe with the increasing digital accessibility encompassing diverse race, class, and geo-political status. Feminist Christian ethicist Kate Ott emphasizes the powerful impact of networked spaces on the terrain of conventional feminist activism: "Feminist movements have historically been plagued by specific acts of appropriation, self-appointment of white women as translators, and

---

89. Slut shaming is a form of sexism conducted in both in-person and virtual spaces. Through this rhetoric, women's body and personal characters are described and derogated to sexualized and stigmatized being. Psychologists Goblet and Glowacz define slut shaming as "the stigmatization of an individual based on of his or her appearance, sexual availability, and actual or perceived sexual behavior and is primarily aimed at women and girls. This stigmatization is reflected in social and relational sanctions, such as rumors, ostracism, or insults, such as "slut" and "fag."" Goblet and Glowacz, "Slut Shaming." Also, see Mendes et al., *Digital Feminist Activism*.

90. Liles, "Sign the Petition."

91. Blair, "Pastor Andy Savage."

geographic limiting of group consultation . . . . What makes social media different from past participatory practices is the extent to which they allow 'audiences to talk among themselves, to critique, remix, and redistribute content on an unprecedented scale.'"[92] Through the #MeToo movement, other women's stories were shared and redistributed, social discourses generated, and critiques of the abuse went viral. Kim who once remained in silence after the assault attained courage by hearing about other participants who spoke up via the #MeToo movement and became the one who generated social discourses by using the hashtag movement as leverage to collect more allies who stand together with victim-survivors. Through this collaborative digital space, Kim found her allies and gained courage to speak the truth. In its dynamically moving virtual discourse relatively without borders and limits of space and time, Kim who was motivated by #MeToo spoke up and her narrative motivated other women who had similar experiences to come forth. She then was one of the earliest women victim-survivors who, in hindsight, ignited #ChurchToo in South Korea.

This *re*-generative function of #MeToo is so powerful that *a story* by *one* individual in #MeToo and #ChurchToo starting at a personal level constructs a virtual community moving across the boundary between personal and communal levels. A story travels beyond the limits of me and my physical relational network and creates a new communal space with many and unspecified people who share the feelings and social cognitions, networked through digital technology. Through the digital network, victim-survivors' severed communal ties are restored through a newly created community which is not built out of commonality but out of solidarity that is composed of the diversity each member of the community brings.

At a meso level, in this sense, #MeToo represents in-between and in-both individuals and communities. The place is created and expanded where individual stories are interwoven and the interwoven stories through empathy construct communities. The narratives of individuals stay in-between and in-both levels.[93] As the stories meet with social cognition and yearnings for social justice, the stories transcend the traditional boundaries of personal stories staying at personal level and disrupts the binary boundaries between the personal and the communal.

92. Ott, "Social Media."

93. In *Marginality*, Lee conceptualizes three categories of marginality that are in-between, in-both, and in-beyond. I only draw on the two terms here that are in-between and in-both. The third notion, in-beyond, will be employed in chapter 4. For more information, see his book, Lee, *Marginality*.

CASE STUDY

One of the biggest contributions of #MeToo and #ChurchToo is that they empower victim-survivors through empathy. At a meso-level, #MeToo creates and reverberates empathy, specifically sympathetic distress, empathic anger, empathy-based feelings of injustice and empathy-based guilt, as I explored in chapter 1, drawing on Martin Hoffman's theory of empathy. In *Digital Feminist Activism: Girls and Women Fight Back against Rape Culture*, Kailtlynn Mendes et al. from a feminist media and cultural studies perspective, pay attention to emotional responses from the readers of hashtag movements such as #BeenRapedNeverReported, whose emotions emerge in response to reading victim-survivors stories. The empathic affect, i.e. vicarious empathic emotions such as empathic anger or empathic disgust arise not only by reading the fact-oriented description of abuse by victim-survivors such as the place, time, and detailed descriptions of the abuse, but also victim-survivors' *responses* to the abuse. By reading a range of emotions of victim-survivors such as fear, anger, disgust, etc. the readers start empathizing with victim-survivors, sharing the responses and forming solidarity that calls forth social change.[94]

This can be understood at a deeper level, when we look into the nature of digital space. Kate Ott in her book, *Christian Ethics for a Digital Society*, asserts that "Digital technology has transformed the way we connect with one another, shape our identity, and form relationships."[95] The ways in which relationships develop and take shape are much different than in a pre-digital era in which relationships tended to be formed in physical encounters, and communities evolved from a rather centralized space with people of shared identities. Now, in the digital era, the scope of relationship is less limited to time and space, thus the boundaries and definition of communities tend to be constructed with greater intersectionality.[96] Through the hashtag movements such as #MeToo and #ChurchToo, victim-survivors in the two case studies were motivated by reading other victim-survivors' shared experiences that were similar to their own stories. Furthermore, when they shared their stories, their stories were heard by others who exist beyond their own physical network and specific affiliated religious communities. Those distant others unbound by time and space then can become the ones who stand with victim-survivors, even when victim-survivors' own proximal community members hurt their dignity,

---

94. Mendes et al., *Digital Feminist Activism*, 56–58.
95. Ott, *Christian Ethics*.
96. See Ott, "Digital Spiritual Embodiment."

emotion, and self-image through various misogynistic means. This was possible because of networked relationships through digital space that exists beyond confined time and space.[97]

At a macro level, let us look at #MeToo from global, societal, and cultural approaches by asking if there is anyone excluded from the #MeToo movement or its derivative movements. Despite the fact that these movements have empowered an enormous number of women, raised awareness of sexual violence worldwide, and motivated bystanders to stand up and participate in the justice-seeking activism, there are still marginalized groups who are left outside the advocacy that these movements offer. Those women who are (im)migrant, asylum seekers, and refugees[98] are one of many groups that we cannot easily hear from or about through #MeToo and #ChurchToo. Intersectional factors such as race, culture, language, nationality, and educational and citizenship status play parts in the ways that the certain groups are excluded from public discourses such as the #MeToo movement.

Lisa Nakamura, a digital humanities scholar, denotes the inequality in digital space and its exclusive tendency by asking a question: "Does the Internet really offer spaces of representations and resistance constructed 'for us' and 'by us'?"[99] The openness and networked nature of digital space may misguide people to develop illusive equality in the space. Digital space can intensify inequality in many ways according to one's social power status, accessibility to digital technology, and other intersectional factors such as language.

With regard to inequality, specifically, of (im)migrant women in #MeToo, the first aspect to explore is the lack of social power and resources among (im)migrant women. Nicole Hallett, in her article, scrutinizes the (im)migrant women's lack of access to the resources that can empower and

97. Ott, "Digital Spiritual Embodiment."

98. Even though there are differences among these terms, I will use (im)migrant women as a term to represent these categories for effectiveness. The term (im)migrant that I use here is to accentuate the liminality immigrants, migrants, asylum seekers, and refugees often have. For example, even when they consider themselves immigrants, their legal status defines their social identity. When asylum seekers feel like they are finally settled in a country, their identity is defined by someone else, an organization, or a system. The discrepancy can be large between their social self-identity and how they are defined by outside sources, especially when they are socially marginalized. This term (im)migrant is to emphasize the marginalization and liminality that those sojourners experience in their daily life.

99. Nakamura, *Digitizing Race*, 176.

CASE STUDY

help them to speak the truth as a part of #MeToo, even though they tend to be more vulnerable to gender-based, sexual and domestic violence in terms of the degree, length, and frequency.[100]

For example, Aura's experience of sexual assault in the detention center that I shared in an earlier section is not something that we can easily find with #MeToo and #ChurchToo. (Im)migrant victim-survivors may be denied access to digital experiences of empathy due to various reasons. When empathy is not mature enough, not equipped with social awareness, immature empathy makes it difficult for (im)migrant victim-survivors to be empathized with. (Im)migrant women's sexual trauma in such abusive institutional environments remains invisible unless one intentionally tries to hear about their voices. Digital movements such as #MeToo necessitate at minimum accessibility to the internet, knowledge of current social trends, and a sense of security in terms of legal residency status, not to mention time and energy that they can spend on truth-telling activism. Thus, the most marginalized even among the marginalized need someone who has access to these digital resources and a willingness to advocate for them.

Another hardship of (im)migrant women to participate in digital discourses is accessibility to the technology and digital literacy, which marginalize the marginalized group of people even further in virtual communities. Nakamura points out the stratification of digital space, arguing that "Relative latecomers to the Internet such as people of color, women, youths, and working- to middle-class users have never owned the means to produce cultural texts on the Internet in the same way that more technically skilled and better capitalized users have."[101] Due to the unique skill sets required to use the Internet and social media, the users' social identities and backgrounds can determine accessibility and aggravate digital inequality by intensifying stratification in the digital space.

The last barrier among others that needs to be investigated is the language barrier. Non-English speaking (im)migrants such as Asian (im)migrants often cannot participate in the discourse of digital activism. Nakamura explains how Asian Americans are excluded and underrepresented in the Census due to their language difference. According to the 2000 U.S Census, seven out of ten Asians were born outside the United States and many of them, Nakamura emphasizes, cannot speak English enough to

---

100. Hallett, "Immigrant Women."
101. Nakamura, *Digitizing Race*, 178.

answer the phone surveys.[102] Then, how can we expect those Asian immigrants who underwent sexual abuse to come forth, describe in English the detailed facts of abuse through #MeToo in the United States—let alone their emotional suffering—to the extent that native English speakers could. Considering that Nakamura's work was written in 2007, there have been significant changes regarding the platforms and technologies. Even though the impact of a language barrier has been reduced as translation technology developed over time in social media platforms, social disparities still impact digital spaces.

These limitations that are induced by one's social identity imply that others who have better access need to advocate for those who do not. As we know, #MeToo was started by Tarana Burke, an African American activist for sexual violence victim-survivors over a decade before it went viral on digital platforms as Alyssa Milano, an actress, used 'Me Too' in her tweet.[103] This is an example of how social disparities impact digital spaces even when individuals have similar access to platforms. #MeToo is grounded on Burke's strong belief in "empowerment through empathy," as she once stated that victim-survivors' healing should not be considered a *destination*, but a *journey*,[104] walking with other survivors and allies together in solidarity. She also stated that:

> What history has shown us time and again is that if marginalized voices—those of people of color, queer people, disabled people, poor people—aren't centered in our movements then they tend to become no more than a footnote. I often say that sexual violence knows no race, class or gender, but the response to it does. "Me too." is a response to the spectrum of gender-based sexual violence that comes directly from survivors—all survivors. We can't afford a racialized, gendered or classist response. Ending sexual violence will require every voice from every corner of the world and it will require those whose voices are most often heard to find ways to amplify those voices that often go unheard.[105]

As Burke emphasized the significance of solidarity in order to see invisible others and to hear unheard voices from "every corner of the world," we

---

102. Nakamura, *Digitizing Race*, 172.

103. Regarding the history of #MeToo and its related criticism, see The New York Times Editorial Staff, *#MeToo*; Colwell and Johnson, "#MeToo and #ChurchToo"; Rodino-Colocino, "Me Too, #MeToo."

104. *Me too. Movement*, "Tarana Burke."

105. *Washington Post*, "Perspective | #MeToo."

CASE STUDY

need "those whose voices are most often heard to find ways to *amplify* those voices that often go unheard."

When George Floyd was murdered by Derek Chauvin and his fellow policemen, people across race, region, gender, class, and nation poured out in the streets, calling for justice as a part of #BlackLivesMatter.[106] Despite the components that may cause inequality in digital platforms such as the users' devices, digital literacy, language differences, and accessibility; people of color and social activists specifically in the United States have found ways in which those spaces can be leveraged for social activism and to overcome the social disparities impacting the movement in digital platforms, in a way that Nakamura or anyone could never have imagined ten years ago. A picture of white women protesters forming a protective line between the police and black protesters went viral, as people gathered, demanding justice as a response to the death of Breonna Talyor.[107] These examples of solidarity and just caring spirit illuminate how far and deep we can expand our circle of caring to distant others, going beyond only significant others through exposure and engagement with digital movements in partnership with mature empathy.

Regarding the invisibility of (im)migrant women victim-survivors in #MeToo, we need to ask why they are excluded and left out of the movement and how we promote more inclusive caring justice within the movement to build a just and caring community. Nicole Hallett points out "If women of color felt pushed to the sidelines by the focus on white middle-class women's experiences, then immigrant women were not in the picture at all."[108] I completely agree that there is race and class issues in the current atmosphere of #MeToo in terms of whose voices are heard and whose are still missing. However, there is more to it than merely race and class. It is the matter of the accessibility to advocacy. At the intersection of gender, race, class, nationality, culture, religion, nationality, (im)migration/citizenship status, and so on; significantly marginalized people do not have accessibility to proper resources that can make their voices heard.

#MeToo should be the most inclusive and caring movement, for it was born out of the belief that no one should be left alone and every suffering voice should be heard and shared. As Burke said, to do that, it requires "those whose voices are most often heard to find ways to *amplify*

---

106. Cave et al., "Huge Crowds."
107. Eadens, "Viral Photo."
108. Hallett, "Immigrant Women."

those voices that often go unheard."[109] The most marginalized women, an example of which are (im)migrant women, do not have the accessibility to the safe channel to speak the truth and power to protect themselves in the process of seeking justice. Because of their lack of accessibility to internet platforms, not to mention the lack of institutional, financial, social, and communal resources, their invisibility will persist unless those who have the accessibility come forward and amplify their voices. So far, in the #MeToo movement, those advocates have been inadequate. Among the brave survivors' stories that we hear in the midst of #MeToo and thus we stand by them, it is hard to find the voices of those whose living environment is simply outside the network. "Empowerment through empathy" is necessary. But before the process of the healing journey starts through empathy, we also need to start with empathy to re-adjust our focal point and widen our perspectives to *proactively* find the stories that did not have a chance to be spoken and heard because of diverse issues ranging from heteropatriarchal cultural backgrounds to lack of accessibility to the internet and other resources. As #BlackLivesMatter taught us, #MeToo also can be invigorated by actively engaging beyond race, gender, citizenship/immigration status, religion, class, nationality, and culture boundaries. It is long past time we ask about the invisibility of immigrant women and LGBTQ+ people even in this inclusive justice-seeking activism. How can we promote and extend this circle of care? I will search for the answer in the following section.

Meta-synthesis of the Responses in Church Communities and Digital Spaces through Empathy

I have demonstrated that the dominant responses in church communities to sexual violence have failed the victim-survivors by showing denial or avoidance, forcing silence or blaming victim-survivors. Culture or theological distortions lie behind these responses, such as purity culture, sexual shame, justification of human sufferings, and abuse of vulnerable people. As Marie Fortune and other Christian feminist scholars such as Traci West, Rita Nakashima Brock, and Rebecca Parker point out, theological distortions can be easily found in the aftermath of sexual violence.[110] The theological distortion of virtuous suffering and forgiveness perpetuates negligence

---

109. *Washington Post*, "Perspective | #MeToo."

110. Fortune, *Sexual Violence*; West, *Wounds of the Spirit*; Brock and Parker, *Proverbs of Ashes*.

CASE STUDY

and societal and communal systemic evil. This process eventually justifies "the abuse of vulnerable people and avoid[s] accountability for those who abuse others,"[111] which perpetuates and spreads violence like a virus.

This section analyzes the findings of the previous two sections of responses from the church community and digital space in order to offer a space to think about how we can participate in promoting just and caring communities through mature empathy. Mature empathy as I have argued has the potential to transform bystanders from passive to active moral agents who can contribute to building a morally mature society. However, when communities respond to disclosure of sexual violence, empathy might or might not be misdirected as pseudo-empathy. What is needed are ways to utilize or maximize the potentials of digital activism through mature empathy. I come to the conclusion that by using digital activism we have a way to expand our circle of care to distant others through mature empathy.

Theological misunderstandings and fallacies of the concept of forgiveness, grace, and repentance as discussed earlier in this chapter lead to expressions of pseudo-empathy by members of a congregation. This happens, for example, when they believe if an offender genuinely repents before God, he should not suffer any social or professional consequences.

Pseudo-empathy is developed through the monopolized power system of clergy who can easily narrate their own stories. Due to the abusive power of monolithic narratives, congregants who are educated in misogynistic and heteropatriarchal culture easily empathize with clergy, the people with power in their religious community. Pseudo-empathy is a manifestation of empathy's dysfunction that feeds off of the silencing of victim-survivors, promotes oppressive theologies, and limits spaces for bystanders to encounter victim-survivors' stories.

In order to explore this further, I first need to remind the readers of what empathy is and how empathy works, as I explained in chapter 1. I construed empathy as *an observer's or observers'—as a community—cognitive and affective inner process and response to another or others in various negative and positive circumstances, which leads the observer(s) to feel congruent and oftentimes matching feelings with the other(s) through mimicry, perspective-taking, imagination, and/or simulation.* Also, empathy generates lingering emotions in the empathizing process such as empathic anger, disgust, shame, and hate as well as sympathy, compassion, love, and joy for the sake of others' well-being, which I called branches of empathic affect. Another

---

111. Fortune, *Sexual Violence*, 142.

element of empathy that I elaborated on was *engagement* and *interaction* with another, which should be accompanied by a cognitive/affective stance which corresponds to the well-being of that other. In other words, any feelings or thoughts based on the empathic process and response should be for the sake of the person with whom one empathizes.

As I contextualize empathy in sexual violence, an example will be helpful to deepen our understanding. When we read about Kim's story, Han made an excuse by claiming he had unstoppable sexual desire, and the other priests and her Catholic community deceptively responded to Kim. When made aware of this we feel angry and disgusted as well as feel sympathy for her. Furthermore, some people may wonder what I can do to help her or prevent this kind of abuse. The whole process is an empathizing process.

However, as other proponents of empathy agree and as I scrutinized in chapter 1, empathy is not a panacea for unjust social issues or moral problems, because we always have moral risks when empathy is *indiscreetly* used or is manifested with personal relationships and preferences. Dysfunctions of empathy, as I called them, imply that empathy can be used against another's well-being. When that happens, the type of empathy that is actualized is what I call *pseudo-empathy*. Actualization of pseudo-empathy then may enhance unjust social systems and heteropatriarchal, white-supremacist, and misogynistic culture and practices.

The quintessence of pseudo-empathy is manipulated empathy. In Han's case, for instance, when he said "I can't control my body. So please understand me," trying to get into Kim's room, he later might argue that he suffers from *uncontrollable* male sexual desire, which deserves empathy from the society. But we know this is a false claim. Behind these cases of dysfunctional empathy, systemic evil and heteropatriarchal misogynistic norms are oftentimes the underlying factors that enable offenders to manipulate empathic responses. In faith-based communities, theological virtues such as forgiveness also play into manipulated responses that work against victim-survivors.

What we see in the stories of Kim and Jules Woodson are striking overlaps and patterns. Andy Savage, manipulating the congregation by using the theological virtue of repentance and forgiveness, plays on a theology of forgiveness as granted by God so no one can blame him anymore. *Without* thinking of community accountability for harms that were done to victim-survivors or of how to build restorative justice generated from the accountability, people start to empathize with him, saying things like: how hard it must be for him to be burdened for a long time and how brave he is to come forth to confess his sin. People even formed a support group for Andy, helping him to found a church named Grace Valley Church.

What makes this manipulation possible is the *asymmetric power structures* that allow the church leader to rewrite or co-opt the offenders' narratives and shift the focus of the community to him. This unilateral communicative way based on heteropatriarchal authority of clergy and distorted theology makes it possible for people in power to manipulate the congregation. Thus, manipulated empathy is realized.

Thinking about how to counterpose the focus of empathy from offenders to victim-survivors is necessary and significant. Here feminist digital activism like #MeToo and #ChurchToo can contribute to building a moral society with the help of mature empathy. If I am right, manipulated empathy feeds off the asymmetric power structure that makes people with power a sole storymaker, hence perpetuating the dualistic power structure of speaker and listeners. In response, we have to dismantle the monopoly of narrative power by *democratizing* the stories, making counternarratives, and disseminating them to every nook and cranny of the land. Let us scrutinize Kim's story as an example.

In Kim's story, we also find manipulated empathy when Kim You-Jung a priest and the president of Daejun Catholic University, published a post on Facebook, spreading an *unverified* and *untruthful* rumor that Han tried to apologize to Kim for the last seven years. Although You-Jung's argument was obviously groundless; he did not provide any legitimate evidence claiming such a bold argument on behalf of Han, he was quite successful in transposing the communal empathic focus from Kim to Han thanks to his position as a priest and the president of the renowned Catholic university. People started to turn their back on Kim and empathize with Han, until Kim's therapist advocated for her, providing a counter-narrative as a resistance via Twitter. The resistance of the counter-narrative seems much more effective, fast, and powerful these days than in the pre-social-media era and specifically pre-#MeToo era. The words spread out in the blink of an eye, generating follow-up news articles. As her therapist spoke up, the asymmetric and monopolistic narratives were disrupted and the communal focus of empathy swung back to Kim with even more powerful empathic anger for this injustice. The public began to develop a supportive community that can stand with Kim and walk with her through the healing process. The therapist's counter-narrative motivated the public to decrease their manipulated empathy for the abuser and to try to hold the abuser accountable.[112]

Of course, the current moral problem of manipulated, pseudo-empathy is much more complicated than a single example where it can be resolved by merely spreading words through social media. Democratizing the narratives alone did not and will not annihilate manipulated empathy that supporters for clergy offenders actualize.[113] The focus here is not on the consequence of the counter-narrative; rather, it should be the ways in which the majority of people transpose their empathic focus from the offender to the victim-survivor.

As I emphasized in chapter 1, we need ethical voices in order to overturn the immoral causation and effect of manipulated, and/or pseudo-empathy; for it often occurs through immoral power systems and immature socio-psychological manipulation along with other factors. One way to fight against pseudo-empathy is to educate members of society to develop their sensitivity to empathy, partnered with social cognition, and to call for systemic change.

I pointed out in chapter 1 that empathy has three different types of weaknesses that are limits, potential risks, and dysfunctions. On top of dysfunctions that are manifested in the cases of sexual violence, we also need to pay attention to the potential risks of empathy. Empathy has a tendency to be realized more easily and more intensely when the other is an in-group member, here-and-now distant others, and/or with intense distress cues on site. For example, in Jules' story, many congregants empathized with the offender, Andy, rather than with Jules. When they have an in-group member struggling, in this case Andy, people tend to empathize with the member more easily and/or more intensely, presenting an inability to empathize with strangers. Because of Andy's profession as a pastor, people find it easier to empathize with him rather than with Jules, who was a distant

---

112. Even though this phenomenon connotes significance in terms of decreasing pseudo-empathy, dehumanization of the abuser in the process is something that we need to try to diminish. In order to do that, we need mature empathy's help to make the caring justice for the abuser, which is holding him accountable while providing him with care. It is a starting point for him to live as a moral and integrative member of the society, without losing his human dignity.

113. This type of empathy is innately unjust and manipulated by the monolithic story by the offender; even though the supporters' empathy was for the sake of well-being of the offender, since Han's well-being is at the cost of the well-being of Kim, the victim-survivor, the lack of moral component in empathy is also considered to be manipulated empathy.

other—*not one of them*—who was not present with the church members, nor showing distress cues in person. This is a *potential* risk since this type of dysfunction might or might not actualize according to diverse factors such as one's psychological maturity, personality, social cognition, ethics, and philosophy just to name a few. Not all church members were empathizing with Andy and some of them even stood with Jules. Hence, we *can* prevent the potential risks by applying a well-developed perspective-taking and considering the possible consequences of one's biased empathic action on all those involved. The dualistic frame of 'us versus them' is often seen in the reactions of faith-based communities where the supporters of clergy offenders only empathize with the offender, which re-harms victim-survivors.

One of the key factors in why the #MeToo movement went viral was because we as human beings have the ability to empathize with distant others; and by empathizing, we recognize the self as situated in a relational network with other fellow human beings. Feeling *connected* and *acknowledged* empowers the victim-survivors and creates solidarity, which makes *ourness*. #MeToo endows a locus where victim-survivors have leverage, break their silence, and where their allies and audience across the globe are exposed to their stories. Sexual violence has always existed. What is different now in this post-#MeToo era is we talk about it more often through digital activism such as the #MeToo and #ChurchToo. Furthermore, social media allows distant others to connect in ways that have never been possible before. It also gives women their own voice since, unlike other media, there are no gatekeepers of heteropatriarchal and misogynistic norms, even though it still carries unjustified personal attacks. The ways in which #MeToo and #ChurchToo were able to make people use mature empathy for the sake of victim-survivors challenge the unjust power structure that church leaders manipulate; and create a public space where power is distributed to every member of the community. The *democratized* digital space helps victim-survivors to break the silence, sharing their side of the story and to disrupt the local congregational space where offenders used to hold power over victim-survivors. Digital platforms provide intersubjective spaces where truth-telling by victim-survivors is shared, even when uncomfortable and empathic affects surge such as empathic anger and disgust toward the offender and his actions as well as compassion and communal mourning for what happened to the victim-survivors.

Empathy generated through #MeToo and #ChurchToo also generates solidarity by looking at the trauma from victim-survivors' perspectives.

#SilenceIsNotSpiritual along with #ChurchToo emphasizes solidarity and breaking silence by responding to the exploitation of doctrine using catch phrases of solidarity calling forth communal empathy: "Violence against her is violence against God"; and "Violence against her is violence against us." At the core of these digital movements is the significance of storytelling and solidarity. This movement helps people to share the concrete lived experience of victim-survivors, the socially oppressed distant others.

Before #MeToo and #ChurchToo, space was lacking for bystanders to be exposed to victim-survivors' narratives so the bystanders could be transformed into listeners and participants in the shared narratives. When #MeToo created the emotional and communal space to share the stories of previously silenced voices, empathy helps the public to form a personal attachment with a distant other since empathy is "the glue that holds communities together."[114] Before being networked through digital activism, physically, and hence emotionally, distanced individuals' narratives may have seemed irrelevant and thus insignificant to each other. The newly formed relationships through digital spaces help people to transform the insignificant or meaningless narratives to an actual person's agony when empathy is properly developed in the process. Once the stories are heard *with empathy*, observers are not bystanders and victim-survivors are not objectified strangers anymore. It is empathy through which diverse individuals intersubjectively encounter one another. If empathizers are mature, they voluntarily open themselves to others' suffering while they temporarily lay aside their own egoistic desire, as they believe that no one in this world can live as a fully detached and independent agent; rather others, regardless of them being significant or distant to the empathizers, intersubjectively entangle and encounter each other. The self is "broken open by the other" and there we find "ourness, that is a community."[115]

Nevertheless, the online community is still far from a "perfectly" mature one and the majority of congregations still choose silence and avoidance over challenging injustice. Many congregations also remain indoctrinated in distorted theology over sharing and making solidarity. Furthermore, many people in online communities often choose solidarity with the abuser. Socio-cultural contextuality of sexual violence and victim-survivors unveils heteropatriarchal, white-supremacist society, a bare face of oppression that the society uses to manipulate the emotions of the oppressed. Empathy in

---

114. De Waal, *The Age of Empathy*, x.
115. Van Nistelrooij, *Sacrifice*. Also, see chapter 2 of this book.

CASE STUDY

this light is the bridge between the testimonies of victim-survivors and the bystanders, generating *personal meanings* between victim-survivors and bystanders. Digital platforms offer a space for that bridge to be built. Empathy amplifies the bystanders' attentiveness to the story, and lets her digest the story as her own, since she walks through what happened at the site of sexual violence through the victim-survivors eyes. What we really need to focus on here is how we encourage people to foster mature empathy and moral sensitivity to issues of justice, so that empathy as an inner response can be transformed to engaging empathic action.

4

Building Blocks of Mature Communal Empathy

I have discussed the moral roles of mature empathy as the bridge of a caring relationship between victim-survivors and bystanders. Also, it was discussed how digital activism provided the space for empathy to be actualized. Now, we need to examine the ways in which we can promote mature empathy in order to motivate people to develop their moral sensitivity at individual, communal, and societal levels. That being said, I will provide a robust picture of mature communal empathy in praxis as well as envisaging a just caring society, an imaginary, as an ethical practice in this chapter.

To better understand mature *communal* empathy, we need to reflect on community and communal empathy first. What does empathy look like at a communal level? How does it relate to resistance against injustice? With such driving questions, I first ponder upon community and communal empathy followed by elements of mature communal empathy in the first section.

In the second section, I encourage the readers to use imagination as a primary tool for us to build a foundation for a just caring society for which mature communal empathy is the predominant building block. As I try to envision a morally mature society, I reflect on three subjects. First, how can we practice mature communal empathy as a resistance to socio-culturally manipulated empathy? Second, what are the Christian values that need to be reconsidered and utilized as a moral value with the aid of mature communal empathy rather than tools that perpetuate social injustice in the grip of dysfunctional empathy? Third, if mature communal empathy is morally significant and effective, how can we foster mature communal empathy at individual, communal, and societal levels? After these questions are answered briefly, I provide a summary of each chapter of this book, highlighting significant points that I made. I will conclude this book by reinforcing my final claims and suggesting future research.

Communal Empathy

What does mature empathy look like when it is actualized at a communal level? Mature communal empathy neither can remain abstract nor be purely derived from reason or emotion. Mature communal empathy by nature should be understood as a praxis.[1] Holding on to this integrative—yet particular—moral understanding of communal empathy, I will reflect on community, the communal, and communal empathy first.

Reflection on Community and Communal Empathy

I use the term community here as an invisible and/or visible group, in which people *share* their values, beliefs, identities, thoughts, emotions, life stories, or goals, and often but not always individually and collectively *care for* one

---

1. My usage of the term praxis is based on two different sources. First, I draw on the denotation on praxis that Visse and Abma used in their work, who articulate praxis as "a particular way of action that is not instrumental or rational (this action leads to that outcome) but morally informed, wise, prudent, and embedded in the traditions of action, reflection, and dialogue on theory and practice. Praxis focuses on "a particular kind of human engagement that involves one's dealings with, or interactions with, others that *unfolds* in view of some particular understanding of substantive rationality appropriate to the practice in question" (Schwandt, 2005, p. 98). We stress the word unfold in italics because it illustrates that we cannot steer or control human engagement or understanding through a rational (evidence-based) approach. We can learn from evidence, but it is impossible to simply transfer evidence gathered in one context to another." Visse and Abma, *Evaluation for a Caring Society*, 4. Also, in Christian ethics, Ott's work, especially drawing on Paulo Freire, resonates with my usage: "Creative moral response is nurtured by a socio-moral pedagogy, what liberation theology terms praxis, defined as 'reflection and action directed at the structures to be transformed.' In the tradition of liberation theology, critical awareness of one's material condition caused by oppression related to economic, racial, or gender disparity is key to transforming the social structures that perpetuate oppression." Ott, *Christian* Ethics, 7.

another. Some communities tend to be inclusive with other communities and their values while others do not. Community can be intentionally or unintentionally *born*.

For example, Jesus never tried to gather people with an end to create a community that was a fixed institution. Rather anonymous people voluntarily gathered and formed a community without an explicit intention to build one or even a recognition that they were a community. In this type of unintentional thus noninstitutionalized community, no one monopolizes power over the community, yet the community continuously forms and evolves its shared ground, with which people often share their feelings, thoughts, gifts, and even possessions as a *caring act*. This type of community is *not created* by one particular person or group; rather it exists, as the shared beliefs and cause collectively motivates people to be intersubjectively connected with one another.[2]

An institutionalized community, on the other hand, often tends to form a power structure through which certain groups of people within the community or the core founder of the community hold control over the community. The gatekeepers of the community then can and often do endow the rules and guides to the members of the community, directing the community.[3]

Community is *a priori* neither moral nor immoral just as empathy *per se* should not be construed as moral or immoral. Yet, I try to pay attention to the moral functions of communal empathy as we desperately need it to realize our moral imaginary. Depending on the ways in which the community was born and evolved, the collective activity may or may not be moral. Some communities can hold a very exclusive and violent culture, hence taking corresponding collective action towards people outside of their own community—or even towards non-compliant members—whereas other communities can exhibit a just, caring, and inclusive nature. As I explored

2. See the prime example of this community in the work of Palmer, especially chapter 7 of *The Active Life*.

3. These are mere examples of different types of communities. It is not my intention to classify the types of the community into the two binary forms here. Categorizing the types of community is beyond my focus in this book. I also do not believe that institutionalized communities are always immoral or non-institutionalized communities are always inclusive. Non-institutionalized communities also have their own vulnerabilities. Furthermore, these two types of community formation can happen at the same time, as Jesus's followers were an unintentional community while the disciples often tried to vie for power by acting as gatekeepers to Jesus. We can find Jesus consistently resisting this attempt.

Building Blocks of Mature Communal Empathy

in the previous chapter, Christian churches, an institutionalized community type, not always but dominantly show its aggressiveness towards sexual violence victim-survivors.

Whereas through the #MeToo movement, caring often takes place among the people in the virtual community, a non-institutionalized type. The #MeToo community that was generated through digital spaces was born out of desperation and the shared suffering of sexual violence victim-survivors and those who had the tendency to maturely empathize with the victim-survivors. The members of the virtual and amorphous community are intersubjectively and interdimensionally connected with one another, acknowledging and recognizing the distant other's cries, providing *just caring*. The victim-survivors were aware that participating in the community by shouting out #MeToo would make themselves vulnerable to targeting and re-victimization. Yet, they voluntarily opened themselves to the vulnerability in trusting the power of community and communal empowerment through empathy. This courageous action and trust make them as *one-caring*, *cared-for*,[4] and *anything in-between*, which makes the caring relationship mutual and symmetric within the community. The severed communal tie of victim-survivors from their institutionalized religious community is re-created with the new community and they are able to begin their healing journey as they are *recognized* for who they are through the eyes of others in the virtual community. The members of the community *collectively* embody the victim-survivors' suffering through empathy, thus the embodied suffering is transformed into empowerment and reassurance. 'Collectively' or 'communally' in this case is defined by a differentiated and diverse collective in which the members can find shared sentiment among each other. These reactions are not uniform nor are they regulated or manipulated by hegemony—a power center that demands a singular reaction. Each individual empathizes with another victim-survivor's sufferings while the collection of the individuals' diverse responses signifies a core message that cares for victim-survivors. 'Collectively' or 'communally' in this sense intrinsically implies reassurance for victim-survivors that they are not the sinners but the survivors, that they are not alone. All these people individually and collectively feel their suffering with them (empathy) and for them (empathic-sympathetic distress). This is an example of mature communal empathy. I come back to this point in the following section.

---

4. Noddings, *Caring*.

Communal empathy is a type of empathy that can be mature or immature—just like individual empathy can be mature or immature. When communal empathy is immature and thus dysfunctional, it tends to contribute to building an unjust society and community as I already explored in the previous chapters. While I carefully oppose a binary distinction between the mature and immature empathy, I constructively described the tendencies of mature empathy and manifestations of dysfunctional empathy over the previous three chapters. If communal empathy is immature hence consequently manifested as immoral, the collective empathic reactions may be destructive and contribute to perpetuating social inequality and injustice. The prime example was the members' collective reaction from the church community to Jules Woodson as I explored in chapter 3. When an individual or community does not morally scrutinize their empathy, and when they act together exclusively for their community's interest, immature communal empathy becomes a very useful tool to reinforce social inequality and institutionally immoral practices. I contextualize this aspect in a later section.

There is a fine line between exclusive and inclusive communal action. For example, some might say #MeToo also seeks their community's own interest, which is the empowerment of sexual violence victim-survivors. The *manifestations* of their communal action might look like the #MeToo movement is exclusively acting for the sake of victim-survivors, ostracizing abusers. When we look in depth, however, it is evident that #MeToo's raison d'être is to build a community where *everyone* is valued and equal—that is by nature moral, thus mature, as it is the developed state. The care carried out through #MeToo is *manifested* differently since the way in which caring is done for victim-survivors is through empowerment and recognition as a practice of just caring, while caring justice[5] for the abusers is evidenced through social accountability, thus constructing a community that contributes to a morally mature society where everyone is included and recognized equally.

If I were to choose only one word that describes mature communal empathy, it would be *inter-connectivity*. Intersubjective connectivity involves relationships between two or more human and non-human beings, where reciprocity is realized. The sense of being *together*, the feeling of *ourness*,

---

5. Some might wonder why I sometimes use these two terms interchangeably. I perceive caring justice and just caring as two sides of the same coin especially in the vein that justice and care should complement each other. As I described the relation of justice and care in chapter 2, their ideas and roles can be distinctive but they are—at least, supposed to be—intrinsically connected to one another.

is founded on a culture in which everyone is *equally recognized*. In this equally recognized relational network (the mature empathic community), the shared feeling of being intersubjectively *connected* charged with morality becomes a very powerful resistance against any kind of subjugation that may happen with-in and with-out the community. The intersubjective and interdimensional connectivity actualizes at affective, cognitive, physical, and spiritual levels. The connectivity transforms individual spirituality and practices into communal resistance based on solidarity. This connectivity brings about action.

Empathy intrinsically is communal for one cannot live a life alone completely detached from another or live only within a dyadic relationship; nor can one generate her empathic feelings toward others without *recognizing* the existence of others. Some type of *communal* interaction has to occur at emotional, physical, cognitive, and spiritual levels in order for empathy to be formed. Communal empathy develops through feelings and thoughts by direct and indirect experiences of the other(s). These interactions enable persons to be intersubjectively connected with significant others or complete strangers through empathy as they adopt others' feelings, thoughts, and views into their perspectives along with other perspectives that they attain from their other relational and experiential network, i.e. interdimensional perspective-taking.

While communal empathy can happen as developed forms, it can also take primordial forms of human instinct that is hard-wired in our brain, which allows human beings to share universal reactions to certain situations. Think about situations in which we see someone getting brutally tortured in a movie. It is a universal reaction to shudder and groan together. We empathize with the character in pain so deeply that we often turn our head away, unable to finish watching the scene. The unavoidable human capacity of mimicry and emotional contagion as very primordial forms of empathy proves how deeply empathy is rooted in and composes humanity, thus so is intersubjective relationality.[6] This existential and non-verbal communicative tool incapacitates the power of the binary conception of I and thou, creating the intersubjective thus liminal space among oneself and others or between communities. In this liminal space created by empathy, it is almost impossible to completely separate my experiences from your experiences as they are intertwined. In other words, we are inseparably *inter-connected,* while individuals or groups keep their own identity

---

6. See chapter 1 for the concept of mimicry and emotional contagion.

(self-other differentiation). Given that our *own* identity as a person, persons, or group(s) keeps being challenged and evolving by the influence of intersubjective connectivity, it is hard to fathom the power and the depth of inter-connective empathy for building an equal society when it is morally well nuanced.

In terms of Christianity, we can also recognize how essential empathy is as a human faculty, and even as one of God's characteristics. Jesus Christ is a prime example. He empathically *embodies* human sufferings, which endows the Christological call for embodying the spirit of Christ in our lives.[7] Think about the Christian teachings to "rejoice with those who rejoice, weep with those who weep,"[8] which is a call for *empathic (re)action* of love and compassion, participation in and embodiment of sorrow and joy as a communal action of empathy.

Then, with this empathic foundation, why do Christian churches often manifest dysfunctional empathy, perpetuating the systemic evil by defending clergy sexual offenders? Why can't we actualize the valuable Christian qualities of embodying the suffering, feeling *together* with those who weep and grieve in social justice activism? This ironic yet significant question will guide us to find ways in which Christian communities can improve and strengthen their moral role in building a morally mature society founded on mature communal empathy. Before diving into the question, I first explore the elements and practices of mature communal empathy.

Elements and Practices of Mature Communal Empathy

While I acknowledge that there is immature communal empathy often actualized in our society, my primary interest here is in how to promote people to develop and actualize *mature* communal empathy as a resistance to social injustice. Thus, as an attempt to imagine mature communal empathy, this section will offer an expanded dialogue with the features of mature empathy detailed in chapter 2. Those features were explored in terms of the nature of mature empathy. In addition to the traits, I attempt to elaborate on specific elements that mature *communal* empathy involves. There are overlaps between the features of empathy and the elements of mature communal empathy, as individual and communal is often—if not always—something that we cannot neatly divide.

---

7. For deeper reflections on this, see Palmer, *The Active Life*.
8. Rom 12:15.

Building Blocks of Mature Communal Empathy

I present five elements, which do not need to be actualized in all cases of mature communal empathy. There are, of course, other elements, which require future research. My intention here is not to provide a standard measuring tool to evaluate communal empathy. Rather, it is a call for imagination of a tendency that we can find in—or even *envisage* for—the dynamics of collective people when mature communal empathy is realized. In other words, this may be a *description* of the current manifestation of mature communal empathy as well as an *imaginative vision* or insight that, we *hope*, would manifest mature communal empathy as we imagine our morally mature society and mature empathic community. Then, through these elements of communal empathy, hopefully, we may be advised how and what to educate for and foster in community and society in order to actualize mature communal empathy and mature empathic community.

The first basic element is heightened branches of empathic affect such as *empathic* anger, disgust, hate, sympathy, joy, and compassion. These affects include four empathy-based moral affects that Martin Hoffman theorized in his work, that are *sympathetic* distress, empathic *anger*, empathy-based *feeling of injustice*, and empathy-based *guilt* in Hoffman's term. These branches of empathic affect should be evident when mature communal empathy is realized. For instance, when Kim's therapist corrected the rumors spread by Kim You-Jung, people collectively felt angry and had the feeling of injustice as they found incongruity between her deed and what she was going through—for she was volunteering to help people in Sudan, yet she is suffering from traumatic sexual violence by the priest. The community was motivated to stand with Kim and fight together against injustice. Anger and feelings of injustice can create synergies, creating a very powerful source of resistance. Also, guilt over inaction would spur a motivation for solidarity for future events as the collective group anticipates future consequences if they do not take any action for similar events now.[9] Sympathetic distress is also a significant element. As I briefly mentioned above, when the #MeToo community fought for victim-survivors, the collective felt empathic (feeling with them) and sympathetic (feeling for them). When the dual distress, that is empathic/sympathetic feeling of distress, is at play, what people go through can be described as we "feel so much of your pain. It hurts [us] so much to see this happen to you."[10] As

---

9. See chapter 1.
10. Hoffman, *Empathy and Moral Development*, 56.

I explored in chapter 1, Hoffman maintains the dual distress develops as children's "first truly prosocial motive."[11]

The second element is the ability to expand the scope of individual and communal perspectives through empathy and to remain vigilant as a result. Mature empathy developed through interdimensional perspective-taking helps us to see unforeseen problems or disturbances. An eye-opening experience may happen when bystanders develop their empathy as they witness others' sufferings before their eyes or through verbal mediation[12]—whether through indirect or direct distress cues. For example, when people watch the movie *Hotel Rwanda*,[13] the common reaction to the movie is empathic anger and empathic disgust at the mass murderers as well as emotional distress that originated from the victims of the genocide in the movie. When viewers are exposed to indirect distress cues[14] by watching what is happening to the Tutsi people in the movie, they come to the realization of the horrible things that happened in the Rwandan genocide. The problem has existed but they never thought about it or were not vigilant about it. Some will investigate further, looking into the genocide and even current relevant issues of racism, ethnic cleansing, or human rights issues with refugees. These problems have always been there but now through empathy, the audience *feels with* the victims and survivors and *thinks through* their eyes. Then the empathizers may remain vigilant against relevant current or future social injustice. This may be stored in their perspectives and can be utilized as the source of supplementary perspective-taking when future events happen that involve shared distress cues.

Another example can be seen in Kim's story. When Kim shared her trauma to the public, narrating it in detail, Catholic believers who never thought about such problems may *realize* the severity of sexual abuse in their community through Kim's narrative. Using their interdimensional perspective-taking based on the resources from their relational network, they may think "That is horrible and disgusting what happened to her. I have a daughter who recently went for a mission trip from her church. Was she fine? What if it happened to her? This is something we as a community shouldn't neglect," or "I have a 15-year-old niece whose parents are Catholic. How would we as adults prevent such injustice? How can we make

---

11. Hoffman, *Empathy and Moral Development*, 88.
12. See chapter 1.
13. Terry George, *Hotel Rwanda*.
14. See chapter 1 for distress cues.

things better so she or other people out there would not suffer from sexual violence like this?" This type of empathy *occurs* when we are exposed to direct and indirect distress cues.

At the point that empathy *occurs* through an involuntary process such as mimicry, classical conditioning, and direct association, it can be a mere emotional reaction to the situation, but when the empathizers are morally mature, empathy may alert them and make them think about issues that they had not thought about much in the past. Even further, they may actively look into the current related issues and stay vigilant against similar social injustices. At this point, empathy becomes a more *voluntary* process, involving cognitive intentions and emotional realization. They can, then, have *empathy for another's experience beyond the immediate situation,* Hoffman's last developmental stage of empathic distress. Even if empathizers were not morally mature, by seeing or hearing someone suffering, their attention may be raised in a new way to already existing problems. As a result, they may question things that have never been questioned before within themselves.

By mature communal empathy, the community and each member of the community can reduce their unintentional negligence of social issues by learning from others' perspectives that are now partially adopted by the empathizers as their own.[15] The empathic learning process not only fosters the community to be more mature, but also a morally mature community is reassured and directed by this process. This element of mature communal empathy as an ability to remain vigilant helps us to address things that may not have been sufficiently addressed as well as to remain alert to any possible unintentional negligence as a check-point. When we try to listen to our empathic process, we may be able to reduce our failure in not doing what we ought to do as an individual in a relational network and a community as a whole.

The third element is a liminal space generated in the empathizing process. It is an *in-between* space of two or more different people or groups, which eventually becomes *in-beyond* space through empathy.[16] A liminal space that is not limited by both worlds, nor merely integrates the worlds. This is a newly created locus, not as a sum of two worlds or subjects; a

15. Murray terms the unintentional negligence as "unwitting omission" in researching on different subjects. See Murray, "Responsibility and Vigilance."

16. I draw on Jung Young Lee's terms from his book, where he introduces the concept of marginality as in-between, in-both, and in-beyond. I also used his work in chapter 3 of this book. See Lee, *Marginality*.

new space where one world/subject learns from the other(s) while keeping as well as *unfolding* and developing its core spirit/self. As theologian Jung Young Lee writes, this is where "the conflict between the margin and the center disappears, and a reconciliation between marginality and centrality takes place."[17] In the "in-beyond" new marginality, "the margin is no longer the margin of centrality, the margin defined by dominant groups, but the new margin, the margin of marginality."[18]

This is also a transitional space in D. W. Winnicott's term, an object relations theorist in psychoanalytic tradition. The space is the area of illusion (in terms of creativity) where a baby experiences in-between the inner and external worlds, where the baby safely meets the mother—whether men or women—without destroying the baby's own capacity, the illusion of omnipotence, where the baby's creativity arouses and her psychical structure develops to become a mature person.[19] Where we as ones with different identities meet safely together, while voluntarily becoming vulnerable as we open ourselves to others; so we can grow and learn together; so we can build a just caring society and mature empathic community *together*.

This liminal space can be understood by examining a recent murder case. A 16-months-old adoptive baby girl was killed by her adoptive mom's torture and abuse from head to toe in October 2020 in South Korea. It was only eight months after she was adopted. The whole country was gripped by communal mourning, rage, and depression. The toddler's main cause of death was deemed to be a ruptured pancreas, which is highly uncommon. Most cases happen in serious accidents such as long falls or car collisions, based on which an autopsy concluded that she might have been hit by an adult with a full blow.[20] In addition to that, an autopsy also found similar kinds of abdominal injuries prior to her death. When she was taken into the emergency room, she had severe bruises and ruptured ribs, a bloated stomach caused by internal bleeding, and both arms broken. Later, it turned out that the adoptive mother and the father starved her often since the mom hated the smell of her feces, locked her in a dark room for hours, often left her unattended for a long time, tore her lips because she refused to eat.[21]

17. Lee, *Marginality*, 61.
18. Lee, *Marginality*, 60.
19. Winnicott, "Transitional Objects," 19–34.
20. Kim, "[Herald Interview] Doctor Asks."
21. Auto, "South Korean Toddler's Death"; Kim, "Adoptive Mother Charged"; Ko, "[Newsmaker] South Korea."

As the result of the communal empathic outrage, a social media campaign *#MiahnhaeJunginah*, which means #SorryJungin, spread as a mourning action. This later developed to *#MiahnhaeJunginahWoorighaBakkulghae*, which can be translated into #SorryJunginWeWillChange followed by a number of protests seeking justice. The communal outrage and mourning motivated legislators to craft a bill for a special law to be passed for child abuse cases. The bill was named after the child.[22]

When communal empathy arose around the whole country, it was not hard to find people crying over, being depressed about, and enraged for Jungin's death. This emotional state, in which empathizers could not completely separate the mingled emotions between what happened to the toddler and to them charged with justice and care principles, helps us to understand the empathic element of liminal space where our empathic reaction to others is not merely the sum of the two different beings; rather it is a newly created state of mind accompanied with actions. After the death of Jungin, the community is not the same community; the spirit of the community has challenged; and the perspectives of the community has expanded; its core spirit was unfolded moving beyond the margin of I and you, and us and them.

When empathy becomes mature, empathizers along with the empathized voluntarily create and stay in this liminal space. In this space, the tension between me and others, or us and them is resolved. This intersubjectively connected two or multiple parties create a new spirit and new identity. The rigid and binary border between the two or multiple subjectivities disappears as the feeling of others is mingled with mine, and their perspectives reverberate in my perspective, while all of the involved parties keep their core spirit or identity. It is a space of openness and imagination as opposed to that of separation and confrontation. Because of mature empathy's strong nature of inter-connectivity, in the liminal space I acknowledge others, admitting that I am not the omnipotent (or singularly important) being and that there are others, 'not-me,'[23] whose existences constantly interact with me, nurture me, and *unfold* me. Through this 'in-beyond' space, the mature communal empathizers undergo transcendental experiences through the diversities that others bring. Through the liminal space that mature communal empathy creates, we realize how we are all inherently relational in our beingness. Even if we do not recognize it fully,

22. Park, "New Legislation."
23. Winnicott's term. See Winnicott, "Transitional Objects."

we actualize the inherently relational beingness in community as it transforms our cognitive and emotional recognition into something concrete. This transformation relates to the following element.

The fourth element is transforming power from empathy to empathic action. This is one of the most significant elements of mature communal empathy. In chapter 1, I described empathy as an affective and cognitive *inner response*. Now, when that inner response is matured enough, the empathizers—whether as an individual or as a community—cannot hold it back solely as an inner response. Rather, they need to find a way to transform that inner state of mind into a practice in order to help out or share the feelings of others, because the empathizers who are now with empathic/sympathetic distress "feel so much of their pain" and "it hurts [the empathizers] so much to see this happen to them."[24] At this empathic/sympathetic level, in the liminal space of empathizers' feelings and the others' feelings are all so interwoven that empathizers cannot separate the feelings of others from their own. They have to do something to make things better for others *and* themselves since the involved parties' beings and feelings cannot be neatly separated. This transformation of empathy into empathic action brings about solidarity—or maybe solidarity based on empathy promotes empathy to be transformed into the action. The liminal space, then, becomes the space of reciprocity and recognition, through which embodied feelings motivate empathizers to intersubjectively engage with others.[25]

The last but not the least element of mature communal empathy is the ethical and caring values that are *working/functioning* as opposed to dysfunctioning. In the previous chapter, I explored how Christian communities carry out unjust double-standards of love, virtuous sufferings, and so on based on manipulated empathy by looking into the stories of Kim

---

24. In the original text, Hoffman puts it: "I feel so much of your pain. It hurts me so much to see this happen to you." Hoffman, *Empathy and Moral Development*, 56. Also, see chapter 1 of this book.

25. In the discipline of care ethics, scholars pay attention to the *recognition* based on reciprocity in relation to caring. I do not think that recognition is a necessary component of care if the form of recognition is expected to be at a cognitive level. If the recognition is presumed to happen in multifaceted levels such as cognitive, affective, and subconscious levels whether explicitly or implicitly, wittingly or unwittingly, recognition may possibly be one of many rewarding occurrences to caretakers. If we can imagine recognition occurring at multidimensional levels, it will be very powerful as an epistemological resource. I will not explore further on this subject despite the significance of the topic, so I can stay focused on mutual communal empathy and its elements. See Noddings, *The Challenge to Care*; Noddings, *Caring*; Kittay, *Love's Labor*.

and Jules Woodson. Now, when empathy is mature and when the mature empathy is actualized at a communal level, we can see collective actions of love, caring, hospitality, sharing, friendship, and empowerment etc.

As I explored in chapter 2, interdimensional perspective-taking as a feature of mature empathy involves an inextricable re-creation of the empathizers' perspectives. In this re-creating process, the empathizers' perspectives are affected with-in and -out of the empathizer. All of the perspectives that the empathizers had seen, noticed, learned, and faced in the relational networks throughout their whole life stages are selectively chosen and mingled, and compel them to develop a mature form of empathy. In this intricate process, if and only if the empathizers are psychologically and morally mature, they examine the possible consequences of their action and take into consideration all of the people or creatures who might be impacted by their empathic action to the best of their ability. They try to avoid limits, risks, and dysfunctions of empathy such as near-and-dear bias, as they develop integrative moral deliberations. This intricate process helps them to prevent exercising pseudo-empathy, and to act against oppressive socio-cultural demands.

When Jules Woodson came forth, there were many Christians who spoke on behalf of Jules instead of standing with Andy. After a two-month long investigation, Andy resigned from his position as a teaching pastor, which the church accepted.[26] Those who stood by Jules saw the *unjust suffering* that Jules had to go through, rather than perpetuating the rhetoric of *forgiveness* and the *gracious redemption* that the supporters of Andy Savage frequently used. When the people fought for Jules, their empathic action was to demand a just caring action for Jules and caring justice for Andy, so Andy can be held accountable, which is the *beginning* of repentance.

In this section, I described actualized elements of mature communal empathy. Since mature communal empathy has not been widely actualized in our society, in order to actively utilize the moral power of mature communal empathy, it requires our imagination to think about a morally mature society and mature empathic community. This whole process of exploring mature communal empathy is to concretize and realize mature empathy as a power of resistance to social injustice. In the following section, I call for imagination to envision a just caring society that is built on mature communal empathy.

---

26. *The Wartburg Watch*, "Jules Woodson"; Johnson "Tennessee Pastor."

Envisioning Just and Caring Society Founded on Mature Communal Empathy

We have learned about elements of mature communal empathy that are intrinsically ethical and political to a great degree. Mature communal empathy is an integral part of mature, holistic, and, most of all, just and caring communities. Not only that, an empathic learning process may *create* a community. This community that never existed before is created as people gather together, who center around morally nuanced empathic inner responses as well as empathic actions and solidarity for the suffering others. Imagining this type of morally mature empathic community, full of mature empathizers in it, our society and the world *will* change to listen to the suppressed, and *repent* what the world has done to them/us. It sounds almost utopian. However, if and only if we become part of the birth of a morally mature community as well as reinforce our community to be grounded on mature communal empathy, the outcomes will be much more radical than we could ever imagine. In order for our community to be a radical imaginary, people must feel with and for others. Consequently they take action to challenge and change the unjust circumstances and practices (micro or particularity), culture (meso), and systems (macro). We should proactively and radically imagine things we ought to do, utilizing an empathic learning process. That being said, empathy may be quite political by nature and in its ways of being used.

Mature Communal Empathy as a Resistance to Manipulated Empathy

I emphasized in chapter 1 that if we can find ways to avoid the moral weaknesses of empathy and even transform them into strengths, the moral function of empathy will be maximized and be a powerful tool for us to fight against social injustice. When we utilize mature empathy in both individual and communal manners, we will be able to find better ways to deal with many moral problems that we are currently facing in our society such as racism, gender violence, gender inequality, economic stratification, inhumane (im)migration and refugee situations, ethnic cleansing, crimes against humanity, animal abuse, and so forth.

For example, we can use mature empathy as a moral tool to attain justice as a resistance to pseudo-empathy.[27] As I said in earlier chapters, pseu-

---

27. I use pseudo-empathy, manipulated empathy, and dysfunctional empathy

do-empathy, within my usage of the term, develops and gets strengthened by monopolized power structure or unjust and unequal socio-cultural and institutional systems. Heteropatriarchal society is one of the examples. Mature communal empathy is a powerful resistance to pseudo-empathy that is the result of an immoral and unhealthy society—and maybe even a partial cause of such a society. When we construct a community in which people value *mature* empathy as their integral part of living, we may encourage every member to turn their empathic attention to the ones who are marginalized and vulnerable in the community and society. When this kind of mature communal empathy is realized in the majority of the community members and in-between communities, pseudo-empathy will decrease. However, it is bitter to acknowledge that it will still be manifested as long as the human race and hence aggression exist.

We have seen such extreme manifestations of immature communal empathy during the Trump administration era. It seemed like white supremacists who employed and utilized political approaches of Donald Trump for their own racist practices, generated and exploited communal pseudo-empathy. However, as time went on, it also seemed like communal pseudo-empathy enlarged and fostered the community of white supremacists. Within their community, it was necessary to *hate* people of color and immigrants to 'make America great again;'[28] it was necessary to oppress people so the country would prosper. When people invest their empathic focus only to their significant others or those who are beneficial for them, it results in people losing their feelings of empathy towards others who are not close or advantageous to them. This generates and maximizes manipulated empathy—a type of immature/dysfunctional empathy, which impacts our society to a great degree.

I am not saying that *mature* communal empathy is the only solution to the problems of pseudo-empathy. Rather, it should be the *foundation* of the resistance. When the community upholds and works together to build mature empathy, the community can help people to transpose their empathic focus from their own people and their own interest to others who are different, hence who also contribute to the beauty of diversity in communities. By seeing those who are different from me/us through the lens of

---

interchangeably since these terms often have overlapping connotations.

28. "Make America Great Again" or so-called MAGA is a political slogan popularized by the formal president of the United States Donald Trump, then the presidential candidate in his 2016 presidential campaign. For more information, see Tumulty, "How Donald Trump Came up with 'Make America Great Again.'"

mature empathy, we also find shared ground with them as human beings and as creatures. Reversing the familiarity bias into the strength that glues us together as the same human beings and creatures who deserve things as equal as I/we do, our community will move and work towards a place where members do not tolerate discriminations, abuse, and inequality. This is thanks to the strong partnership with justice and care principles inherent in mature empathy.[29]

Christian Values That Can Be Re-conceptualized and Strengthened

Through mature communal empathy, we can also maximize values that we already appreciate in our society, but have not actualized fully, properly, and morally. When we look at Christianity, we can find examples of these values. It is unfortunate, however, that Christianity has throughout history contributed to quite destructive and distorted understandings of values such as anger, love, sacrifice, repentance, etc. Despite that fact, Christian theology *within* itself indeed also has various resources to criticize, repent, and purify the wrongs that are done in the name of those values. In this section, I will briefly exemplify the Christian values of love, anger, and sacrifice through which mature communal empathy can help our community to maximize their moral values and resist the dysfunctions of them.

Beverly Wildung Harrison, a feminist theologian and Christian ethicist, argued that anger should be seen as an energy that can be used as a practice of love in her article "The Power of Anger in the Work of Love: Christian Ethics for Women and Other Strangers."[30]

> It is my thesis that we Christians have come very close to killing love precisely because anger has been understood as a deadly sin. Anger is not the opposite of love. It is better understood as a feeling-signal that all is not well in our relation to other persons or groups or to the world around us. Anger is a mode of *connectedness* to others and it is always a vivid form of caring. To put the point another way: anger is—and it always is—a sign of some resistance in ourselves to the moral quality of the social relations in which we are immersed. Extreme and intense anger signals a deep

---

29. See chapter 2.
30. Harrison, "The Power of Anger."

reaction to the action upon us or toward others to whom we are related.[31] [italics added]

In her short article, she challenges not only the misconstrued Christian notion of anger but also the understanding of love. She goes on to say, "I believe we have a very long way to go before the priority of activity over passivity is internalized in our theology, and even further to go before love, in our ethics, is understood to be a mode of action."[32] I already addressed anger in chapter 1. Anger needs proper channels through which it can be aimed morally. One of the channels is, I argue, mature empathy. When anger is revealed through pseudo-empathy, it may cause immoral and destructive outcomes as we have witnessed in the event of 2021 United States Capitol attack under the Trump administration. When and only when anger is morally nuanced, mature empathic anger can be a very powerful way of practicing love. Such as anger that is against injustice: anger against discrimination that the marginalized have had to undergo in their everyday life, anger against politicians who did not do their job properly to help out the refugees and change unequal social systems, and anger against those clergy abusers who hurt and harm their congregants in the false name of love. Empathic anger is a powerful way of loving others as long as it remains mature.

Sacrifice is another value that we can think about in relation to empathy. Unfortunately, it is easy to find sacrifice being exploited against women and those who tend to be given much less authority than what they deserve in our society. When pseudo-empathy is a predominant mechanism of a community or society, this type of unjust sacrifice is fostered and *perpetuated*. On the contrary, when the ethos of our community and society is founded on mature communal empathy, sacrifice can be understood very differently.

The sacrifice that I explore involves three different types. One is the most prevalent type of sacrifice that is imposed on women and the marginalized in current society. The second one is an unavoidable outcome of our mature empathic actions in an *immoral* society. The last one is our voluntary sacrifice in our daily life out of our love—as a practice—and empathy. For the first two types of sacrifice, Harrison's work is quite helpful.

> Jesus's death on a cross, his sacrifice, was no abstract exercise in moral virtue. His death was the price he paid for refusing to

---

31. Harrison, "The Power of Anger," 49.
32. Harrison, "The Power of Anger," 46.

abandon the radical activity of love—of expressing solidarity and reciprocity with the excluded ones in his community. Sacrifice, I submit, is *not* a central moral *goal* or virtue in the Christian life. Radical acts of love—expressing human solidarity and bringing mutual relationship to life—are the central virtues of the Christian moral life. That we have turned sacrifice into a moral virtue has deeply confused the Christian moral tradition.

Like Jesus, we are called to a radical activity of love, to a way of being in the world which deepens relation, embodies and extends community, passes on the gift of life.[33]

Feminist theologians and care ethicists have criticized the unjust sacrifice that burden women and subalterns, including Harrison and Joan Tronto, who I drew upon in chapter 2.[34] When sacrifice becomes a virtue that we need to seek, it becomes a tool to perpetuate heteropatriarchal and white supremacist systems. Traci West reinforces that "Assertions of self-sacrifice and suffering as the chief virtue for Christians, for example, can reward denial of the significance of the harm of intimate, gender abuse."[35] As West and Harrison point out, sacrifice perceived as a moral virtue has been one of the dysfunctional values that perpetuates unjust and unequal society. We saw how destructive this dysfunctional view of sacrifice can be in the examples of Kim's Catholic church community's response to her, asking her to remain silent, and how she herself felt the pressure to sacrifice her agency and dignity at the moment of sexual abuse for the Sudanese mission in chapter 3.

The second type of sacrifice—an outcome followed by our empathic action in an *immoral* society—is what Harrison described as Jesus's sacrifice on the cross, for he refused to submit to injustice and "loveless power."[36] I deeply agree with Harrison to the extent that this type of sacrifice is not and should not be "a central moral goal." In this case, sacrifice is not a virtue that we need to follow. It should be *de facto* our goal to build a community where we do not have to sacrifice ourselves to practice empathic actions for the *systematically* marginalized. If sacrifice is necessitated by institutional, systemic, and socio-cultural injustice, it should be our goal to *un-necessitate* the sacrifice in the process of our *radical activity of love*,

33. Harrison, "The Power of Anger," 52.

34. Also, West's exploration of (self-)sacrifice is very helpful. See West, *Wounds of the Spirit*.

35. West, "Ending Gender Violence," 201.

36. Harrison, "The Power of Anger," 52.

an empathic action. In other words, as we practice our empathic action out of mature empathy and as we refuse to stop our caring practice—based on reciprocity—the outcome should not be *sacrifice* at least in the just caring society that we are envisaging.

Harrison reminds us, "The aim of love is not to perpetuate crucifixions, but to bring an end to them in a world where they go on and on and on! We do this through actions of mutuality and solidarity, not by aiming at an ethic of sacrifice."[37] For this type of sacrifice, our Christian goal of justice is to dismantle the system that requires the moral empathizers to be punished and sacrificed due to their caring actions. Perhaps, then, empathic sacrifice is a necessary outcome in an unjust society that we are asked to embrace as we commit to *empathic care* of others and to change the status quo; as Jesus had to sacrifice himself on the cross by *choosing* to refuse "to abandon the radical activity of love—of expressing solidarity and reciprocity with the excluded ones in his community."[38] This kind of sacrifice is an antipode to the sacrifice that current dominant Christianity values. The sacrifice that is imposed on marginalized people is one that causes immoral qualities—requiring our empathic action to fight against it. When mature communal empathy is realized, sacrifice should be manifested as the latter not the former of the first two types of sacrifice.

However, the third type of sacrifice also needs to be acknowledged. In our daily life, another type of sacrifice, i.e. empathic sacrifice, is often necessary as we practice caring for people who need our help as individuals and as a community. When we have a daughter who is disabled and requires caring in her everyday life, sacrifice is necessary not as a socially imposed burden but out of love as a *practice*—while I fully acknowledge the difficulties of caring, which need to be supported and shared by social institutions. This caring practice, the activity of love, should be shared by social programs and assistance, communities and institutionalized care that do not erase the sacrifice, but promote *solidarity* with the caregiver along with *recognition* of care at a communal and social level. Moreover, this is not only about our fellow humans, when we see a stray dog who is injured and starved, we should sacrifice our time and money for the dog's well-being out of empathy as we all are intersubjectively connected. Our voluntary sacrifice out of mature empathy should extend to the care of the environment as we face massive climate impacts. These necessary empathic

37. Harrison, "The Power of Anger," 49.
38. Harrison, "The Power of Anger," 52.

sacrifices in our daily life will still be necessary and even more so in a just caring society that we imagine.

How Can We Foster Mature Communal Empathy?

I constantly emphasized that empathy *per se* is not moral nor immoral. When empathy is in a mature form, empathy may be manifested as a strong resistance to injustice. Empathy then should be transformed from inner response to *empathic action* since empathy as an inner response is not strong enough for us to fight against injustice and build a just caring solidarity and society. When we actualize mature communal empathy as individuals and as a community, the power of empathy and empathic action can create radical differences. This radicality through mature communal empathy is something we should fully imagine and seek.

Then, what are the possible practical strategies in order to promote mature communal empathy as a first step toward a just caring society? For this, Martin Hoffman's induction theory from the psychological domain will be helpful and viable for us to imagine this moral society. He emphasizes the significance of parental technique in developing prosocial empathy. "[I]n situations in which the child has harmed others, the parent's use of discipline techniques that call attention to the victim's pain or injury or encourage the child to imagine him- or herself in the victim's place, i.e., inductive techniques, should help put the feelings of others into the child's consciousness and thus enhance the child's empathic potential."[39] Parent(s) can teach children to *think* about the possible impact of their behaviors on other people's feelings and lives. Children in this type of learning environment then not only develop their ability for moral deliberation based on empathy but also have a moral motive through which they meet others' needs, putting aside their own egoistic needs and wants.

This is in fact a core part of the gospels that Christ embodied in everyday life. We can find Jesus's strong calling in the scripture, "for I was hungry and you gave me food, I was thirsty and you gave me something to drink, I was a stranger and you welcomed me, I was naked and you gave me clothing, I was sick and you took care of me, I was in prison and you visited me."[40] In a Christian context, when we promote mature empathy in our daily lives, pedagogy based on the spirit of mature empathy will be a great resource for

---

39. Hoffman, "Development of Prosocial Motivation," 306.
40. Matt 25:35–36.

Christian education, as it resonates with the core spirit of Christianity. The Christian value of care and love as praxis will be synergistic with empathy education, while this pedagogy is not limited to Christianity.

Based on this induction theory, education is the most essential part of promoting mature communal empathy. It should be education not just for children but also for adults and each and every community. Let's use our imagination here. What if we proactively include the inductive technique in every curriculum that we have not only for our children at school but extensively for higher education institutions, religious communities, organizations, and even secular companies? What if clergy and lay leaders prioritize mature empathy as the utmost principle of the community building process? What if a government makes a policy based on mature empathy regarding issues such as refugees, resource allocations for infrastructure, building institutions and managing institutional systems, and so on? What if mature empathy becomes one of the most significant values in the culture?

Over ten years ago, when I came to the United States as an international student at Candler School of Theology at Emory University in Georgia, despite the seemingly welcoming atmosphere, I was struggling with such overwhelmingly different cultures, ethos, expectations, and systems in the US from those of South Korea. While some cultures did not make sense, and some systems were inconvenient, and some chronic pathological problems were scary and shocking such as racism, I still vividly remember the awe-inspiring impression when my 1.5 generation Korean American friend told me about America's "honor system." She told me that, sometimes, there is no supervisor who regulates and monitors the students to make sure that nobody is cheating during midterm exams in the classroom based on the honor system. The system values honesty, trust, and honor based on the members of the society's voluntary contribution to keeping the system running. When I was in South Korea, I had never heard of such values with an actual name and truly at play as a foundation that people are *expected* to live up to. What if we make mature empathy as significant as those values at the communal level? If we can demand that our community make mature empathy—through the inductive technique—as one of those foundational values that people are socially expected to live with and up to, our society will begin to see the difference that actualized intersubjective connectivity makes in our daily lives. What name can be attributed to such a system? Can you imagine someone saying 'you are ruining the empathy system' instead of 'you are ruining the honor system'?

Conclusion

Mature communal empathy as a political and moral resource will offer a very powerful source of solidarity and caring activity. To articulate the significance of mature communal empathy, I explored empathy through psychological findings in chapter 1. In the following chapter, feminist care ethical perspectives were used to envisage a morally mature society to which our mature empathy can contribute. Based on this exploration, I provided the features of mature empathy, which is a foundational concept for this book. In chapter 3, after examining the socio-cultural and systemic cause of the prevalence of sexual violence and the hardships victim-survivors underwent, I introduced two case studies through which Christian and social responses to sexual violence victim-survivors were explored and demonstrated how empathy was realized in digital activism such as the #MeToo movement. In the final chapter, I offered elements of mature communal empathy and a way to systematically promote mature empathy while imagining the moral society in which mature empathy is one of the foundational moral values. In the following section, I will summarize each chapter, underlining important arguments that need to be remembered. After the summaries, I finalize the chapter by presenting my final claims and suggesting possible future research.

Summary of Chapters

This section is designed to recapitulate what I have explored and also to invite the reader to think about the communal power mature empathy brings. Whereas each chapter has its own focus, they should be read from the perspective of moral and political potentials that mature communal empathy has. The potentials can only be realized when we as moral agents actualize it on a daily basis in our moral encounters as a community, creating a liminal space between the different existences, nurturing and recognizing one another and being vigilant of urgent needs we are facing and of underlying moral problems.

A History of the Scholarship of Empathy

In chapter 1, I intended to provide a psychological understanding of empathy in depth, exploring its nature, significant concepts in the scholarship, developmental aspects of empathy, and its possible connection to morality. I delineated empathy as *an observer's or observers'—as a community—cognitive and affective inner process and response to another or others in various negative and positive circumstances, which leads the observer(s) to feel congruent and oftentimes matching feelings with the other(s) through mimicry, perspective-taking, imagination, and/or simulation.* As I examined the strengths of empathy as a moral resource, in addition to the view of empathy as "a source of altruism,"[41] I also further maintained that empathic action as an engaging action, which was transformed from empathy as *inner response,* may create the space of reciprocity and *transitional space,* where different individuals or communities intersubjectively encounter and expand their perspectives. Empathic action is fostered by branches of empathic affect such as shame, guilt, the feeling of injustice, anger, sympathy, and many more.

I concluded that empathy has rich potentials to be utilized as a moral resource, providing moral motivations to communities as well as expanding the parochial caring circle to the circle for distant others. Yet, we need to be cognizant of its weaknesses that I categorized into three, i.e. limits, risks, and dysfunctions of empathy. I asserted that if someone tries to judge whether empathy *a priori* is morally helpful or harmful, they are *either too naive or too ignorant* to see the extremely complicated and nuanced contexts of moral encounters of human beings. With that in mind, I emphasized that we need to find a way that we can avoid the weaknesses while we pay attention to the ways in which we all can urge members of our society and communities to find ways in which the members are explicitly and implicitly educated to develop mature empathy, so each member can contribute to building a just and caring society with their morally-nuanced empathy.

Mature Empathy and Its Moral Implications

In chapter 2, I defined *mature* empathy as the most developed form of empathy which accompanies a balanced judgment based on the empathizer's or the empathizing community's individual or collective cognitive and affective experiences, moral deliberation, and integrative and balanced perspectives that are composed of one's own and other human and non-human beings' perspectives through perspective-taking. In this light, mature empathy, I maintained, should be understood as a normative

---

41. Batson, *The Altruism Question*, 58; Batson, *A Scientific Search for Altruism*, 28.

moral faculty. Thus, mature empathizers cannot tolerate social injustice, needless to say, they cannot foster any forms of discriminatory and unequal socio-cultural demand; for they who take the most developed form of perspective-taking, which I call interdimensional perspective-taking, from other fellow beings feel with and for other beings' sufferings, i.e. dual empathic/sympathetic distress.[42]

With this definition of maturity and mature empathy as a moral resource, I envisioned a morally mature society, i.e. a *just and caring society*, out of a social imaginary that can be developed by mature empathizers as moral agents. In this society, moral agents both as an individual and a community embrace the fact that everyone is a care-giver *and* a care-receiver in the caring network. No one can survive without being cared for, hence refusing the asymmetrical caring relationship and unjust power structure. In this society, members are encouraged to understand how intersubjectively they are interwoven with other beings. Furthermore, a social consensus exists that the vision of care is a foundational component of justice and the foundation of the society and communities. In that, a social climate would be formed in which every member of the society has the responsibility of caring for the vulnerable and the marginalized. Thus, correspondingly, they should eagerly take action to disrupt the social, legal, cultural, and institutional systems that perpetuate the status quo. In the process of developing the imaginary and building the morally mature society, mature empathy is to be the greatest motivational resource.

Based on this imaginary, I concretized the six features of mature empathy: (1) *inter*subjective understanding of self, others, and the community, (2) *inter*dimensional perspective-taking with the help of *supplementary* perspective-takings, (3) ability to make a strong partnership with justice and care principles, (4) metacognitive ability and self-reflexivity, (5) willingness to make extra emotional, cognitive, and behavioral effort on behalf of both significant and distant others resonating with interdimensional perspective-taking, and (6) active and heightened ability of empathic affects such as empathic anger, guilt, shame, and so forth that concur with didactic moral principles for other fellow human and non-human beings.

A noteworthy implication of these features is that when mature empathy is well developed hence equipped with these features, it will be transformed to empathic *engaging* action in various moral encounters for those who are oppressed in society, and who need a community who can

---

42. See the section of "Four Empathy-Based Moral Affects" in chapter 1 of this book.

rejoice or weep together with them. The mature empathizers move one step further to transpose the focus of supportive communal empathy toward the vulnerable and marginalized from the ones with power, while providing caring justice for the ones with power out of mature empathy. The realization of praxis, i.e. the state of integrating the knowledge and practice, ideas and action, and education and actualization, occur among mature empathizers who do not stay only at the level of the inner process of empathy but move beyond their thinking and feeling, transforming themselves from bystanders to active participating moral agents. These moral agents become *engaged* and *interconnected* with the other(s) and form *solidarity* with the other(s) and allies. With solidarity formed through cognitively and affectively mature empathy, moral agents who are from diverse backgrounds can expand the caring scope and make changes, bringing in interdimensional perspectives to the personal and public discourses.

Mature empathizers are neither flawless nor fearless. Rather, they are open to accepting their limits and trying to correct themselves by being *voluntarily broken open* by others' voices, challenges, joyful laughter, and suffering cries, as they construct their knowledge and moral deliberation based on interdimensional perspective-taking. They have the ability to put extra effort to understand other beings' existence and situations, and to prioritize the impending need of action by putting aside their own egoistic desires while they *recognize* what their desires are, i.e. self-other differentiation. This is distinguished from oppressive selfless sacrifice demanded by unequal social systems disproportionately to those who are relatively vulnerable in society and communities, as Joan Tronto pointed out.[43] This aspect of mature empathizer—prioritizing others' suffering over their egoistic needs—is important since without a healthy construction of self-other differentiation and genuine voluntariness, the empathizer(s) as individuals *and* communities will only comply with the oppressive society's norms that reproduce the unequal status of caregivers. One of the most important features of mature empathizers is the ability to utilize perspective-takings from oneself (self-oriented perspective-taking), the other (other-oriented perspective-taking), and their extended relational network. I conceptualized this as interdimensional perspective-taking, which helps the empathizers to think beyond the dyadic relationship and bring in all of their integrative experiences from direct and indirect, and immediate and distant

---

43. See the section "Intersubjective Understanding of Self, Others, and the Community" in chapter 2 of this book.

situations to their moral deliberation. The interdimensional perspective-taking allows empathizers to come to an extensive understanding of others' situations and unique recognitions and feelings of the others. One's entire life experiences become the source of empathy, taking all the factors that they can think of and the perspectives of everyone currently involved or beyond the situation into consideration.

Sexual Violence in Christian Communities and Empathy in Digital Activism

Chapter 3 was intended to provide a concrete example of a moral context, i.e., sexual violence, through which I was able to analyze and learn about empathy's moral value and its detailed actualization process. In the first section, I scrutinized three main factors that are intersectionality, systemic evil, and misogynistic beliefs and norms. The intersection of multiple marginalized identities as well as the other two factors sustain and promote the prevalence of sexual violence against women victim-survivors, and silence and re-harm them. Through exploring Aura's story, I demonstrated how marginalizing intersectional factors work against victim-survivors and how perpetrators exploit the factors to manipulate the lack of socio-political power of victim-survivors. The second factor, systemic evil, is explored to prove that sexual violence is not merely a person-to-person matter, rather it is perpetuated by systemic injustice. The third factor is misogynistic beliefs and norms that generate emotional, social, and communal injuries to victim-survivors, which I included, but not exclusively, victim-blaming,—shaming, and –guilt; humiliation; and misogynistic stereotypes of women.

With this misogynistic socio-cultural environment, I examined how church communities responded to sexual violence victim-survivors by taking the clergy offenders' side, and what the underlying reasoning and theological distortions were. I found that people's collective responses to victim-survivors often diverged into two extremes, for some people empathize with sexual crime offenders and reharm victim-survivors based on pseudo- and/or dysfunctional empathy, while others show empathic affects, supporting and empowering victim-survivors, and forming solidarity with them. Looking into such a prevalent manifestation of injustice in our society and various collective responses to victim-survivors, I analyzed *why* church communities' dominant responses were against victim-survivors and *how* people responded in digital space to them and why. I came to a conclusion that even with the pitfalls of the digital space, it can be a powerful tool for

Building Blocks of Mature Communal Empathy

us to utilize to dismantle monopolized power and dysfunctional theologies in church communities and democratize the appropriated power of story-making without gatekeepers of heteropatriarchy, thanks to its spreadability, searchability, regenerative features, and extensive networked nature.

Through this case study, I tried to see how empathy is actualized in a moral context, why it is actualized in certain ways and what the underlying social, political, cultural factors and norms are that impact people's empathizing process and moral deliberation. Digital activism with these features are a very helpful way in which mature empathy can be spread out and can transform bystanders into actively involved moral agents. Varied empathic affects can be developed such as empathic anger, guilt, disgust, and collective mourning, just to name a few, as bystanders are exposed to the narratives of distant others' suffering cries and vivid descriptions of their emotional and cognitive responses in the aftermath of sexual violence.

Ultimately, I maintained that through digital activism distant individuals can build an empathetic relationship, which can transpose the focus of empathy from offenders to victim-survivors, expanding their circle of caring. Empathy, especially in mature form, may infuse intersubjective meanings into the event of distant others and provide personal engagement with the others. Members of society equipped with mature empathy partnered with digital activism will be able to effectively disrupt oppressive society and contribute to fostering a just and caring moral society.

Building Blocks of Mature Communal Empathy

In this final chapter, I tried to visualize or imagine what it will look like when mature communal empathy is realized in our lives and communities. I first contemplated the meaning of 'communal' and 'collective' and its relation to empathy. In #MeToo, the collective empathic response was founded on the moral agents' shared sentiment and moral judgment, which were *not* uniform or regulated reactions by a power center. In this type of collective response, the manifestations of each participant's reaction may seem similar but they were not deliberately homogeneous responses.

I also argued that empathy is intrinsically communal since it cannot stay only in dyadic relationships—thanks to interdimensional perspective-taking—and is generated by *recognizing others' beings*. Based on this communal quality, I emphasized that the essential disposition of communal empathy is intersubjective *inter-connectivity*. If we can develop a mature empathic community by acknowledging we are all equally in the relational network, it becomes a powerful resource to seek justice against any type of subjugating culture or system.

I provided five significant elements of mature communal empathy. The first element is four empathy-based moral affects suggested by Martin Hoffman, which include sympathetic distress, empathic anger, empathy-based feeling of injustice, and empathy-based guilt. The second element is the expansion of the range of social awareness and the ability to stay vigilant as a result. By fostering this element, we may question things that have not been questioned enough, and hence reduce our unintentional negligence in what we ought to do in our moral encounters. The third element was a liminal space coming into being in the empathizing process. I accentuated that in this space the margin between I and you, and us and them can be dismantled, and openness and imagination overtake the spirit of separation and confrontation. The fourth is mature communal empathy's transforming ability from empathy as an inner response to empathic engaging/intervening action. Thanks to the features of mature empathy such as interdimensional perspective-taking, empathic/sympathetic distress, and intersubjectivity, mature empathizers cannot continue to ignore others' pain as the pain is embodied in them. These embodied feelings motivate empathizers to take action with regard to the situation. I offered working/functioning values as the last element as opposed to morally dysfunctional values. Especially in Christian contexts, I exemplified communal actions of love and caring as a resistance to virtuous suffering. For example, *unjust suffering* shown in Jules Woodson's case reminds us of the need of the just caring for Jules and caring justice for Andy. The caring justice for the offender will be requisite for the *beginning* of repentance and holding him accountable.

In the second section, Envisioning Just and Caring Society Founded on Mature Communal Empathy, I contemplated three different applications of mature communal empathy, calling for imagination. I maintained that mature communal empathy is not only an indispensable part of a holistic and just caring community, but also it may *create* a just caring community in the empathic process. Mature communal empathy equipped with the above-mentioned elements will become a powerful resistance to dysfunctional empathy which is provoked by unjust social, cultural, institutional power systems. I underlined that mature communal empathy is not the *only* solution to social problems that pseudo-empathy induces. Rather, mature communal empathy should be the *foundation* of such resistance.

Secondly, I exemplified a few Christian values, i.e., love, anger, and sacrifice, which needed to be re-conceptualized and whose ethical function can be maximized through the lens of mature communal empathy. Drawing on the work of Beverly Wildung Harrison and Traci West, I offered that love as a radical caring activity can be strengthened by mature empathic anger that can help anger to be morally aimed. As to sacrifice, I categorized it into three types: two that are unjust sacrifice, an unavoidable outcome of our empathic action in an *un*just society, and lastly voluntary sacrifice as a caring practice that will be *promoted* in a just caring society.

The section was finished by imagining how we can foster mature communal empathy in our society, where mature communal empathy becomes the utmost moral value. By introducing Martin Hoffman's induction theory, I maintained that if we can find ways to apply the inductive technique to promote mature communal empathy in every nook and cranny of our society, the outcome will be radical. We have never experienced the just caring society I propose, thus, I call for radical imagination to envision it.

Final Claims about Mature Communal Empathy and Future Research

This whole book was written in hope. It was a very hopeful and wonder-full experience to radically imagine a society where the majority of people care for others; where they are ready to voluntarily sacrifice themselves to practice care for one another, not forced through socially imposed burdens. A society where there is a prevailing social consensus that moral agents need to include the vision of care as a foundation of justice in a sense that care and justice are supposed to be complementary to one another. The kind of society where the majority of people are mindful of and motivated to act for the vulnerable and the marginalized, and always remain alert to inequality and the systems perpetuating injustice.

Some people might argue that this is too utopian to come true. This kind of hope in the social imaginary might be perhaps one that we need to be most vigilant about, since staying hopeful not followed by plausible plans and corresponding actions will make us nothing but idealists. In this vein, envisioning a mature empathic society and staying radical about it is a *beginning* step towards the moral society where mature communal empathy is promoted in each and every community through education as well as through building proper institutions and cultural attitudes. I do believe that mature communal empathy exists since we have already seen it realized.

The question is what we are going to do to spread it farther until it becomes the bedrock of our society.

I tried to concretize the concept of mature communal empathy as a moral resource in this book. Conceptualizing—or I would say envisaging—the power of mature communal empathy is and should be the very first step towards studying the moral potentials of mature communal empathy. Thus, a range of research should be sought in the future. First of all, *applicable* practices need to be studied. How would we be able to popularize it writ large and to apply the inductive technique to working education policies specifically? How are we going to build caring institutions and systems of mature empathy? Are there any empathic caring model based on which we can develop viable caring institutions, policies, and systems?[44] What kind of institutions and regulations would we need for mature communal empathy to become an actual possibility? Investigating workable systems and institutions is a very significant subject for fostering the empathic community and society. While I appreciate the hope that our social imaginary can bring in, through the future studies, we need to keep focusing on how to foster the caring vision charged with mature empathy to be actualized and become an integral part of our institutions and political arenas.

Also, studying moral and political implications of mature empathy will be enriched when researched from the perspective of affect theory. Particularly, it will be worthwhile to study the types of affects that can be morally synergetic with mature empathy. There are many kinds of affects that have been downplayed as having moral quality because of their possible diverse manifestations. As I exemplified, while anger can be destructive without mature empathy's moral guidance, it can also be a valuable moral resource when it meets mature empathy as mature empathy provides cognitive moral motivations and guidance. What other affects can become moral resources that may be conferred as resistance to injustice? Furthermore, what are other elements of mature communal empathy that can be helpful to build a morally mature society?

I might offer more questions than solutions to the problems that we are facing in our immoral society. Yet, I hope that this specific imaginary that I propose can contribute to accelerating a just and caring society where the majority of people believe that we should build a community where everyone is equally appreciated and receives help when they/we need it.

---

44. In this sense, Tronto's article on how to create care-based institutions provides insights. See Tronto, "Creating Caring Institutions," 158–71.

Bibliography

Adams, Sarah LaChance. Mad Mothers, Bad Mothers, and What a "Good" Mother Would Do: The Ethics of Ambivalence. New York: Columbia University Press, 2014.
Agence France-Presse, "South Korea Catholic Church Apologises over Sexual Harassment Accusation." *New Indian Express* (February 2018). https://www.newindianexpress.com/world/2018/feb/25/south-korea-catholic-church-apologises-over-sexual-harassment-accusation-1778798.html/.
Ahmed, Hauwa. "How Private Prisons Are Profiting under the Trump Administration." *Center for American Progress* (August 2019). https://www.americanprogress.org/issues/democracy/reports/2019/08/30/473966/private-prisons-profiting-trump-administration/.
Auto, Hermes. "South Korean Toddler's Death Sparks Call for Stiffer Penalties for Abuse." *The Straits Times* (January 2021). https://www.straitstimes.com/asia/east-asia/south-korean-toddlers-death-sparks-call-for-stiffer-penalties-for-abuse/.
Baron-Cohen, Simon. *Zero Degrees of Empathy: A New Theory of Human Cruelty*. New York: Allen Lane, 2011.
Batson, C. Daniel. *The Altruism Question: Toward a Social-Psychological Answer*. Hillsdale, NJ: Erlbaum, 1991.
———. *A Scientific Search for Altruism: Do We Only Care About Ourselves?* New York: Oxford University Press, 2019.
———. "These Things Called Empathy: Eight Related but Distinct Phenomena." In *The Social Neuroscience of Empathy*, 3–15. Cambridge: MIT Press, 2009.
Batson, C. Daniel, Shannon Early, and Giovani Salvarani. "Perspective Taking: Imagining How Another Feels Versus Imagining How You Would Feel." *Personality and Social Psychology Bulletin* 23 (1997) 751–58.
Battaly, Heather D. "Is Empathy a Virtue?" In *Empathy: Philosophical and Psychological Perspectives*, edited by Amy Coplan and Peter Goldie, 277–301. 2011. Reprint, New York: Oxford University Press, 2014.
Blair, Leonardo. "Pastor Andy Savage Launches New Church as Beth Moore Offers Comfort to His Sexual Assault Victim." *Christian Post* (October 2019). https://www.christianpost.com/news/pastor-andy-savage-launches-new-church-as-beth-moore-offers-comfort-to-his-sexual-assault-victim.html.
Bloom, Paul. *Against Empathy: The Case for Rational Compassion*. New York: Ecco, 2016.

Bibliography

Brock, Rita Nakashima, and Rebecca Ann Parker. *Proverbs of Ashes: Violence, Redemptive Suffering, and the Search for What Saves Us.* Boston: Beacon, 2001.

Cave, Damien, Livia Albeck-Ripka, and Iliana Magra. "Huge Crowds around the Globe March in Solidarity against Police Brutality." *New York Times*, June 6, 2020. https://www.nytimes.com/2020/06/06/world/george-floyd-global-protests.html/.

Chodorow, Nancy J. The *Reproduction of Mothering: Psychoanalysis and the Sociology of Gender.* Berkeley: University of California Press, 1978.

Collins, Patricia Hill. "Truth-Telling and Intellectual Activism." *Contexts* 12 (February 1, 2013) 36–41.

Colwell, Kelly, and Sheryl Johnson. "#MeToo and #ChurchToo: Putting the Movements in Context." *Review and Expositor* 117 (2020) 183–98.

Cooper-White, Pamela. *The Cry of Tamar: Violence against Women and the Church's Response.* 2nd ed. Minneapolis: Fortress, 2012.

Coplan, Amy. "Understanding Empathy: Its Features and Effects." In *Empathy: Philosophical and Psychological Perspectives*, edited by Amy Coplan and Peter Goldie, Reprint ed., 3–18. New York: Oxford University Press, 2014.

Coplan, Amy, and Peter Goldie, eds. *Empathy: Philosophical and Psychological Perspectives.* Reprint ed. New York: Oxford University Press, 2014.

———. "Introduction." In *Empathy: Philosophical and Psychological Perspectives*, edited by Amy Coplan and Peter Goldie, ix–xlvii. Reprint ed. New York: Oxford University Press, 2014.

Decety, Jean, and Andrew N. Meltzoff. "Empathy, Imitation, and the Social Brain." In *Empathy: Philosophical and Psychological Perspectives*, edited by Amy Coplan and Peter Goldie, Reprint ed., 58–81. New York: Oxford University Press, 2014.

Decker, Michele R., Anita Raj, and Jay G. Silverman. "Sexual Violence Against Adolescent Girls: Influences of Immigration and Acculturation." *Violence against Women* 13 (2007) 498–513.

DeMuth, Mary E. *We Too: How the Church Can Respond Redemptively to the Sexual Abuse Crisis.* Eugene, OR: Harvest House, 2019.

de Waal, Frans. *The Age of Empathy: Nature's Lessons for a Kinder Society.* New York: Broadway, 2010.

Eadens, Savannah. "Viral Photo Shows Line of White People between Police, Black Protesters at Thursday Rally." *Courier-Journal*, May 29, 2020. https://www.courier-journal.com/story/news/local/2020/05/29/breonna-taylor-photo-white-women-between-police-black-protesters/5286416002/.

Eisenberg, Nancy. "Empathy and Sympathy." In *Handbook of Emotions*, edited by Michael Lewis and Jeannette M. Haviland-Jones, 677–91. 2nd ed. New York: Guilford, 2000.

Eisenberg, Nancy, and Janet Strayer. *Empathy and Its Development.* Cambridge: Cambridge University Press Archive, 1990.

Erickson, Camille. "Detention Center Contractors Will Keep Reaping Profit Even after DHS Upheaval." *Open Secrets* (April 2019). https://www.opensecrets.org/news/2019/04/detention-center-contractors-keep-reaping-profit-after-dhs-upheaval/.

Everhart, Ruth. *The #MeToo Reckoning: Facing the Church's Complicity in Sexual Abuse and Misconduct.* Downers Grove, IL: InterVarsity, 2020.

Fortune, Marie. *Sexual Violence: The Sin Revisited.* Cleveland: Pilgrim, 2005.

George, Terry, dir. *Hotel Rwanda.* Santa Monica, CA: Lions Gate Films, 2005.

Gibbs, John C. "Toward an Integration of Kohlberg's and Hoffman's Moral Development Theories." *Human Development* 34 (1991) 88–104.

Bibliography

Gibbs, John C., and Martin Hoffman, "In Defense of Empathy and Justice." Oxford University Press (Blog) (August 13, 2015). https://blog.oup.com/2015/08/hillary-clinton-in-defense-of-empathy-and-justice/.

Gilligan, Carol. *In a Different Voice*. Cambridge: Harvard University Press, 1982.

———. "In a Different Voice: Women's Conceptions of Self and of Morality." In *The Psychology of Women: Ongoing Debates*, edited by Mary Roth Walsh, 278–320. New Haven: Yale University Press, 1987.

Gish, Elizabeth. "'Are You a "Trashable" Styrofoam Cup?': Harm and Damage Rhetoric in the Contemporary American Sexual Purity Movement." *Journal of Feminist Studies in Religion* 34 (2018) 5–22.

Goblet, Margot, and Fabienne Glowacz. "Slut Shaming in Adolescence: A Violence against Girls and Its Impact on Their Health." *International Journal of Environmental Research and Public Health* 18 (2021) 1–15. https://www.mdpi.com/1157858.

Goldscheid, Julie, and Richard Caldarone. "#MeToo and Sexual Assault of Immigrants by Federal Officials." *Tahirih Justice Center* (November 2019). https://www.tahirih.org/news/metoo-and-sexual-assault-of-immigrants-by-federal-officials/.

Guenther, Lisa. "Resisting Agamben: The Biopolitics of Shame and Humiliation." *Philosophy & Social Criticism* 38 (2012) 59–79.

Haag, Matthew. "Memphis Pastor Admits 'Sexual Incident' With High School Student 20 Years Ago." *New York Times*, January 9, 2018. https://www.nytimes.com/2018/01/09/us/memphis-megachurch-sex-assault.html/.

Hallett, Nicole. "Immigrant Women in the Shadow of #MeToo." *University of Baltimore Law Review* 49 (2019). https://scholarworks.law.ubalt.edu/ublr/vol49/iss1/3.

Hamington, Maurice. "Empathy and Care Ethics." In *The Routledge Handbook of Philosophy of Empathy*, edited by Heidi Maibom, 264–72. Abingdon, UK: Routledge, 2017.

Harrison, Beverly Wildung. "The Power of Anger in the Work of Love: Christian Ethics for Women and Other Strangers." *Union Seminary Quarterly Review* 36 (1981) 41–57.

Held, Virginia. "Care and Justice, Still." In *Care Ethics and Political Theory*, edited by Daniel Engster and Maurice Hamington, 19–36. New York: Oxford University Press, 2015.

———. *The Ethics of Care: Personal, Political, and Global*. New York: Oxford University Press, 2007.

———. *Feminist Morality: Transforming Culture, Society, and Politics*. Women in Culture and Society. Chicago: University of Chicago Press, 1993.

Herman, Judith. *Trauma and Recovery: The Aftermath of Violence: From Domestic Abuse to Political Terror*. New York: Basic Books, 1997.

Hoffman, Martin L. "The Contribution of Empathy to Justice and Moral Judgment." In *Reaching out: Caring, Altruism, and Prosocial Behavior.*, edited by Bill Puka, 161–94. Moral Development: A Compendium 7. New York: Garland, 1994.

———. "Development of Prosocial Motivation: Empathy and Guilt." In *The Development of Prosocial Behavior*, edited by N. Eisenberg, 281–313. New York: Academic Press, 1982.

———. *Empathy and Moral Development: Implications for Caring and Justice*. Cambridge: Cambridge University Press, 2000.

———. "Empathy, Social Cognition, and Moral Action." In *Handbook of Moral Behavior and Development 1: Theory*, edited by William M. Kurtines and Jacob L. Lamb, 275–302. New York: Psychology Press, 2014.

Ickes, William, ed. *Empathic Accuracy.* New York: Guilford, 1997.
Jaggar, Alison M. "Love and Knowledge: Emotion in Feminist Epistemology." In *Feminist Theory Reader: Local and Global Perspectives,* edited by Carole McCann and Seung-kyung Kim, 487–501. 3rd ed. New York: Routledge, 2013.
Johnson, Alex. "Tennessee Pastor Andy Savage Resigns Weeks after Admitting 'Sexual Incident' with Minor." *NBC News* (March 2018). https://www.nbcnews.com/storyline/sexual-misconduct/tennessee-pastor-andy-savage-resigns-weeks-after-admitting-sexual-incident-n858541/.
Kaplan, E. Ann. "Empathy and Trauma Culture: Imaging Catastrophe." In *Empathy: Philosophical and Psychological Perspectives,* edited by Amy Coplan and Peter Goldie, 255–76. 2011. Reprint, New York: Oxford University Press, 2014.
Keenan, Marie. *Child Sexual Abuse and the Catholic Church: Gender, Power, and Organizational Culture.* New York: Oxford University Press, 2011.
———. "The Institution and the Individual: Child Sexual Abuse by Clergy." *The Furrow* 57 (2006) 3–8.
Kim, Arin. "[Herald Interview] Doctor Asks Prosecutors to Consider Murder Charges in Toddler's Death." *The Korea Herald* (January 2021). http://www.koreaherald.com/view.php?ud=20210106001007/.
Kim, So-hyun. "Adoptive Mother Charged with Toddler's Murder." *Korea Herald* (January 2021). http://www.koreaherald.com/view.php?ud=20210113000751/.
Kittay, Eva Feder. *Love's Labor: Essays on Women, Equality and Dependency.* New York: Routledge, 1998.
Klein, Linda Kay. *Pure: Inside the Evangelical Movement That Shamed a Generation of Young Women and How I Broke Free.* New York: Atria, 2018.
Ko, Jun-tae. "[Newsmaker] South Korea Gripped by Anger and Remorse over Toddler's Death." *The Korea Herald* (January 2021). http://www.koreaherald.com/view.php?ud=20210113000786/.
Kristeva, Julia. *Powers of Horror: An Essay on Abjection.* Translated by Leon Roudiez. European Perspectives. New York: Columbia University Press, 1982.
Kukmin Ilbo. "'Junginah Miahnhae' Sipyookghaewol Ipyangah Samangeh Gongboonhan Nitezen." Kukmin-Ilbo (January 2021). https://m.kmib.co.kr/view.asp?arcid=0015384441/.
Kwok, Pui-lan. "The Image of the 'White Lady': Gender and Race in Christian Mission." In *The Power of Naming: A Concilium Reader in Feminist Liberation Theology,* edited by Fiorenza Elisabeth Schüssler, 250–58. Maryknoll, NY: Orbis, 1996.
———. "Unbinding Our Feet: Saving Brown Women and Feminist Religious Discourse." In *Postcolonialism, Feminism and Religious Discourse,* edited by Laura E. Donaldson and Kwok Pui-Lan, 62–81. New York: Routledge, 2002.
Larrabee, Mary Jeanne, ed. *An Ethic of Care: Feminist and Interdisciplinary Perspectives.* Rev. ed. New York: Routledge, 1992.
Light, Sharee, and Carolyn Zahn-Waxler, "Nature and Forms of Empathy in the First Years of Life." In *Empathy: From Bench to Bedside,* edited by Jean Decety, 109–30. Cambridge: MIT Press, 2011.
Liles, Amy. "Sign the Petition: Support Andy Savage!" *Change.org* (2018). https://www.change.org/p/highpoint-church-memphis-support-andy-savage/.
Maibom, Heidi, ed. *Empathy and Morality.* New York: Oxford University Press, 2014.
———, ed. *The Routledge Handbook of Philosophy of Empathy.* Routledge Handbooks. Abingdon, UK: Routledge, 2019.

Bibliography

Manne, Kate. *Down Girl: The Logic of Misogyny*. Illustrated ed. New York: Oxford University Press, 2019.

Margalit, Avishai. *The Decent Society*. Translated by Naomi Goldblum. Cambridge: Harvard University Press, 1996.

Masto, Meghan. "Empathy and Its Role in Morality." *Southern Journal of Philosophy* 53 (March 2015) 74–96.

Maumjari [@mirboristar]. Tweet. *Twitter* (February 26, 2018). https://x.com/mirboristar/status/968160787075186689/.

Me too. Movement. "Tarana Burke, Founder." https://metoomvmt.org/get-to-know-us/tarana-burke-founder/.

Mendes, Kaitlynn, Jessica Ringrose, and Jessalynn Keller. *Digital Feminist Activism: Girls and Women Fight Back Against Rape Culture*. New York: Oxford University Press, 2019.

Merton, Rebecca, and Christina Fialho. "Civil Rights Complaint, RE: Sexual Abuse, Assault, and Harassment in U.S. Immigration Detention Facilities." *A Letter of Complaint to U.S. Immigration and Customs Enforcement*. Department of Homeland Security (April 2017). https://static1.squarespace.com/static/5a33042eb078691c386e7bce/t/5a9da297419202ab8be09c92/1520280217559/SexualAssault_Complaint.pdf/.

Morrison, Andrew P. *Shame: The Underside of Narcissism*. Hillsdale, NJ: Analytic, 1997.

Murray, Daisy. "Everyone Meet Tarana Burke, The Woman Who Really Started The 'Me Too' Movement." *ELLE* (October 2017). http://www.elleuk.com/life-and-culture/culture/news/a39429/empowerment-through-empathy-tarana-burke-me-too/.

Murray, Samuel. "Responsibility and Vigilance." *Philosophical Studies* 174 (2017) 507–27.

Nakamura, Lisa. *Digitizing Race*. Minneapolis: University of Minnesota Press, 2007.

Nam-Joo, Cho. *Kim Jiyoung, Born 1982*. Translated by Jamie Chang. 1st American ed. New York: Liveright, 2020.

Nathanson, Donald L., ed. *The Many Faces of Shame*. New York: Guilford, 1987.

The New York Times. "Opinion: I Was Assaulted. He Was Applauded." *The New York Times* (March 2018). https://www.nytimes.com/2018/03/09/opinion/jules-woodson-andy-savage-assault.html/.

The New York Times Editorial Staff. *#MeToo: Women Speak Out Against Sexual Assault*. New York: Rosen, 2018.

Nickel, Dana. "Who Profits From Migrant Detention in the US?" *The Globe Post* (August 2019). https://theglobepost.com/2019/08/19/profit-migrant-detention/.

Noddings, Nel. *Caring: A Relational Approach to Ethics and Moral Education*. 2nd ed. Berkeley: University of California Press, 2013.

Oliver, Kelly. *Reading Kristeva: Unraveling the Double-Bind*. Bloomington: Indiana University Press, 1993.

Ott, Kate M. *Christian Ethics for a Digital Society*. Lanham, MD: Rowman & Littlefield, 2018.

———. "Digital Spiritual Embodiment: Power, Difference, and Interdependence." *Cursor_Zeitschrift für Explorative Theologie* (November 2019). https://cursor.pubpub.org/pub/3lsdep9t/release/5.

———. "Social Media and Feminist Values: Aligned or Maligned?" *Frontiers: A Journal of Women Studies* 39 (2018) 93–111.

Overgaard, Søren, and Dan Zahavi, "Empathy without Isomorphism: A Phenomenological Account." In *Empathy: From Bench to Bedside*, edited by Jean Decety, 3–20. Cambridge: MIT Press, 2011.

Bibliography

Oxford English Dictionary. s.v. "mature (adj.)." *Oxford English Dictionary Online* (December 2021). https://doi.org/10.1093/OED/8470565006/.

Oxley, Julinna C. *The Moral Dimensions of Empathy: Limits and Applications in Ethical Theory and Practice*. New York: Palgrave Macmillan, 2011.

Palmer, Parker J. *The Active Life: A Spirituality of Work, Creativity, and Caring*. San Francisco: Jossey-Bass, 1999.

Park, Boram. "New Legislation Toughens Punishment for Perpetrators of Fatal Child Abuse." *Yonhap News Agency* (February 2021). https://en.yna.co.kr/view/AEN20210226011300315/.

Parker, Rozsika. Mother *Love/Mother Hate: The Power of Maternal Ambivalence*. New York: Basic Books, 1995.

Poulson, Chris. *Shame: The Master Emotion?* Hobart, Australia: University of Tasmania, 2000.

Preston, Stephanie D., and Frans de Waal. "Empathy: Its Ultimate And Proximate Bases." *The Behavioral and Brain Sciences* 25 (February 2002) 1–71.

Prinz, Jesse J. "Is Empathy Necessary for Morality?" In *Empathy: Philosophical and Psychological Perspectives,* edited by Amy Coplan and Peter Goldie, 211–29. 2011. Reprint, New York: Oxford University Press, 2014.

———. "Against Empathy." *Southern Journal of Philosophy* 49 (2011) 214–33.

Pulcini, Elena. Care of the World: Fear, Responsibility and Justice in the Global Age. Studies in Global Justice. Dordrecht: Springer, 2013.

Rodgers, Julie. "Maternal Abject (Kristeva)." In *Encyclopedia of Motherhood*, 694–95. Thousand Oaks, CA: Sage, 2010.

Rodino-Colocino, Michelle. "Me Too, #MeToo: Countering Cruelty with Empathy." *Communication and Critical/Cultural Studies* 15 (January 2018) 96–100.

Ruether, Rosemary Radford. "Sexual Ethics in Church History." In *Professional Sexual Ethics: A Holistic Ministry Approach*, edited by Patricia Beattie Jung and Darryl W. Stephens, 57–66. Minneapolis: Fortress, 2013.

Ryu, Ran et al. "*Cheonjugyodo* 'MeToo.' *Chimmook ggaen 7nyun ahkmong . . . Gyeolko Izeulsoo upsseotda.*" *KBS News* (February 2018). //news.kbs.co.kr/news/view.do?ncd=3609848/.

Schwartz, Lita Linzer, and Natalie K. Isser. *Endangered Children: Homicide and Other Crimes*. 2nd ed. Boca Raton, FL: CRC Press, 2011.

Sevenhuijsen, Selma. "Care and Attention." Paper presented at the conference "*A Meaningful Life in a just Society: Investigating Wellbeing and Democratic Caring*." Utrecht, IL: University of Humanistic Studies (January 2014). http://selmasevenhuijsen.nl/wp-content/uploads/2015/12/Active-attention.pdf.

Silence is Violence. "Sign the Petition: Force Andy Savage to Resign from Highpoint Church." *Change.org* 2018. https://www.change.org/p/megachurch-pastor-receives-standing-ovation-after-admitting-to-sexual-assault-resign/.

Simner, Marvin L. "Newborn's Response to The Cry of Another Infant." *Developmental Psychology* 5 (1971) 136–50.

Smith, Amy. "Silent No More: A Survivor of Sexual Assault by Prominent Memphis Pastor Andy Savage Shares Her Story #metoo #churchtoo #silenceisnotspiritual." *Watchkeep* (blog) (January 2018). https://watchkeep.org/2018/01/silent-no-more-a-survivor-of-sexual-assault-by-prominent-memphis-pastor-andy-savage-shares-her-story-metoo-churchtoo-silenceisnotspiritual/.

Bibliography

Smith, Sharon G., Xinjian Zhang, Kathleen C. Basile, Melissa T. Merrick, Jing Wang, Marcie-jo Kresnow, and Jieru Chen. "The National Intimate Partner and Sexual Violence Survey (NISVS): 2015 Data Brief—Updated Release." *National Center for Injury Prevention and Control Centers for Disease Control and Prevention*, Atlanta, GA: Centers for Disease Control and Prevention (June 2020). https://www.cdc.gov/violenceprevention/datasources/nisvs/2015NISVSdatabrief.html/.

Steele, Meili. "Social Imaginaries and the Theory of the Normative Utterance." *Philosophy & Social Criticism* 43 (2017) 1045–71.

Steinem, Gloria. "Challenges Facing Women" Speech presented at *the Feminist Majority Foundation Summit* (October 5, 2009). https://www.c-span.org/video/?289286-82/challenges-facing-women/.

Stueber, Karsten. "Empathy." In *The Stanford Encyclopedia of Philosophy*, edited by Edward N. Zalta. Stanford: Stanford University, 2019. https://plato.stanford.edu/entries/empathy/

Taylor, Dianna. "Humiliation as a Harm of Sexual Violence: Feminist versus Neoliberal Perspectives." *Hypatia* 33 (2018) 434–50.

———. *Sexual Violence and Humiliation: A Foucauldian-Feminist Perspective*. New York: Routledge, 2019.

Tronto, Joan C. *Caring Democracy: Markets, Equality, and Justice*. New York: New York University Press, 2013.

———. "Creating Caring Institutions: Politics, Plurality, and Purpose." *Ethics and Social Welfare* 4 (2010) 158–71.

———. "Democracy Becomes Care; Care Becomes Democracy." *Ethics of Care* 1 (2011) 33–50.

———. *Moral Boundaries: A Political Argument for an Ethic of Care*. New York: Routledge, 2015.

Tumulty, Karen. "How Donald Trump Came up with 'Make America Great Again.'" *Washington Post*, January 18, 2017. https://www.washingtonpost.com/politics/how-donald-trump-came-up-with-make-america-great-again/2017/01/17/fb6acf5e-dbf7-11e6-ad42-f3375f271c9c_story.html/.

van Dijke, Jolanda, and Inge van Nistelrooij, Pien Bos, and Joachim Duyndam. "Care Ethics: An Ethics of Empathy?" *Nursing Ethics* 26 (2019) 1282–1291.

van Nistelrooij, Inge. *Sacrifice: A Care-Ethical Reappraisal of Sacrifice and Self-Sacrifice*. Leuven, Belgium: Peeters, 2015. https://www.researchgate.net/publication/285593755_Sacrifice_A_care-ethical_reappraisal_of_sacrifice_and_self-sacrifice.

Visse, Merel, and Tineke A. Abma, eds. *Evaluation for a Caring Society*. Charlotte: Information Age, 2018.

Walsh, Mary Roth. *The Psychology of Women: Ongoing Debates*. New Haven: Yale University Press, 1987.

The Wartburg Watch. "Jules Woodson Responds via The New York Times: Shame on Andy Savage, Chris Conlee and Highpoint Church." *The Wartburg Watch* (March 2018). https://thewartburgwatch.com/2018/03/09/jules-woodson-responds-via-the-new-york-times-shame-on-andy-savage-chris-conlee-and-highpoint-church/.

Washington Post. "Perspective: #MeToo Was Started for Black and Brown Women and Girls. They're Still Being Ignored." *Washington Post*, November 9, 2017. https://www.washingtonpost.com/news/post-nation/wp/2017/11/09/the-waitress-who-works-in-the-diner-needs-to-know-that-the-issue-of-sexual-harassment-is-about-her-too/.

West, Traci C. "Ending Gender Violence: An Antiracist Intersectional Agenda for Churches." *Review & Expositor* 117 (2020) 199–203.

———. "Is Christian Political Theology Too Conservative to Undermine Sexual Violence?" *Political Theology Network* (October 2018). https://politicaltheology.com/is-christian-political-theology-too-conservative-to-undermine-sexual-violence/.

———. *Solidarity and Defiant Spirituality: Africana Lessons on Religion, Racism, and Ending Gender Violence*. New York: New York University Press, 2019.

———. *Wounds of the Spirit: Black Women, Violence, and Resistance Ethics*. New York: New York University Press, 1999.

Winnicott, D. W. *Playing and Reality.* 2nd ed. London: Routledge, 1971.

Wispé, Lauren. "History of The Concept of Empathy." In *Empathy and Its Development*, edited by Nancy Eisenberg and Janet Strayer, 17–37. Cambridge: Cambridge University Press, 1987.

Yang, Yeon-Hee. "Daejeon Catholic-dae Kim You-Jung Chongjang, Han Man-Sam shinboo Sungpokryuk ongho nonran." *Pen and Mike* (February 2018). http://www.pennmike.com/news/articleView.html?idxno=2800.

Index

actualize/actualization, 2, 4, 11, 24, 37, 46, 49–50, 54, 57, 73, 92, 94, 117–18, 130, 132–33, 136–37, 142–44, 148–49, 152, 156–57, 161–63, 166
affect match, 16, 20, 26, 34–35
anger, 13, 15, 21, 27, 29, 37, 152–54. *See also* empathic anger
association, 22, 34–37, 105, 145

Batson, Daniel, 8, 14n–17n, 18, 19, 22, 27n, 29, 159n
behavior
    abusive, 120
    aggressive, 39
    altruistic, 24
    helping, 35
    moral, 20
    prosocial, 25
    sexual, 121
behavioral, 75, 80, 88–89, 93, 160
bias, 4, 25, 30–31, 42, 46–48, 52–53, 64, 67–69, 80, 83–85, 87, 89, 92, 106, 133
    egocentric, 30
    familiarity, 46–48, 50, 80, 83, 85, 152
    friendship, 47
    hear-and-now, 46–48
    in-group, 47. *See also* in-group
    near-and-dear, 47, 50, 56, 80, 84–85, 149
    racial, 32. *See also* racial
    racial and xenophobic, 32
    self-centered, 30
    similarity, 46, 47
branches of empathic affect, 23, 55, 129, 143, 159
Brock, Rita Nakashima, 5, 9, 106, 128
bystander guilt over inaction, 40–41, 56, 143
bystander(s), 13–15, 33, 39, 40, 42, 45, 56, 82, 84, 94–95, 100, 124, 129, 134–36, 144, 161, 163

care ethics/ethics of care, 2, 7–15, 43–45, 56–76, 91, 111, 148
caring justice, 25, 72–73, 90–92, 120, 127, 132, 140, 149, 161, 164
Christian value(s), 13, 117, 136, 152, 157, 165. *See also* sacrifice, anger, love
#ChurchToo. *See* ch. 3
collective, 2, 7, 104, 137–40, 143, 149, 159, 162–63
communal tie, 95, 122, 139
community
    caring, 13, 91, 95, 127, 164
    digital. *See* digital, communities
    faith, 5, 12, 107–8, 111
    institutionalized, 138–39. *See also* institutionalized care
    institutionalized religious, 139. *See also* institutionalized community; faith community
    just caring, 91, 95, 164. *See also* caring community

Index

community (*cont.*)
  new, 23, 139
  non-institutionalized. (*see* institutionalized community)
  transnational, 6
  virtual, 122, 139
compassion, 17–19, 23, 25, 38, 44, 55, 78–79, 129, 133, 142–43
conditioning, 22, 33–37, 145
congruent emotions. *See* congruent feelings
congruent feelings, 16, 18–25, 32, 36, 54, 56, 73, 86, 129, 159
Coplan, Amy, 8, 16–18, 24–25, 30–31, 79
cue(s)
  (in)direct, 34, 36, 56
  distress, 34, 37, 46–47, 52–53, 88, 132
  imagery, 36f
  immediate, 35–36

de Waal, Frans, 4, 18–19, 27–28, 134
deliberation, 3, 23, 41, 56, 61, 73–74, 80, 84, 91–92, 97, 149, 156, 159, 161–63
detention center, 98–99, 125
digital
  accessibility, 121
  activism, 11, 32–33, 56, 92–93, 121, 125, 129, 131, 133–34, 136, 158, 162–63
  communities, 117
  discourses, 125
  era, 83, 121, 123
  experiences, 125
  humanities, 7, 9, 95, 118, 124
  inequality, 125
  literacy, 125, 127
  movement, 92, 118, 125, 127, 134. *See also* activism, digital
  platforms, 118, 126–27, 133, 135
  resources, 125
  space, 13, 55, 95, 118–19, 122–25, 129, 133, 162
distant. *See* distant others
distant others, 12, 15, 41–44, 50–51, 55, 57–58, 64, 70–71, 73, 75, 83–85, 88–89, 91, 94, 96, 123, 127, 129, 132–34, 139, 159–63

distress
  cue(s) (*see* cues, distress)
  dual, 38, 143–44
  empathic (*see* empathic distress)
  sympathetic, 17, 20, 33, 37, 38, 42, 56, 78–79, 86, 88, 91, 123, 139, 143, 148, 160

egoistic drift, 24, 37, 56
Eisenberg, Nancy, 8, 16, 17, 24
elements of mature communal empathy, 10, 13, 136, 142, 148, 149, 150, 158, 164, 166
embodied. *See* embody
embodiment, 116, 123n, 124n, 142
embody, 4, 11, 66, 139, 142, 148, 154, 156, 164
emotional
  contagion, 18, 26–29, 33–34, 42, 55, 141
  state, 15, 27, 35, 147
emotional contagion, 18, 26–29, 33–34, 42, 55, 141
emotions, 9, 12–28, 31, 33–34, 37, 41–42, 45, 55–56, 62, 64–67, 69, 74, 90, 91, 99–101, 103, 123, 129, 134, 137, 147
empathic
  (in)accuracy, 20, 46–47, 49, 52
  action, 23, 55, 79, 80, 84–85, 88–89, 91, 133, 135, 148–50, 153–56, 159
  affect, 23, 55, 75, 86, 88, 89, 92, 123, 129, 133. 143, 159, 160, 162–63
  anger, 17–20, 23, 25, 37–40, 55–56, 86, 88, 123, 129, 131, 133, 143–44, 153, 160, 163–65
  arousal, 22, 28, 33–39, 44, 48, 56. *See also* primitive modes of empathic arousal
  community, 141, 143, 146, 149–50, 163–64, 166
  distress, 20, 31–48, 56–57, 79, 91, 145
  duality, 39
  guilt, 5, 33, 40. *See also* guilt
  interaction, 23, 84
  overarousal, 31, 31n, 32, 37n, 41, 46–48, 79

Index

process, 3, 18, 23, 42, 49, 51, 56, 61, 82, 130, 145, 164
  relief, 35
  thinking process, 59, 74, 108
empathic arousal
  automatic involuntary, 35, 42
  preverbal, 28, 35, 43–44
empathic just caring society, 73, 91
empathy
  as universal experience and ability, 7, 26, 35, 64, 67, 141
  communal, 1–16, 23, 26, 29, 32–37, 41–44, 54–59, 64, 68–69, 92, 94, 111, 117–18, 134–66
  definitions of, 16–25
  definition of, 25
  dysfunctional, 5, 52–53, 84, 130, 137, 140, 142, 150–54, 162–64
  dysfunctions of, 46–53, 57, 81, 84–85, 102, 130, 132, 149, 152, 159
  ethic(s) of, 74, 81
  genuine, 24, 24n, 30–31, 51–55, 74, 75, 78–79, 129, 161
  immature, 7, 50–51, 79, 88–89, 125, 140
  involuntary (*see* involuntary)
  limitations of, 2, 4, 10, 31, 37, 42, 46, 47, 49, 57, 119, 126
  limits of, 30–31, 48–50, 53, 56–57, 69, 79, 85, 122, 129, 132, 149, 159, 161
  manipulated, 5, 49, 120, 130–32, 136, 148, 150
  mature, 1, 3–8, 11–15, 24–30, 33, 43–44, 50, 52–63, 68–69, 72–95, 117–20, 125–66
  morally nuanced and psychologically mature, 4, 45, 49, 50
  potential risk(s) of, 2, 4, 8, 10, 30, 32, 46, 48–53, 57, 79, 81, 85, 130, 132–33, 149, 159
  pseudo, 13, 24n, 31, 49, 52–55, 92, 129–32, 150–53, 162, 164
  weaknesses of, 15, 32, 45–58, 64, 79, 132, 150, 159
empathy-based
  affective and cognitive reaction, 41
  anger-at-aggressor component, 39

emotion(s), 37, 42
feeling(s) of injustice, 37, 123, 143, 164
guilt, 37, 41, 88, 123, 143, 164
moral affects, 37–38, 40, 56, 143, 160, 164
resistance, 118
empower, 2, 4, 6, 10, 119–20, 123–24, 126, 128, 133, 139–40, 149, 162, ix
empowerment. *See* empower
engagement, 6, 23, 54, 84, 91, 121, 130, 137, 163
engaging action, 23, 51, 84, 128, 135, 159, 160, 164
envision. *See* vision
epistemic. *See* epistemological
epistemological, 29, 31, 49–51, 62, 65, 67, 69, 72–73, 87, 90, 92, 148
epistemology. *See* epistemological
expression(s)
  facial, 27, 34, 55
  posture, 27, 34–36
  vocal, 27, 34–35, 36

features of mature empathy, 11, 15, 33, 55–57, 60–62, 69, 73–75, 87, 89, 91, 142, 160, 164
Fortune, Marie, 5, 96, 104, 116, 128–29

gatekeeper, 133, 138, 163
gendered, 4–5, 40, 44, 69, 100–101, 126
Gibbs, John, 8, 73, 87
Gilligan, Carol, 61–63
guilt, 5, 8, 17–21, 33, 37, 40–42, 56, 86, 88, 91, 101–2, 108, 112, 123, 143, 159–64

Harrison, Beverly Wildung, 9, 39, 152–55, 165
Held, Virginia, 8, 61, 63–75
Hoffman, Martin, 8, 10, 73, 75, 78–80, 85–91, 123, 143–45, 148, 156, 164. *See also* ch. 1.
humiliated, 82, 103
humiliation, 5, 101–3, 162
humiliator, 102–3

Index

ignorance, 104–5
imagination, 10, 13, 21–25, 45, 49, 54, 61, 73, 84–85, 117, 129, 136, 143, 147–49, 157, 159, 164–65
(im)migrant, 3, 9, 11, 12, 21, 30, 62, 80, 83, 94–98, 124–28, 151
in-group, 47, 50, 53, 64, 132
institutionalized care. See institutionalized community
intentional stance, 22, 74, 88
intercultural, 7, 54
interdependence, 6, 62, 67, 70–73, 92
intersection, 2, 11–12, 45, 51, 62, 64, 66, 74, 80, 83, 84, 87, 91, 93, 96–97, 104–5, 109, 111, 115–16, 118–19, 123–24, 127, 162
intersectional. See intersection
intersectionality. See intersectional
intersubjective, 2–3, 6, 23, 55, 74–94, 133–34, 138–42, 147–48, 155, 157, 160, 163
intersubjectivity, 3, 23, 80, 84, 164
intrinsically caring 74
intrinsically communal, political, 140n, 141, 150, 163
invisibility, 11, 127–28
invisible, 60, 125–26, 137
involuntary, 26–28, 33, 35, 42, 47, 55, 115, 145

judgment. See moral judgment
just caring, 2, 4, 7, 10, 13, 25, 70–74, 85–95, 116, 118, 127, 136–40, 146, 149, 155–56, 164–65
just caring society, 2, 4, 7, 10, 13, 72–74, 86, 91, 92, 94, 136, 146, 149, 155–56, 165

Kwok, Pui-lan, 9, 110

language, 35, 36, 42, 56, 63, 72, 82, 108–9, 113, 124–27
Lee, Jung Young, 145–46
liminal, 124, 141, 145–48, 158, 164
liminal space. See liminal
liminality. See liminal

love, 13, 23, 25, 50, 103, 106–16, 129, 142, 148–49, 152–57, 164–65

macro, 68, 118, 124, 150
Maibom, Heidi, 8, 18, 28, 31, 66, 71, 79, 80
Manne, Kate, 99–101
marginalization, 72, 76, 80, 124
marginalize, 2, 4, 11–12, 60, 66, 70, 71, 73, 77, 94, 96, 99, 102, 104, 106, 111, 120, 124–28, 151, 153–55, 160–62, 165
marginalizing, 97, 99, 162
mature
    definition of, 61–62, 159–60. See also maturity
mature empathizer, 11, 61, 76–77, 80, 85–90, 111, 147, 150, 160–61, 164
mature society, 4, 8, 10–11, 15, 41, 58–62, 68, 73–74, 85, 89, 91, 117, 129, 136, 140, 142–43, 149, 158, 160, 166
maturely, 46, 53, 76, 139
maturity, 51, 59–60, 62, 133, 159–60. See also mature, definition of
meso, 118, 122–23, 150
#MeToo. See ch. 3
micro, 68, 118–19, 150
mimicry, 22–23, 25–27, 29, 33–37, 54–55, 73, 129, 141, 145, 159
misogynist, 100–101, 108
misogynistic, 52, 92, 99–107, 116, 121, 124, 129–30, 133, 162
misogyny, 99–101
    definition of, 99–100
moral agent(s), 51, 54, 60–61, 66, 70–74, 83, 85–86, 89–92, 94, 117, 129, 158, 160–61, 163, 165
moral judgment, 42, 49–50, 52, 59, 61, 63, 67, 73–75, 78, 86–87, 90, 159, 163

Nakamura, Lisa, 9, 124–27
negligence, 39, 104, 128, 145, 164
networked, 119, 121–22, 124, 134, 163
Nistelrooij, Inge van, 8, 75–77, 81, 91, 134
Noddings, Nel, 45, 50, 65, 81, 139, 148

Index

oppressed, 4, 44, 48, 66, 70, 97, 134, 160
oppressing, 106
oppression(s), 12, 117, 134, 137
oppressive, 67, 77, 100, 106, 109, 116–18, 129, 149, 161, 163
Ott, Kate M., 9, 121–24, 137
Oxley, Julinna, 3, 8, 16, 21–23, 32, 55, 80

parochial, 45, 57–58, 159
parochialism. *See* parochial
parochiality. *See* parochial
particular. *See* particularity
particularity, 4–7, 9, 11–12, 15, 21, 27, 35, 39, 45, 47, 48, 61–62, 64, 67–69, 90, 92, 94, 97, 109, 111, 137, 150, 166
people of color, 111, 125–27, 151
people with power, 129, 131, 161
perspective-taking
    dual, 32, 55–57, 79–80, 82
    interdimensional, 32, 56, 74–75, 80–85, 88–92, 109, 139, 141, 144, 149, 160–64
    other-oriented, 16, 19, 22, 29–32, 56, 79, 80, 82, 161
    self-oriented, 29–32, 36, 56, 79, 80, 82, 161
    supplementary, 82–83, 144, 160
pity, 19, 76
powerless, 77, 77n, 79n, 111n
praxis, 1, 6, 13, 136–37, 157, 161
    definition of, 1, 6n
pre-digital era, 121, 123
primitive modes of empathic arousal, 22, 33, 35. *See also* empathic arousal
the process model, 18
Pulcini, Elena, 8, 61, 66–67, 70–71

race, 2, 9, 12, 35, 45, 47, 62, 80, 84, 87, 90, 93, 96, 97, 110n, 119, 121, 124, 126–28, 151
racial, 32, 43, 51n, 62, 80, 83, 94, 126n, 137
racialized, 126
rape, 21, 95, 96, 101, 105, 108, 110, 123
resistance, 2, 4, 5, 13, 53, 95, 118, 124, 131, 136, 141–43, 149–52, 156, 164, 166

role-taking, 21, 35–37, 43, 56. *See also* perspective-taking

sacrifice, 5, 13, 76–80, 105–11, 120, 152–56, 161, 165–66
self-other differentiation, 31, 38, 78–90, 142, 161
Sevenhuijsen, Selma, 8
sexual
    abuse, 2, 44, 50, 66, 98, 101, 105–7, 112, 116, 126, 144, 154
    abuser, 39, 50, 52, 97, 104, 107, 108, 120, 132, 134, 140, 153
    harassment, 25, 52, 96
    offender, 5, 14, 21, 38–39, 52–53, 96, 98–99, 103–7, 111–16, 120–21, 129–33, 142, 162–64
    violence, 4–12, 22–26, 32–33, 44, 92, 162–62. *See also* ch. 3
shame, 5, 15, 21, 56, 101–2, 112, 116, 128, 129, 159–60. *See also* victim-shaming
significant other(s), 25, 29, 32, 50–51, 83, 89, 91, 103, 127, 141, 151
simulation, 21–23, 25, 32, 54, 61, 73, 129, 159
social imaginary, 57, 91, 160, 165–66
solidarity, 3–4, 6, 12, 15, 23, 26, 34, 45, 55, 71, 84, 91, 95, 119, 122, 123, 126–27, 133–34, 141, 143, 148, 150, 154–56, 158, 161–62
spiritual, 11, 21, 97, 103, 106, 108–9, 111, 113, 115–16, 123–24, 134, 141
stimulate, 90
stimulus/li, 33, 34, 88
stranger(s), 6, 29, 32, 48, 83–85, 89, 95, 100, 132, 134, 141, 152, 156
sympathetic, 21, 24, 40
    atmosphere, 113
    dimension in empathy, 78
    distress, 17, 20, 33, 37–38, 42, 56, 78–79, 86, 88, 91, 123, 139, 143, 148, 160, 164
    empathic/sympathetic distress, 38, 91, 139, 148, 160, 164
    feeling, 143
    level, 148

sympathy, 8, 16–19, 23, 25, 28, 33, 37–38, 42, 55, 129–30, 143, 159
    definition of, 16–17
systemic evil, 11, 92, 97–99, 104–5, 129–30, 142, 162

transform, 23–24, 31, 33, 37–38, 40, 42, 47, 54–55, 59, 79, 84, 88–89, 91–92, 94, 123, 129, 134–35, 137, 139, 141, 148, 150, 156, 159–61, 163
Tronto, Joan, 8, 66, 76–81, 109, 111, 154, 161, 166

verbal, 21, 26, 35–37, 56, 82, 141, 144
victim-blaming, 41, 100–101, 103–4, 107, 114–16, 119–20, 128, 162. *See also* victim–shaming and shame
victim-blaming culture. *See* victim-blaming

victim-shaming, 100–101, 107, 114, 116, 121, 162. *See also* victim–blaming
victim-shaming culture. *See* victim-shaming
victim-survivors, 4–6, 9, 11–12, 21, 24–26, 32–33, 38–39, 44, 53, 83, 92, 136, 139, 140, 158, 162–63. *See* also ch. 3
vision, 11, 45, 57–63, 67–68, 70–74, 117, 136, 143, 149–50, 160, 164–66
Visse, Merel, 6, 137
vulnerability, 11, 36–37, 47, 51, 80, 89, 96–97, 138–39
vulnerable, 2, 6, 11, 31, 48, 70–71, 74, 77, 79–80, 83, 91–92, 97, 102, 106, 111, 125, 128–29, 139, 146, 151, 160–61, 165

West, Traci C., 4, 5, 9, 95–96, 100, 103–4, 106–9, 117, 128, 154, 165

www.ingramcontent.com/pod-product-compliance
Lightning Source LLC
Chambersburg PA
CBHW062046220426
43662CB00010B/1675